James Fergusson is a freelance journalist and author who began reporting on Afghan affairs more than twelve years ago. His first book, the acclaimed *Kandahar Cockney*, told the story of his friendship with Mir, an Afghan asylum-seeker in London. From 1999 to 2001 he worked in Sarajevo as a press spokesman for OHR, the organization charged with implementing the Dayton peace accord that ended Bosnia's civil war in 1995.

D0988245

www.**rbooks**.co.uk

Also by James Fergusson

Kandahar Cockney
The Vitamin Murders

A MILLION BULLETS

The Real Story of the British Army in Afghanistan

James Fergusson

BANTAM PRESS

LONDON • TORONTO • SYDNEY • AUCKLAND • JOHANNESBURG

TRANSWORLD PUBLISHERS
61–63 Uxbridge Road, London W5 5SA
A Random House Group Company
www.rbooks.co.uk

First published in Great Britain
in 2008 by Bantam Press
an imprint of Transworld Publishers

This book is a work of non-fiction. In some limited cases names of people, places,
dates, sequences or the detail of events have been changed solely to protect the privacy
of others and for reasons of operational security. The author has stated to the publishers
that, except in such minor respects not affecting the substantial accuracy of the work,
the contents of this book are true.

A CIP catalogue record for this book
is available from the British Library.

ISBN 9780593059029 (cased)
9780593059036 (tpb)

Addresses for Random House Group Ltd companies outside the UK
can be found at: www.randomhouse.co.uk
The Random House Group Ltd Reg. No. 954009

The Random House Group Limited supports The Forest Stewardship
Council (FSC), the leading international forest-certification organization. All our
titles that are printed on Greenpeace-approved FSC-certified paper carry the FSC logo.
Our paper procurement policy can be found at www.rbooks.co.uk/environment

Typeset in 12/16pt Granjon by
Falcon Oast Graphic Art Ltd.
Printed in the UK by CPI Mackays, Chatham, ME5 8TD

2 4 6 8 10 9 7 5 3 1

Mixed Sources
Product group from well-managed
forests and other controlled sources
www.fsc.org Cert no. TT-COC-2139
© 1996 Forest Stewardship Council
FSC

For Melissa

Contents

Acknowledgements

The project could not have gone ahead without the approval of Brigadier Ed Butler, commander of 16 Air Assault Brigade in 2006. I am indebted to him, as well as to Colonel Ben Bathurst and his team at the Public Relations Directorate in the Ministry of Defence.

My thanks also to Susan Aird, Colin Ball, Jane Bonham Carter, Chloe Breyer, Rupert Chetwynde, Tim David, Adam Fergusson (both of them), Robert Fox, Phil Goodwin, James Hanning, Tania Kindersley, Alastair Leithead, Tif Loehnis, Anthony Lloyd, David Loyn, Flora Maclay, Jenny McVeigh, Martin Melia, Peter Merriman, Gulalai Momand, Dave Muralt, Ian Nellins, David Ramsbottom, Simon Reade, William Reeve, Chris Riley, Toby Smart, Edward Smyth-Osborne, Rory Stewart, 'Stonker', Miriam Swift, Ray Whitaker, Piers Wickman, Doug Young and all at Transworld – and to all those whose names for one reason or another I cannot mention.

I heard so many extraordinary stories from the troops who took part in Operation Herrick 4 that it has not been possible to tell all of them here. My main purpose in writing this book was, and remains, polemical; it was never intended as an exhaustive history. But to Nick Wight-Boycott's Pathfinders, Gary Wilkinson and the men of 7 Para RHA, the OMLT officers and all the others whose voices I know also deserve to be heard, I apologize.

Finally, I am deeply grateful for the coooration and understanding of the families of the killed, not all of whose names appear in these pages. A percentage of the profits from this book will go to Combat Stress, the ex-Services mental welfare society.

Introduction

The war had been running for more than a month before the public properly woke up to it. It was not until early July 2006 that the first images of the fighting in Helmand began to filter on to our television screens. In retrospect it is clear that the news had some serious competition that summer, the hottest in Britain since records began in 1772. Those still indoors were mostly tuned either to *Big Brother*, the seventh series of which had begun in May (the competition was eventually won by Pete Bennett, a ketamine addict from Camberwell who suffered from Tourette's Syndrome), or, more likely, the closing stages of the World Cup in Germany. (England was knocked out by Portugal on 1 July after a penalty shoot-out. The final eight days later, won by Italy, attracted an estimated global audience of 715 million people – the most-watched event in television history.)

Yet even for those paying attention it was hard to make out what was going on in Helmand – or 'Hell Manned' as the BBC persistently called it. Chinook helicopters touched down in violent sandstorms of their own making. Hoarse squaddies, their tattooed arms and chests exposed to the burning desert sun, dropped mortars into firing tubes with the speed and precision of robots on a production line. They crouched behind sandbagged machine-guns that spat torrents of tracer fire, or zig-zagged towards mud buildings and an unseen enemy to a soundtrack of explosions, curses and heavy breathing.

Our senses were tantalized. As the news anchors solemnly explained, most of the 'unique footage' on our screens had been filmed by the troops themselves. This sounded almost like a coded apology for the poor quality of the clips, which tended to be short, jerky and badly pixelated. And though the names of the battlefields changed – Now Zad, Sangin, Musa Qala, Kajaki – the crash-bang footage soon took on a disturbing sameness. As viewers we relied on the presenters to impose any sense of continuity or rationality. We could see that a military crisis was unfolding on the other side of the world, yet the more we watched, the less the pictures seemed to offer an explanation of how or why this was happening.

One thing, at least, was clear: there were many members of the Armed Forces who would be missing the World Cup Final. This was not some blip in a benign peace-keeping campaign that we were watching, but a full-blown battle. The British, it seemed, were cut off and under siege in at least three southern Afghan market towns, manning the sangars* of fort-like local government district centres – or 'platoon-houses' as they were sometimes known – against a well-armed enemy determined to throw them

---

* A sangar, the Persian word for 'barricade', is a small temporary fortified position usually built of sandbags. The term was first appropriated by the British Indian Army in the nineteenth century and is still in use. There is a town called Sangar in Ghazni province in central Afghanistan.

out. Rorke's Drift came to mind. It was as though a whole new front in the War on Terror had opened up while we were looking the other way. General David Richards, the British commander of ISAF, Nato's International Security Assistance Force in Kabul, later appeared to confirm our groggy impression. The military, he said, was engaged in the most 'persistent, low-level dirty fighting' undertaken by the British since the Korean War, half a century ago. A professor at the Royal Statistical Society declared that British soldiers in Afghanistan were precisely six times more likely to be killed than their comrades in Iraq.

My concern was personal. As a journalist I had been reporting on Afghanistan for over a decade. My first book, *Kandahar Cockney*, documented the travails of Mir, a Pashtun interpreter with whom I once worked, and whose family I helped to gain political asylum in London in 1998. We are still close friends. Yet it now looked, dispiritingly, as though our two countries were at war again for the first time since 1919. The potential consequences of this renewed fighting, both for our friendship and for the peace and security of the country he loved and to which he and his family fervently hoped one day to return, were serious.

My feelings were further complicated by indirect family involvement. My wife's cousin Tom Burne, a lieutenant in the Household Cavalry, had been deployed as part of the Helmand battle group. He was twenty-five and had been out of Sandhurst for little more than a year when he was called upon to swap his horse and bearskin for the turret of a Scimitar light tank. Tom was tall, fair-haired and good-looking. We had recently spent Christmas with him in New York, at the home of his marketing-director sister. He was a sunny, easy-going person, the kind who laughed so often that he seemed almost impervious to the troubles of life.

I recalled his free-wheeling gait on a walk through Williamsburg, his red socks and beaten-up loafers scuffing the graffitoed tarmac, his hands stuffed comfortably into his overcoat against the crisp winter air. Williamsburg, a chic but still up-and-coming neighbourhood of Brooklyn, could be mildly threatening at night, but it was no match for Tom, who wore his confidence like a suit of armour. That, like the real armour of his tank, was soon to be sorely tested.

Like everybody else in the battle group, Tom was sent first to Camp Bastion, the British Task Force's £1 billion Helmand headquarters. Bastion was located deep in the remote Dasht-i-Margo, the poetically named 'Desert of Death'. In a few short months this enormous military base had risen from the empty sands, and now housed thousands of British troops. They had a gym there, and air-conditioning, and access to computers with email. Tom and I corresponded, and for a few short weeks he became my inside track on what was going on.

'A pleasure to hear from you, and yes, there is sand in my i-Pod!' he wrote. 'In fact there is bloody sand everywhere!'

I'd written to ask him about a report by Christina Lamb, the *Sunday Times* correspondent, who had recently gone out with a patrol that had been ambushed. Her account had been widely noticed at home, and was an important milestone in the public's growing realization that all was not well in Helmand. Tom had to choose his words carefully for security reasons, yet it was still evident that the situation was actually worse than we knew. The incidents reported in the media were 'the tip of the iceberg', he wrote. 'In reality we are dealing with around three Christina Lamb-type incidents per day.' Morale among the battle group, he reported, was extremely high despite some recent British deaths.

Their mission to win hearts and minds, he said, was not just clear but 'simple', and was being 'successfully received' across the province. He was proud that they had 'not had one collateral damage casualty throughout all the engagements', a result he attributed to the restraint and professionalism of the troops, who had been issued with a 'robust set of Rules of Engagement'.

I admired but did not share Tom's optimism. I was already hearing quite a different story from Mir about collateral damage. Afghan contacts had told him that many innocents were dying. The problem, he said, was not the troops on the ground so much as the Coalition bombers and helicopters flying in their support. Mir was filled with angry gloom. When 1,000lb or 2,000lb bombs are dropped into built-up areas, he reasoned, bystanders were bound to get caught sooner or later. His prediction was tragically accurate. By the end of the year international forces had unintentionally killed at least 320 non-combatants, and Hamid Karzai, the President of Afghanistan, publicly wept as he called on the Coalition to stop 'killing our children'.

Of course, Tom was still acclimatizing at Camp Bastion in July and had yet to see action in the forward areas. It was a relief to learn that he had been assigned a job as a liaison officer, which would no doubt entail some dangerous reconnaissance work but not, his family hoped, the full-on combat of the outstations. His first fortnight in Afghanistan was spent drinking ten litres of water a day – disgustingly warm, he complained, because there were as yet no fridges – and preparing his troop for forthcoming operations. His was a modern mechanized unit that spent long days training and adjusting their vehicles, but some of the camp's off-duty activities sounded weirdly Victorian. 'I have been unable to enthuse the locals with a game of cricket,' Tom wrote. 'For some reason they are wary of the outfield on our pitch. Probably the mine tape is keeping them away! However, Afghan ponies have been found so polo could be introduced. The volleyball with the nurses is also something I feel strongly should be a regular thing! Good morale for the boys.'

I was disquieted by this. I didn't necessarily agree with the fashionable opinion that the Afghan mission was doomed because history was bound to repeat itself. One heard this all the time in London: had Britain learned nothing from her adventures there in the nineteenth century, or, for that matter, from the disastrous Soviet occupation in the 1980s? Pubs and dinner parties were full of armchair critics who spoke with scant knowledge of Afghanistan, and I thought I knew better. Our soldiers were surely more than mere hamsters in the wheel of history. This was not the 1840s. ISAF had a mandate from the United Nations, and was in no way comparable to the Soviet occupiers, whose counter-insurgency was based on a scorched-earth policy rather than winning hearts and minds. The Russians had condoned torture and murder in their time in the country. In the 1980s, 20,000 Afghans were said to have died in jail in Kabul alone. I felt patriotically certain that the British would never become involved in brutality like that.

Even so, the echoes of the past were impossible to ignore. In 1841, during the First Afghan War, a much bigger British force under William Elphinstone set itself up in isolated cantonments not unlike Bastion. Its nucleus was the 44th Regiment of Foot, which, like the 16th Air Assault Brigade from which Tom's battle group was drawn, was once headquartered at Colchester in Essex. The men of the 44th were suffused with the same irrepressible confidence, the same feeling of invincibility based on the certainty of

6

technological superiority. They also tried and failed to persuade the locals to play cricket, just as Tom had. 'They looked on with astonishment at the bowling, batting and fagging out of the English players,' according to one contemporary account, 'but it does not appear that they were ever tempted to lay aside their flowing robes and huge turbans and enter the field as competitors.' Elphinstone's army was, of course, annihilated in one of the greatest defeats the British have ever known.

At the end of July there was a period of worrying silence from Bastion. It could mean only one thing: Tom's troop had been deployed forward. His family and his girlfriend Katie began listening to the news even more avidly than before. We told ourselves that he would be protected from the bullets by the armour of an eight-ton tank. But then, on 1 August, came the worst possible news: a British armoured vehicle had been destroyed at Musa Qala with the loss of three lives. In line with Ministry of Defence (MoD) protocol, the names of the dead were not officially released until the following day. It was two days before we heard from Tom himself. His email was short and businesslike; the jaunty tone of his earlier messages had vanished.

Dear All,

Just writing to let you all know that things here are absolutely fine. We obviously had a pretty terrible 24 hours but everyone has pulled together and worked tirelessly to ensure things run positively.

Much thanks must go to Dad and Katie who seemed to inform everyone and if the situation arises again the same channels of communication will probably be followed.

Lots of love to you all, can't wait to see you all soon, can't come too soon.

Tom

The family's relief at his escape was short-lived. Among those killed was the troop leader, 2nd Lieutenant Ralph Johnson, a twenty-four-year-old South African and a friend of Tom's, which was bad enough; worse was the news that Tom had been ordered to take over the troop. The relative safety of the liaison officer job was no more. Ten days later he was deployed to Sangin, and the sporadic emails from Bastion dried up altogether, for there were no soft email facilities in the outstations. We didn't hear from him again for fifty-two days.

We did, however, see him. On 20 September an ITN news crew was at last permitted to fly into Sangin. The landing site came under attack the moment their Chinook landed. The cameraman dived to the ground, cracking his lens. Dust swirled madly from the rotor blades. Rocket-propelled grenades (RPGs) whooshed past at head height. Paratroopers stood or knelt in the open alongside soldiers of the ANA, the Afghan National Army, and blazed back with their own weapons, the deafening pop-pop-pop confounding the journalists' microphones, as it always did. And there unmistakably in the background was Tom, perched on the turret of a Scimitar, his tall physique bent as though huddling against rain rather than horizontal metal, directing cannon and machine-gun fire at the enemy-infested tree line.

His family were not the only ones who were shocked by the

ferocity of the fighting. This, surely, was a war that was never supposed to happen. Operation Herrick 4,* as the Helmand deployment was called, was supposed to secure economic development and reconstruction in the region. It was, in the terminology of the planners, a 'hearts and minds' operation, not a search-and-destroy one. The intention was to spread the Karzai government's remit into the recalcitrant south of Afghanistan, the Pashtun heartlands and one-time spiritual home of the Taliban – a force that, barring a handful of hardliners, was confidently assessed to have been defeated in 2001.

As late as March 2006, during a visit to a squadron of RAF Harriers stationed at Kandahar, the then Defence Secretary, John Reid, told a reporter that 'if we came for three years here to accomplish our mission and had not fired one shot at the end of it, we would be very happy indeed'. By October, however, the Para-based battle group whose lot it was to launch the campaign had fired more than 480,000 shots. They had also expended 31,000 cannon rounds, 8,600 artillery shells, 7,500 mortars, 1,000 hand grenades and 85 anti-tank missiles – and sixteen British soldiers had been killed as a direct result of enemy action. Given the intensity of the fighting it was astonishing that more had not died. The toll on the other side was unknown but was undoubtedly much higher. The Taliban naturally disputed it, but the British estimated they had killed as many as 700 of their number even by mid-July.†

* Like most major British Army operations, the name was computer-generated, and nothing to do with the seventeenth-century English poet and cleric Robert Herrick.
† The difficulty of collating accurate figures in Afghanistan is notorious. Brigadier John Lorimer, commander during Operation Herrick 6, remarked that trying to extract meaningful statistics from Afghans was 'like speaking one of those African languages that only has three numbers: one, two, and "lots"'.

Reid's remark was not quite the hostage to fortune it was later made out to be. What he also said during that notorious interview, on a crackling uplink between Kandahar and a London BBC studio, was that he expected the mission to be 'complex and dangerous' because 'the terrorists will want to destroy the economy and the legitimate trade and the government that we are helping to build up'. He added that 'if this didn't involve the necessity to use force, we wouldn't send soldiers'. But the media weren't interested in this context. Six months later the MoD's Director of News, James Clark, was still issuing angry clarifications, although by then it was too late: John 'not one shot fired' Reid was already entrenched in the public mind as the man responsible for leading Britain into its fourth Afghan War since the mid-nineteenth century.

The British, officers on the ground conceded, were facing a 'major and highly organized insurgency'. An extra 960 troops were hastily announced on 6 July, amid accusations that the initial deployment of 3,300 – a Task Force that included a battle group of only 650 fighting troops – had never been enough for the job in hand. For the first time in decades, Britain's Armed Forces were now fighting on two fronts at once, in Iraq and Afghanistan, and the signs were that they were struggling to cope. Even General Sir Richard Dannatt thought so, and he was the Chief of the General Staff, the most senior officer in the Army. 'We are running hot, cer-tainly running hot,' he told one newspaper, before adding, 'Can we cope? I pause. I say "just".' In a later interview with the BBC he confirmed his belief that the tempo of current operations was not sustainable. 'I am not a maverick,' he said, 'I am a soldier speaking up for his army. I am just saying, come on, we can't be here for ever at this level . . . I have got an army to look after which is going to be successful in current operations, but I want an army in five years' time and ten years' time. Don't let's break it on this one.'

The theme of military 'overstretch' had been bubbling in the media for some time, and now it boiled over. One by one, a gaggle of ex-generals and other senior figures came forward in the press to agree with the CGS. The whole question of military funding rose to the top of the agenda. The Shadow Defence Secretary, Liam Fox, pointed out that only 2.2 per cent of the national income was being spent on defence – the lowest proportion since 1930. The Helmand Task Force, it was said, was not just undermanned as a consequence of operations in Iraq, but also scandalously under-equipped after decades of under-investment. There were not enough helicopters, ammunition, body armour, radios or night vision goggles, while the troops' vulnerable Snatch Land Rovers were desperately inappropriate for the job, and their rifle grips were melting in the heat.

It was hard to discern the truth of all this from London. The media, initially denied access to the fighting by the MoD, had relied all summer long on unverified evidence gathered from the soldiers at the front, often at second hand via blogs or private emails. Squaddies are famous whingers, which made me suspect that the reports were exaggerated or distorted, a convenient stick for the press to beat the government with. It seemed inconceivable to me that the modern Armed Forces were fighting with equipment that was actually sub-standard. I was wrong, though. As I was to dis-cover, there were many instances in Helmand when they had to do exactly that.

But even in 2006 it was clear that not all was well with the military. Alongside the reports about inadequate equipment were others about low levels of pay, scrofulous housing for soldiers'

families, soaring insurance premiums, and inadequate compensation and healthcare for the wounded. On top of all that, the
chances of getting killed or seriously injured were now higher than
at any time in half a century. No wonder the military had a recruitment and retention problem. In November 2007 the Army was
3,600 short of its required strength of 101,800. Some older soldiers
also blamed the Army's reorganization in the late 1990s, when
dozens of historic regiments were abolished or amalgamated into
faceless new 'super-regiments'. The move had been intended to
improve efficiency but it also greatly weakened the traditional
recruiting system, with its dependence on local and family ties.

In his comments to the press, Dannatt had launched a critical
debate. Who or what was the British Army? What values did it
represent, and what was it really fighting for in Iraq and
Afghanistan? This crisis of identity clearly troubled the CGS – as
well it might, since 'knowing yourself' is one of the foundations of
a successful army, a precept laid out by Sun Tzu in *The Art of War*,
the oldest and best-known military treatise in the world. Dannatt,
a church-going Christian, spoke of the spiritual dimension to
soldiering and worried that Britain's moral compass was spinning.
'I am responsible for the Army, to make sure that its moral compass
is well aligned and that we live by what we believe in,' he told the
Daily Mail on 13 October 2006. 'It is said that we live in a post-
Christian society. I think that is a great shame. The broader
Judaic-Christian tradition has underpinned British society. It
underpins the British Army.'

But did it do that? The General's remark must have surprised
the family of Lance Corporal Jabron Hashmi, twenty-four, a Royal
Signalman from Bordesley Green, Birmingham, who was killed at
Sangin on 1 July. Hashmi, who was born in Peshawar in Pakistan,

was the first British Muslim to die in the prosecution of the War on Terror. According to his devastated family, he had wanted to be a military commander 'ever since he was a little child' and had seen the Afghan posting as 'a chance to build bridges between the East and the West'. Within hours of his death, an extremist British group called Al Ghurabaa' posted a photograph on their website of Hashmi surrounded by flames, labelling him a 'home-grown terrorist'. 'I don't see how any Muslim can be in the British army, not with all the shit that's happening in Muslim countries,' a twenty-five-year-old Muslim in Bordesley Green told one reporter. 'It doesn't make sense. It's not right. Of course it's a tragedy and I feel for his family, but what was he doing over there? He was an Asian dude fighting a white man's war. Basically, we can't be like the *goreh* [white people] and they can't be like us.'

The British Army is neither as Christian nor even as British as it used to be. Hashmi was one of about 330 Muslims serving in the Armed Forces. Of Britain's 99,000 ground troops, 6,600 are now recruited from Commonwealth countries – up from 300 a decade ago. Almost 2,000 of them come from Fiji; there is a particularly high proportion of Fijians in the new Scottish super-regiment, the Royal Regiment of Scotland. The change worried Dannatt so much that he was later reported to be considering limiting the intake of Commonwealth recruits to 10 per cent of the total.*

---

* The press predictably made much of this proposal (see, e.g., *Mail on Sunday*, 1 April 2007, 'Race uproar over Army troop quota'), but missed its real point. This was not about protecting the Army's 'Britishness' so much as finding a way to reduce the ability of foreign governments to influence British security interests. In 2006, for instance, the South African government was considering legislation that would ban its citizens from serving in foreign armies. If such legislation were passed, up to 1,200 South Africans now serving in the British Army could be forced to leave suddenly.

Meanwhile, there was a suspicion throughout the military that neither the British government nor the public fully appreciated the sacrifices that soldiers were being asked to make in Helmand. Dannatt spoke eloquently of a 'military covenant', the compact of trust between the country and its armed forces that he evidently felt was at risk of being breached. Most of the public seemed to know little and to care less about why young Britons were fighting and dying in Afghanistan. The most dismaying example of this came in 2007 when the military hospital at Headley Court, near Epsom in Surrey, applied for planning permission to convert a nearby house into badly needed lodgings for visiting family members. Local residents objected, eighty-three of them, claiming the conversion would 'adversely impact the quiet, peaceful nature of the existing area', and the application was turned down. The objectors' self-interest was widely condemned, and planning permission was eventually granted; but the episode still revealed an unsettling public indifference towards the suffering of the modern military. To the patients across the road, it felt like damning proof of how disconnected the civilian world had become from the fighting in Iraq and Afghanistan.

Headley Court's history underlined the extent to which times had changed. The former home of Walter Cunliffe, the Governor of the Bank of England during World War One, it was bought for the nation in the 1940s with donations by the public in grateful tribute to the injured pilots of the RAF. An Elizabethan mansion set deep in London's commuter belt, and surrounded by eighty-four acres of prime parkland, it was what the MoD liked to call a 'legacy asset' – shorthand, perhaps, for the kind of facility that nowadays they could only dream of acquiring.

'We owe [our soldiers] a great debt of gratitude,' said the new

Defence Secretary Des Browne in an address at Camp Bastion in October 2006, 'and we need to make sure they get all the support they need . . . from those at home.' But what could Browne really do to ensure support among a public who, in Surrey at least, proved to be unprepared even to allow a military hospital some new visitor accommodation? His rhetoric was empty, and many soldiers knew it.

Browne himself did not exactly inspire confidence on his many subsequent visits to the troops in the field. On one occasion at Bastion he was rumoured to have fallen asleep during a briefing. On another he was introduced to a unit fresh back from the front, and who had been specially assembled to meet him, yet he was unable to find anything to say to them. An officer who witnessed it thought it was appalling. 'He didn't ask a question. He was looking down at the floor, kicking stones. It was left to one of the boys to go, "So, er, did you have a good trip out here then, sir?"'

The troops made some allowances for Browne. He was, after all, newly appointed to his role and still coming to terms with the demands of the job. Nevertheless, it was clear how little of his new brief he had really mastered; and with Britain effectively at war on two fronts for the first time in more than half a century, it was unsurprising if many soldiers felt that this was unacceptable in a Secretary of Defence. At Bastion he refused to engage with their questions about equipment, steering them instead towards one of the 'procurement expert' officials accompanying him. Introduced to some Scimitar crews, the minister jabbed a thumb at a pair of 'Sisus' that happened to be parked nearby and asked, 'Are those yours?'* Such stories reflected a widespread perception in the

---

* A Sisu is a six-wheeled, Russian-built armoured car used by ISAF's contigent of Estonians; it looks nothing like a Scimitar, which is tracked.

Army that here was a leader who lacked the necessary stardust, the force of personality required to motivate tired troops engaged in the fight of their lives. A former solicitor from Glasgow with a thick Scots accent and a bureaucrat's manner, Browne's previous government roles had included Work and Pensions, Citizenship and Immigration, and Chief Secretary to the Treasury. His was the curriculum vitae of a box-ticking apparatchik – ambitious and clever, no doubt, but a man nevertheless who had risen to power on the coat-tails of New Labour since becoming an MP only nine years before. No wonder soldiers felt that he was not up to the unique and exacting task of representing an army at war. Could such a man possibly understand the importance and fragility of the 'military covenant'?

If Browne seemed over-promoted, he was also under-supported. At the Labour Party conference at Bournemouth in September 2007, much was made of the fact that he was placed in the back row of ministers seated behind the new Prime Minister, who then proceeded to devote just 126 words to the Armed Forces in his main conference speech – 'one word', as Shadow Defence Secretary Liam Fox observed, 'for every two servicemen or women killed in Iraq and Afghanistan'. Three months earlier, Gordon Brown had actually increased his Defence Secretary's burden by adding Scottish affairs to his ministerial portfolio, allowing the Opposition plausibly to claim that fighting the Taliban was no more important to the Labour leader than battling Alex Salmond and the Scottish National Party.

Soldiers often pointed out that not one member of Brown's Cabinet – or, for that matter, of David Cameron's shadow cabinet – had any first-hand military experience, and that this state of affairs was unprecedented in the 800-year history of Parliament. I asked Peter Merriman, a lieutenant colonel in the Royal Fusiliers, whether he thought that Blair, Brown or anyone in government really understood the meaning of military sacrifice.

'That's a highly political point, isn't it?' he said, after a pause. 'Do you think politicians have ever understood it?'

'Winston Churchill?'

'But that's a generational issue, isn't it? Although I do think there's a very good case to be made for a wider understanding of what the military, particularly now, is actually doing. The nature of the military commitment has changed.'

Dannatt was right: these were the symptoms of a very serious military crisis indeed. If things went on in this vein it seemed perfectly possible that the Army could eventually 'break'. Thanks to Tony Blair's belief in interventionism, Helmand was the fifth time the Armed Forces had been sent to war in a decade. 'It's the man who is the first weapon of war,' warned the retired brigadier and historian Allan Mallinson. 'He can be worn out by misuse and even quicker by overuse.'

I was becoming deeply curious about the personnel who had been ordered to deploy on Herrick 4. What mood were they really in? The answer had vital implications for the future of the British military and, by extension, for the successful prosecution of the War on Terror itself.

From a pure soldiering point of view, the military were understandably proud of their performance in Helmand. Brigadier Ed Butler, the Task Force commander, wrote afterwards of his men's 'unsurpassed achievements that will go down in history as one of the most intense periods of combat for a generation'. Older soldiers who had worried that the 'i-Pod generation' of recruits was not up to the danger and hardship of all-out combat were emphatically silenced. Butler declared himself humbled. In the Queen's New Year's honours list at the end of 2006, seventy-seven people received awards for gallantry and other outstanding service in Afghanistan, including one Victoria Cross.

The majority of the main gallantry awards went to members of the 3rd Battalion, The Parachute Regiment – unsurprisingly, given that 3 Para formed the nucleus of the battle group – but men from many other units were honoured as well, and I found myself more drawn to their stories. The Paras are the attack dogs of the British Army. They are tougher and more rigorously trained by far than the average squaddie, and they join up in the frank antici-pation of a fight. In the exceptional circumstances of Helmand in 2006, however, there simply weren't enough Paras. The shortage of manpower meant that, over and over again, soldiers who had deployed in the expectation of little more exciting than training ANA recruits, guarding Camp Bastion or repairing a vehicle, were thrust into the front line. Artillery men, mechanics, military policemen, a Chinook loadmaster – and, yes, my wife's cousin Tom – were all forced at times to take up a rifle and fight as infantrymen.

Herrick 4 was extraordinary, too, for the reinforcements hastily flown in from the beginning of July 2006. Unlike the Paras, who had months to train for Afghanistan, some of these units were deployed at a few days' notice; in some cases they were given only a few hours. This, it seemed to me, was the true meaning of 'over-stretch'. It was also an example of what Brigadier Butler later described as 'ordinary people doing extraordinary things'. Who were these 'ordinary' people, and what was Herrick 4 like for them? What did it mean for them in psychological terms – and, by extension, for the future of the military? And was this the kind of thing that Dannatt was talking about when he warned that the tempo of current operations could break his beloved British Army?

In the spring of 2007 I began the first of dozens of interviews with the men and women involved, from the earliest planning stages of Herrick 4 to its controversial conclusion, a fragile truce in the district of Musa Qala. Sixteen Air Assault Brigade headquarters in Colchester did not smile on my project to begin with. The Paras, it seemed, had already commissioned their own account of Operation Herrick 4. There was therefore no need for another book on the subject – or so I was told. I countered that my book, by focusing on the non-Para elements of the battle group, would be quite different to theirs. Eventually the MoD agreed, on the strict understanding that I was not to speak to any Para, with the exception of the battle-group commander Lieutenant-Colonel Stuart Tootal. The battle group and all its constituent parts and supporting units had finished their six-month tour in October 2006. It took more than three months to obtain permission to talk to anyone, and by then the relevant troops were scattered. The Gurkhas were mostly in their barracks in Kent, but some were in Brunei. The Fusiliers were mostly in Cyprus, although some were on a training exercise in Jordan. Still others, astonishingly, had already been sent on a second tour to Afghanistan. The Royal Irish were in Inverness, the Household Cavalry in Windsor, the Royal Air Force at Odiham in Hampshire. It took months to track them all down. I met them singly, in pubs, restaurants, railway stations and hospitals across the country, or else in groups on officially sanctioned visits to their barracks at home and abroad.

They were keen to talk, on the whole. Most of them were frankly anxious that their stories should be told. The feeling that the public did not properly appreciate their efforts was a potent one. That, indeed, had been the principal motivation for many of those soldiers who filmed themselves in action and passed their helmet-cam footage to the media. For others, the Helmand experience was still recent enough for talking about it to be cathartic. A few even described to me the most intensely personal act in any fighting man's career: the moment when he is first called upon to take the life of another human being.

What impressed me first and most was how shockingly young they were – not the privates so much, whom I expected to be twenty or so, but the officers in charge of them. Even the company majors were generally in their early thirties. My civilian pre-conception of a major was of an older, fustier figure, like the fictional Major Gowen, perhaps, the character played by the actor Ballard Berkeley in the comedy series *Fawlty Towers*. Gowen, a xenophobic old buffer who was forever enquiring if the bar was open or the newspapers had arrived yet, was about as different as it was possible to be from the dynamic men in charge of the besieged garrisons. Each of these thirty-somethings was responsible for the lives of about a hundred men. The decisions they took were routinely a matter of life or death, and they took them for months on end, using equipment and munitions worth millions of pounds. I could think of few other professions that involved such fearful pressure at so early a stage in life.

Gradually, however, my admiration gave way to something else. Part of it was straightforward anguish at the terrible human cost of so much violence. Mental trauma was often visible beneath the surface bravado, though never so obviously as on a visit to Headley Court military hospital. Ten years ago this establishment contained a mere handful of patients, most of them the victims of sporting accidents. Now the wards are full to bursting with veterans of Iraq and Afghanistan; a new ward has just been completed, increasing the number of beds to 200. I saw young men and even one or two women with one arm, with one leg, with limbs hanging scarred and useless at their sides. There were fretful teenagers with protuberances on their heads the size of croquet balls, or monstrous scars where their bodies had been unzipped by mortars, mines and rockets. The corridors were clogged with their wheelchairs. They shuttled up and down them, bored and petulant, to a flat-roofed fire escape where they were allowed to smoke. Here, some of them showed off their wounds like trophies; others stared out across the parkland, brooding in silence upon their truncated bodies and careers. It was a hellish vision of a generation of soldiers newly blooded, a throwback to Dunkirk, to Flanders, to Florence Nightingale and the Crimea. It is a side of Blair's wars the public are seldom permitted to see.

The more I spoke to the troops, the more convinced I became that the fight in Helmand could and perhaps should have been avoided. I was to become more than a little familiar with the maxim of the nineteenth-century Prussian Field Marshal Helmuth von Moltke that 'no battle plan survives first contact with the enemy'. For apologists for the conflagration it was often their first line of defence. No doubt there was some truth in it, yet I couldn't help wondering quite how we had managed to deviate so far, so fast, from the plan.

The move into southern Afghanistan was no ad hoc decision, but part of a carefully phased international strategy to extend the remit of Nato's ISAF to areas of the country it had yet to reach. Afghanistan's Loya Jirga, or Grand Assembly, had overwhelmingly voted for Hamid Karzai as head of state in June 2002, but three years on, his authority beyond the capital was so limited that he was nicknamed 'the Mayor of Kabul'. The south and east of the country were particularly lawless. ISAF's mission was clear. Without security in the outlying regions there could be no economic development, no law and order, no proper governance. Unless something was done, the entire democratization project in Afghanistan could fail.

The British plan resembled the 'inkspot' strategy devised in the Malaya campaign of the 1950s, the last truly successful counter-insurgency operation conducted by the British. Back then, some 600,000 peasant Chinese were brought in from the countryside and rehoused in heavily defended 'New Villages' complete with schools, clinics and all the other trappings of development. The strategy was designed to drain the swamp of poverty that formed the insurgency's main recruiting ground. The policy had its critics – it was expensive and difficult to implement, and the forced relocation programme had uncomfortable human rights impli-cations – but it did work. The surrender of the guerrilla leader Chin Peng followed, and then independence for Malaya on British rather than Chinese Communist terms.

The idea now was for the military to establish a secure zone in the centre of Helmand between Lashkar Gah (the provincial capital), Gereshk (the second biggest town) and Camp Bastion in the west. The northern limit of the Area of Operations was supposed to be delineated by Highway One, the vital national ring road that crossed the province from west to east. Civilian agencies, the Foreign Office and the Department for International Development (DfID) would then pour into this 'development triangle', as it was later called, bringing money for infrastructure projects, opening schools and supporting small businesses. Lashkar Gah, in particular, would provide what one planner described as a 'gentle beacon' of peace. Once established, the triangle could be slowly pushed out across the region, spreading like an inkspot as neighbouring communities got to hear about the possibilities of a better economic future, and embraced the Karzai government and the foreigners supporting it out of choice rather than coercion.

Something had gone awry, though. The military were fighting in remote market towns far to the north of the development triangle, cut off from Helmand's centre by miles of enemy-controlled desert. This was not an inkspot so much as an ink splatter. Operation Herrick 4, furthermore, had begun as a programme of steady reconstruction, yet by the end of it large parts of the towns the British had garrisoned lay in spectacular ruins. How had that been allowed to happen?

Many of the soldiers I spoke to, even some of the senior officers, had only the haziest idea of what Herrick 4 was supposed to achieve. In this they were no different to most of the British public. Some of them thought the fighting was about poppies, and the need to curtail and control the world's biggest source of opium. Some thought it was about the War on Terror, and conflated the Taliban with al-Qaida in the most general way. Others were closer to the mark when they said it was about policing the world, and bringing democracy and governance to a benighted nation. Uncertainty of purpose was anticipated by Brigadier Butler, who was bothered enough by it to circulate an explanation of what he thought the mission was about to all his commanders at the start of the deployment. 'Everyone should be entirely clear as to why we are here,' he wrote. 'If we fail to deliver a pro-Western Islamic state in the post-9/11 era then I would suggest that the War on Terror will become untenable.' Towards the end of Herrick 4, however, the very phrase 'War on Terror' had been disavowed at the most senior British military levels, on the grounds that it didn't suit the supposedly benign nature of the Afghan mission.

Some within the military were ignorant not just of why they were fighting, but of whom. Even the official name for the enemy kept changing. To start with they were all 'Taliban'. Then they were called 'Anti-Coalition Militia', or ACM, a convenient catch-all for everyone from al-Qaida hardliners and foreign jihadists to disgruntled poppy farmers, co-opted villagers and adventurers looking for a bit of fun. Intelligence officers later began to speak of 'Tier 1' and 'Tier 2' Taliban, in an attempt to distinguish between the committed ideologues who would probably never surrender, and the opportunists who might be persuaded of an alternative. To the soldiers on the ground, though, the distinction usually meant little. The squaddies' nickname for their opponents was 'flip-flops' – which in itself was a mark of the failure of the British plan. There was a discussion about this on arrse.co.uk, the unofficial but immensely popular Army Rumour Service website, and a reliable indicator of rank-and-file opinion. A contributor called 'Dilfor' got the point. 'I think we need to be very careful about how we characterize those we are purporting to help,' he wrote. 'I know this sounds like some God-awful PC nonsense, but in the battle for hearts and minds, the first thing to do is to recognize that these people have hearts and minds too, and not just amusingly silly clothing.'

It was over four years since my last visit to the country, soon after Karzai's election to the presidency, and I knew I was out of touch with what was going on in Pashtun hearts and minds. In February 2007, therefore, I decided to visit Kandahar, Afghanistan's second city and the Taliban's spiritual home.

1

In Kandahar

I flew to Kandahar from Kabul with the UN. My plan was to take advantage of the winter season, when snow prevents troop movements in the high passes and Afghanistan traditionally enjoys a cessation of hostilities. An uneasy calm had indeed returned to the south since the end of Herrick 4 in November 2006. In Kabul, however, there had been indications that the hiatus was coming to an early end this year. In the bar of the Gandamak Lodge, a default location for journalists, there had been rumours of a new Coalition offensive specifically designed to deny the Taliban the chance to regroup. Was I already too late to make this trip?

My plane, a white-painted, propeller-driven Dash-8, was essentially an expensive taxi-service for international aid workers for whom the roads were deemed too dangerous. The main Kabul–Kandahar highway, a distance of 500 kilometres, had recently been repaved at vast expense by the Americans, who judged the project essential to the economic development of the nation. The driving time between the cities had been cut from fifteen hours to four and a half, yet the highway was still little used. Five years after the overthrow of the Taliban, it was considered foolhardy to travel on it past Ghazni, a mere 140 kilometres south of the capital. Beyond that was bandit country.

Despite its being only a twice-weekly service, the flight was only half full. There were two Bengalis, a Japanese man and a Filipino, all clutching laptops. There were two Americans, one of them nodding off over a copy of *The Fragmentation of Afghanistan* by Barnett Rubin. There was an Italian based in Sri Lanka who worked for Handicap International, and two German journalists from *Der Spiegel*. The mood among these displaced foreigners was sombre. Nobody talked much, apart from the pilot, who sounded South African, and the stewardess, whose name was Joyce, from Kenya. 'Have you been to Nairobi?' she beamed as she served fizzy drinks from a trolley, as though we were on a safari tourist flight up the Great Rift Valley. 'You should go some time. It's really a nice place.'

The landscape beneath us was Tolkienesque. Jagged, icing-sugared peaks stretched to the western horizon. Giant, dirty glaciers meandered eastwards, to disgorge on the plains leading to Pakistan. The occasional road or an ice-bound river snaked in between. It took a bird's-eye view like this one to appreciate how truly insurmountable this country's terrain could be. Soon, however, the mountains receded and we were flying over desert, its dun-coloured folds familiar from countless television news bulletins. Out on the ground beyond the starboard wing, the plane's shadow grew larger as we dropped gently towards Kandahar.

Six people got off, three of whom were journalists – confirmation, of a kind, that international aid agency activity in the south was as negligible as the critics claimed. The other passengers were flying on to Herat in the far north-west of the country. A large barrack town had grown up around KAF, as the military called Kandahar Airfield. It covered 400 square kilometres and was home to some 12,000 foreign military personnel. The facilities here were legendary among the troops – they included a Pizza Hut, a Kentucky Fried Chicken, a Subway sandwich shop and a Green Bean Café – but none of this was visible as our little party made its way across the tarmac from the plane. The civilian part of the airport, clean and recently redecorated in pretty blues and yellows, was separate and almost deserted. Only the clatter of passing Black Hawk helicopters betrayed the foreign military presence.

I had arranged for an unmarked car to come out from the hotel to meet me as a precaution. The twenty-five-kilometre road between KAF and Kandahar proper was a well-known 'choke-point', notorious for IEDs (improvised explosive devices) and suicide attacks on patrolling Coalition vehicles. KAF itself still came under attack about once every ten days. Indeed, the first thing I saw was a truck park which had been attacked the previous evening. Five long vehicles, once gaudily painted and tassled with chains of hammered tin in the regional fashion, had been subjected to tremendous and sudden heat. They lay alongside one another like the bag of a big game hunt, their articulated carcasses fused and twisted, their tyres reduced to skeletal strands of woven steel.

They were ex-fuel tankers whose loads had been destined for KAF, and a baleful reminder of the Coalition's vulnerability in this land-locked nation. Everything needed to supply ISAF's enormous military machine had to be brought up from Karachi, 750 kilometres away on the coast of the Arabian Sea. Sabotage was not the only problem. A million dollars' worth of fuel was said simply to have been stolen en route to KAF in the first six weeks of Herrick 4 alone. Now I learned that, for security reasons, fuel deliveries were permitted only between seven and eight o'clock in the morning. The mostly Pakistani truckers who missed this time slot were obliged to park where they could and wait until the following day, presenting an irresistibly soft target for the Taliban.

The drive into town was a quick one. Everyone drove fast on this stretch of road. We passed a lazily manned police checkpoint, and then a bombed-out mosque complex, its elegant dome shattered and open to the elements. This was where al-Qaida fighters had made a last stand late in 2001. Three camels ambled in the foreground. There was a crazily tilted Russian tank, burned out a quarter of a century ago, its gun barrel still pointing at the sky. Here and there on the horizon, weird saw-toothed mountains rose sheer out of the desert. We crested a hill and suddenly the city was spread before us – a low-rise, mud-coloured conurbation, semi-obscured by a pall of pollution.

For a city with such a menacing reputation, Kandahar is not a big place. Its population in 2002 was put at a mere 316,000. Nor is it an ancient city, at least by Afghan standards: its modern foundations were laid only in the 1760s. But to the Durrani Pashtuns, the leading Pashtun group in Afghanistan, it is the centre of the world. This was the headquarters both of the Taliban and of al-Qaida before 2001. It was the last place to fall when the Americans invaded, as well as the prize the insurgents now sought to recapture most of all. At Kandahar's spiritual centre, just north of a series of bazaars once famous for their fruit, lies the octagonal mausoleum of Ahmad Shah Durrani, the eighteenth-century ruler who made Kandahar the capital of Afghanistan. Next to it is the Shrine of the Cloak of the Prophet, a relic invested with quasi-supernatural powers that is almost never put on public display. Shah Amanullah brought it out in 1929 in an attempt to rally the tribes. Mullah Omar did the same thing in 1996, when he declared himself the Supreme Prince of Islam and set himself on the present collision course with the West.

The bazaars looked busy and normal as we inched our way to the hotel through the city's milling and flowing – the usual urban Afghan scene of beggars and hawkers, mud and rubbish and rickety traffic. This was not, however, a good time for tourism. Most Westerners here were Canadian soldiers, and even they were seldom seen. Their heavily fortified base on the edge of town was a former fruit-canning factory – the perfect symbol of how the priorities of war had overtaken those of development and peace. When they did venture out on patrol they did so in armoured vehicles with all the hatches down, as sealed off from the populace they had been sent to safeguard as it was possible to be. The urge to protect themselves was understandable. Even in my few days in Kandahar there were six assassination attempts, some of them successful, on local politicians and mullahs in and around the city. There were also two suicide attacks, one against the Canadians, the other against some local security guards hired to accompany a supply convoy bound for Bastion. The Canadians were unscathed, but six Afghans died in the second attack, in which explosives were hidden in a motorcycle. The insurgents were here all right, hidden among the population. The normality of the bazaars was an illusion. Kandahar was living in constant expectation of sudden and disastrous violence.

I was glad to reach the Hotel Continental. The veranda-fronted rooms were arranged around a patch of lawn bounded by rose-beds and a pair of swing seats, although it was too early in the year to enjoy these things: the lawn was mostly mud, and the flowerless rose bushes stank heavily of manure, which I suspected was human in origin. It was cold when I arrived, and it grew colder the following day when heavy rain set in.

I was not alone at the hotel. The Germans from *Der Spiegel* had checked in, as had James Bays, the Kabul-based correspondent for al-Jazeera television, along with his fixer from Kabul and a Turkmen cameraman. It seemed a certainty that we were all being closely watched. I was asked more than once what I was doing in Kandahar by the under-employed hotel staff. There seemed to be dozens of these retainers, lounging around in the lobby, watching lurid Bollywood videos or playing raucous games of cards on the dining-room floor. The card-players scattered unnervingly at my approach, sweeping up their cards and melting silently into the interior of the hotel, deferentially switching the Bollywood channel over to BBC World as they went.

Bays was an energetic and experienced newsman, and kind enough to let me tag along with his crew as they went about their work in the city. I was grateful for the sense of security in numbers, however illusory this might have been. We made quite a party in the evenings, downing plates of chicken and rice in the dining-room, swapping notes and the news. Things were beginning to heat up in Helmand. Assadullah Wafa, the new governor, had announced that 800 fighters had crossed the border from Pakistan, although the report could not be verified. Bays was considering a trip to Helmand to try to establish what was really going on. In the meantime he was working on a story about Kandahar's newly recruited police force, a part of the ANP, the Afghan National Police. He had arranged to go out on a routine patrol with them, and I went along for the ride.

The ANP story was an important one for the future of Afghanistan. Across the south they had an unsavoury reputation for extorting money from road users at unofficial vehicle checkpoints. So endemic was the problem that in early 2007, following the assassination in his home of a local import-export magnate, the region's trucking companies briefly went on strike. This mattered. Never mind that the Coalition's military effort was scarily dependent on the trucking trade to bring in heavy supplies from Karachi; banditry by uniformed men represented a public relations catastrophe that threatened to wreck ISAF's mission altogether.

Public 'security' was at the heart of the myth about the Taliban's creation. The reappearance of highwaymen between Kandahar and the Pakistani border was particularly disastrous, for this was the exact stretch of road on which the Taliban had first appeared in 1994, pledging to rid the province of the freelance bandits then blighting ordinary farmers' lives. In those days it was hardly possible to drive a mile without encountering a chain across the road, manned by some Kalashnikov-toting militiaman demanding money. Farmers were unable to get their crops to market, ordinary trade was paralysed and the local economy was stalled. The Taliban put a stop to the thievery by the swift and sometimes instantaneous application of sharia law. However harsh, hanging or amputation was also popular with many people. And now, banditry was creeping back, and being practised by the very policemen responsible for preventing it – policemen, moreover, who were supported, trained and equipped by the international community.

I was later to meet a member of the Household Cavalry Regiment (HCR) who described how, early in Herrick 4, his patrol of Scimitars had come across an ANP checkpoint not far from

Camp Bastion. The policemen manning it were wearing civilian clothes, but on the HCR's approach they were spotted hurriedly putting their uniforms on again; they had been stopping vehicles and extorting money from the drivers while pretending to be bandits. The bitter symbolism of the return to lawlessness was not lost on any Afghan. It was a propaganda coup for the Taliban and a dreadful case of *plus ça change*, while the damage by association to the British Army's reputation was another blow to the campaign for hearts and minds.

We were picked up by three open-backed trucks packed with gun-toting policemen, and we lurched off to a large roundabout on the west side of town, the main entry point into Kandahar from the Helmand badlands beyond. The men all leapt out, forming a ring around the junction to secure it, while others set about stopping and searching incoming vehicles for illicit weapons. The air grew heavy with diesel fumes as a long tail-back built up. Cars and rickshaws hooted impatiently, trying to queue-jump the idling trucks and buses. Bays and his crew began to film the tumult, while I picked my way across the squelching ground to chat to the policemen on the perimeter.

The bored young men I found there were evidently not local. Most of them had the high cheekbones and clean-shaven features of Tajiks and Uzbeks from the north. They wore uniform, which was something: blue fatigues, a white shoulder-cord that looped to the right breast-pocket, grubby white puttees over muddy black boots. They were pleased to be photographed – the presence of a clutch of Western journalists provided welcome relief from a normal dull day – and I detected at least some *esprit de corps* in the way they posed for my camera, legs apart and shoulders back, a studiedly mean expression on their faces as they brandished their weapons.

Yet there was no hiding their lack of discipline. They were the beneficiaries of a German-run training programme, but there was nothing Teutonic about their perfunctory search technique. Their guns were festooned with stickers. Some of their Western-supplied uniforms were so ill-fitting that they looked borrowed. The future security of the country depended on such people, but it looked to me as though they were really only playing at being policemen. I sensed that it would be an easy thing for them to shed their new clothes and return to the distant villages they had come from. Dozens of uniformed police had been killed by the Taliban the previous year. Just by mounting a routine checkpoint at the edge of the city the police were undoubtedly making targets of themselves. President Bush had recently requested an extra $8 billion from Congress to fund Afghanistan's new security forces, but for now these men were paid a pittance, even on the irregular occasions when their pay-packets arrived: about $70 a month for a job that involved both hardship and great personal danger. Was it any surprise if some of their number were guilty of bribe-taking and extortion?

About halfway through the day's patrol, which moved to another roundabout when the tail-back at the first one became unmanageable, the big boss himself, the Chief of Police, General Ismatullah Alizai, turned up to see how things were going. He was a portly man of about fifty, taller than the average Afghan, who exuded confidence and authority in his neat grey serge uniform and military-style webbing. Unlike most of his officers he was a local Pashtun. He was clean-shaven apart from a neat moustache – the mark of a functionary trained by the Communists in the 1980s. His men obviously liked him, and I could see why. He stood in the middle of the roundabout like a proud, benevolent uncle, his belly out and his hands on his hips, surveying his men with twinkling eyes. The courage his sortie from headquarters required was not in question. As a prominent emissary of central government, Kandahar's Chief of Police was a prize target for the insurgency. Indeed, Alizai's predecessor, Akrem Khakrezwal, was killed by a suicide bomb in June 2005.* Alizai was new in his job – unsurprisingly, it had taken some time to find a replacement for Khakrezwal – and he looked terribly vulnerable out on the street.

'Dangerous?' he said, shouting above the noise of the traffic, his black eyebrows beetling. 'Yes, this is dangerous. But I couldn't do my job if I didn't have courage.'

'Rather you than me,' I said.

'But you're here too, aren't you?' He smiled.

Later, when the patrol was over, the stop-and-search operation having drawn a total blank, I followed Alizai back to police head-quarters to speak to him alone. The walls by the sandbagged entrance were gouged by shrapnel splash – the result, according to the guards there, of another recent suicide bomb. His office, deep inside the compound, was lined with sofas in the usual way, although these ones were made of leather. There were rich red carpets, a neat row of glitzy glass coffee-tables, a big map of Kandahar, a framed picture of Hamid Karzai, huge sprays of plastic roses arranged in vases the size of standard lamps, and a fake miniature apple tree. The smell of chemical air-freshener was almost overpowering. I spied the spray-can responsible later on, a product called *Lotion Anity* that claimed to come from Paris. The other oddity was the pile of books on the General's enormous desk.

* For a full account of this tragic episode, see Sarah Chayes's excellent *The Punishment of Virtue* (Portobello Books, 2006).

Sandwiched between two hefty treatises on global drugs policy was a copy, in English, of *Revolt in the Desert*, T. E. Lawrence's 1927 abridgement of *Seven Pillars of Wisdom*.

'Are you reading that?' I asked, surprised.

The General had not so far revealed any ability to speak English; until now we had communicated entirely through the al-Jazeera crew's interpreter.

'With some help . . . I am trying,' he replied, shyly.

He threw himself down in the armchair next to me, the over-stuffed cushions exhaling in protest, and examined me over a pair of half-moon spectacles which made him look more avuncular than ever.

His biggest problem, he confirmed, was corruption within his force. 'Bribery and extortion are habitual to the people here, and policemen are no different.' He sighed. 'It is in their bones. There are people who would extort their own mothers for money.' He was cracking down on it, though. His conviction that the matter was too important to be allowed to fester sounded genuine. 'The police are vital to the health of the nation. They are like the soul of the body: they must be clean, or the country will go to hell. I've told my men that if I catch them taking bribes, I'll expose them.' He slapped the arm of his chair for emphasis and added, 'I'll put them on TV.'

'Why don't you just pay them better? Wouldn't that remove the temptation to abuse their positions?'

'It would. And they will get more money soon, insha'allah. Reform is in progress. We are waiting for orders from Kabul.'

His other problem was the lack of training. Things were slowly getting better, he said, but as things stood, some of his men had received as little as four weeks' instruction before being let loose on

Kandahar's streets. 'Keeping the peace here is complicated,' he told me quietly. 'Four weeks' training isn't really enough.'

That was an understatement. Kandahar was probably the most unstable city in one of the most over-armed nations in the world. Decades of war had left Afghanistan flooded with guns and ammunition – according to one estimate* there were more than 720 million rounds at large in the country for Kalashnikovs alone – and suicide bombs had been going off in Kandahar province at the rate of five a week for the last four months.

General Alizai's courage and quiet dedication to duty were impressive, yet I left his office feeling dismayed by the West's lack-lustre support for what he was trying to do. The foreigners had had five years to set Afghanistan on the right path, and spent billions. Yet legislation designed to bolster law and order was still pending in Kabul, and police training programmes had clearly been done on the cheap. It was baffling how such an opportunity could have been so badly squandered. The reforms now in progress seemed too little, too late, the Taliban come-back perhaps no more than our just deserts.

The following day I telephoned the local offices of the Senlis Council, a new non-governmental organization (NGO) which operated outside the established aid community in Afghanistan. Perhaps as a consequence they were not much liked in Kabul; 'amateur' and 'maverick' were two of the more polite terms I had heard used to describe them. Their solution to the opium problem was certainly unorthodox. They were lobbying, vigorously and

* by the HALO Trust, the British mine clearance organization. Since starting operations in 1988 in Afghanistan, HALO (Hazardous Areas Life-Support Organization) have cleared more than 570,000 mines and disposed of 43.7 million bullets.

quite effectively, for the entire poppy harvest to be channelled into the licit manufacture of medical morphine, of which, they claimed, there was a global shortage.

Senlis had agreed to take me to a poppy farm. I was picked up from the hotel by Akhtar, the mild-mannered station chief, and his driver, Izzatullah, who turned out to be the nephew of Akrem Khakrezwal, the assassinated Chief of Police. Akhtar wore a shiny black and blue leather motorcycle jacket with the word 'Technoiogy', deliciously misspelled, picked out in bold white letters across its back. Both men, I couldn't help noticing, were packing a Makarov – the small, heavy, standard-issue service pistol used by the Soviets for more than forty years.

'I get scared when I leave Kandahar,' Akhtar said simply.

It was then that I found out where we were going: Arghandab. I knew of this fertile valley region, a few miles north of the city. It took its name from the river that ran through it, a tributary of the Helmand. It was the home territory of the powerful Alokozai tribe, led by Mullah Naqib, to whom the Taliban had handed control of Kandahar when they retreated in 2001 – although he subsequently lost it again to an American-backed rival.

Despite his earlier accommodation with the Taliban, Naqib was no great believer in their cause but a professed supporter of Hamid Karzai and the central government, a rare moderate who advocated reconciliation with the insurgents instead of military suppression. He was still a political force in the province, and it was significant that our driver was related to the murdered police chief Khakrezwal, who had been one of Naqib's allies. It meant that I was effectively travelling under Alokozai patronage, which in Arghandab was better than any life insurance policy. I was beginning to appreciate the encompassing nature of the Pashtun tribal system. Its reach extended even to the breakfast table in my hotel, which was adorned each morning by a yellow box of teabags labelled 'Alokozai Tea', a product manufactured in Dubai by an enterprising tribesman under the slogan 'Celebrate the Winning Taste!'.

The road to Arghandab traversed an enormous cemetery. It was a bleak and alien spot, devoid of the tranquil greenery of a country churchyard at home. Many of the graves were marked by tattered scraps of black or green cloth on poles of cane which bent and quivered like aerials in the sharp wind. In Afghanistan, such flags are reserved for those who have died violently in the name of Islam. Here and there a widow hunkered by the remains of a loved one, living blobs of pleated blue who pulled their burkas closer against the cold. I watched a gust throw up a mini-tornado of dirt and rubbish – a *djinn*, as the superstitious locals called it. Off to the right was a concentration of flags and rough white stones with more mourners around them than elsewhere: the last resting place, Akhtar said, of several dozen Arab al-Qaida fighters who died in 2001. To the embarrassment of the authorities, who tried to prevent it, the spot had become a popular shrine. Whatever the locals thought of bin Laden's politics, the magic of holy martyrdom was not to be denied. The people were credulous, and tended the Arab graves with loving care. They even licked salt scraped from the earth above the corpses, seeking proximity to Allah by primitive osmosis.

The road rose gently towards a narrow pass between two steep outcrops of rock. Just before the pass was another famous land-mark of the old regime: the former compound of Mullah Omar himself. Omar had survived a direct hit from an American bomb here by covering his roof with seven metres of earth, rubble and tyres. With exquisite irony the ex-*Führerbunker* was now in use as the southern headquarters of the US Special Forces, and just as off-limits to the public as it ever was. The construction workers who reinforced it for Omar were said to have been diverted from a giant new mosque, the size of a city block, which he had once ordered for the centre of Kandahar. That project was never finished; I had seen the building site the day before, with its cranes standing idle, and ugly clumps of rusting reinforcing rods protruding from its naked concrete arches. No one knew what to do with this eyesore. To pull it down would be just as provocative as finishing it. Kandahar was full of such uneasy symbols of transition.

There was yet more symbolism around the corner as we topped the pass and the Arghandab valley came into view. On 12 January 1842, a British force of 3,500 met an Afghan one of perhaps 20,000 in this place, and routed them. The regiment who led the attack, the 40th Queen's Lancashires, was led by Major General William Nott (an ancestor of John Nott, Britain's Secretary of Defence at the time of the Falklands War), who marched out from Kandahar to meet the enemy along this very road. 'As we cleared the pass,' wrote Captain John Martin Bladen Neill of the 40th, 'a most beautiful spectacle presented itself. The sun gleamed brightly on a forest of sabres, and the whole valley glittered with the pomp of war.'

The battle was not a long one. The enemy, led by a Ghilzai chief called Akhtar Mohammed Khan, took up a position beyond a swamp, which the British assaulted frontally. 'The infantry columns were directed to advance, and proceeding slowly and steadily through the swamp up to our knees in mud, we neared the enemy's position, who welcomed us with a heavy, but fortunately for us exceedingly ineffectual fire. Their line began to waver as we approached, and when at length the bayonets were brought to the charge, and the British cheer struck upon their astonished ears, they fell back, broke, and retreated in complete disorder across the plain.'

Nott's was not the only British victory in this valley. In its own way, Arghandab was as significant a British battlefield as Agincourt or Waterloo. In 1880, following an exhausting – and, in Victorian times, legendary – three-week summertime march from Kabul, a force of 11,000 under Lieutenant General Sir Frederick Roberts defeated the army of Ayub Khan, who had earlier beaten the British at Maiwand, forty miles to the west. It was the last and decisive encounter of the Second Afghan War. British and Indian casualties amounted to 248 killed and wounded, against an estimated 2,500 on the Afghan side.

The valley was empty of armies now – at least the visible kind – but otherwise the view was unchanged. A pretty patchwork of ploughed fields and mud-walled orchards, neatly separated by avenues of trees, stretched for miles across a rolling plain. The line of the river was discernible in the middle-distance, with mountains beyond beneath a leaden sky. This land was richly irrigated, the soil thick and loamy. You could tell that in the summer the place would resemble a garden paradise.

We drove a short way to the local police station, the centre of municipal authority, to pay a courtesy visit to the chief, Hajji Ismarai. Senlis was on good terms with him; that winter, the NGO had donated fifty blankets to his village. The station was a dismal, echoing place. Most of the windows had no glass, and pools of water had collected on the rough concrete floors. We found Hajji Ismarai in his office at the end of a lightless corridor. The room contained a safe, a single-bar electric heater and an outsized double-bed with a mirrored headboard. The only window had been coated in red paint. He sat in blood-coloured gloom in the far corner with a colleague, huddled beneath a large, pink-edged rug decorated with flowers. He welcomed the three of us in, turning up one corner of his rug and inviting us to join him (an offer we politely but unanimously refused).

Ismarai looked embattled, and with some reason. He had a serious Taliban problem. He sent out his seven-year-old son to fetch us something to eat and began to explain how, the previous autumn, eighteen local men had volunteered for the insurgency in the firm belief that the government would fall within two months. They had fought ISAF for three weeks in the nearby districts of Panjwayi and Pashmul, but had been soundly defeated by the Americans and Canadians during Operation Medusa. They were now back in their homes, where a neighbour had recently spotted one of them burying anti-tank mines in his garden for future use. Ismarai promptly arrested this man and two others, and was 'investigating' the rest of the troop. His difficulty was that the Alokozai tribal elders, Mullah Naqib included, were in favour of reconciliation with the Taliban, and had ordered Ismarai to release the arrested men.

'But how can I release them?' he sighed. 'They could make a lot of trouble for me. I'm appealing to Naqib to see sense.'*

He wasn't exaggerating the threat. The previous year, the local headmaster had been assassinated in a nearby bazaar. 'He was out

---

* Mullah Naqib died – of natural causes – in October 2007. Within weeks, Taliban forces exploited the resulting power vacuum by sweeping into Arghandab and occupying several villages; they headquartered themselves in Naqib's house for maximum psychological effect. It took a concerted effort by Canadian forces to push the Taliban back again.

on a walk with the young children,' Ismarai told us, nodding at his son, who had returned with some oranges. 'You don't kill people in front of children. That's not a part of our culture. They have no mercy or decency.'

Ismarai himself had been targeted the previous year, twice. By way of proof he produced a small roll of photographs from beneath his blanket and tossed it to us across the room. The pictures were close-ups of a bearded young man laid out on a floor, clearly dead. Everyone whistled in fascinated horror as they were passed around. One of the dead man's arms was twisted back at an unnatural angle, and his face and *shalwar qamiz* were caked in congealed blood.

'I never wanted to be a policeman, you know,' Ismarai muttered. 'I'm a farmer by nature, like my father and grandfather before me. I really just want to go back to the land.'

The dead man was a would-be suicide bomber. No one knew who he was or where he had come from. Ismarai recounted how, the previous summer, he had been picnicking with friends at a nearby shrine, one of the *zyarats* dedicated to local saints that dot the country. This one, commemorating a fifteenth-century holy man called Baba Wali, had been a popular tourist-spot in happier times, with its lovely views and shaded terraces of pomegranates. The bomber had leapt on them from an outcrop of rock above shouting 'Allahu Akbar!' but his bomb had misfired. It was still visible in one of the photographs: two clear plastic bags of explosive taped to his chest and back, connected by wires to a detonator on his hip. Ismarai wrestled with his attacker, overpowering him. But as a bodyguard rushed to help, the bomber reached for his hip again, revealing four hand-grenades. He succeeded in pulling the pin on one of them, severely injuring himself and the bodyguard, before a second bodyguard arrived and shot the bomber through the head. No wonder Ismarai was hiding beneath a blanket.

'We never used to have suicide bombers in Afghanistan,' Izzatullah the driver muttered. 'First there was Massoud. Then there was my uncle. Nowadays they've got training camps for them in Pakistan. Everything has changed.'

His claim was not quite true – suicide bombs were used occasionally against Soviet targets in the 1980s – but what certainly had changed was the frequency of them. In the preceding two years, 'not-so-smart bombs', as a Canadian officer I met called them, had become routine.

The formalities over, Ismarai assigned us an armed guard, and his deputy led us out to a large and muddy field to meet some farmers. It was late afternoon by now, and the wind blasting across the open ground had turned icy. Despite this the farmers, their faces cracked and leathery from a lifetime out of doors, were work-ing shoeless in the freezing slime. A dozen of them quickly gathered round, curious and happy to talk. The field they were working on was for wheat, but they grew many other things in the orchards and meadows near by: apples, plums, peaches, pomegranates, melons – and poppies.

The farmers' attitude to opium was ambivalent. They were growing poppies, they said, because nothing else they grew was anything like as valuable. On the other hand they were growing less of them this year because in 2006 government soldiers had come to Arghandab and eradicated their crop. 'We were promised compensation but so far we have received nothing at all,' one said. In 2007 they were hedging their bets. One said he hoped the government might simply overlook Arghandab this time – which, actually, was perfectly possible, since the authorities could not hope to eradicate everywhere. Hajji Ismarai had echoed this position earlier. 'If I'm ordered to eradicate this year, I will obey,' he told me with bitter sarcasm, 'but I might just be a little bit late in carrying out the instruction.' Arghandab's loyalty to the central government was clearly not cast in iron.

'The Taliban have protected poppy-growers,' I said to the farmers. 'Aren't the people around here tempted to turn to them?'

They shook their heads vehemently. 'No one wants the Taliban around here.'

'What about in other districts?'

'I'm sure, if you went over those mountains there,' said the lead farmer, nodding to the south, 'you'd find some Taliban supporters.'

'Or over there,' said another, pointing in the opposite direction.

'But not here?'

'Definitely not here,' they all agreed.

'But if you support the government, why are you still growing poppies?'

They looked around at one another as if my question was daft.

'Of course we'd prefer not to grow it,' came the answer, 'but we are poor and have to feed our families. What else can we do? We have received no help from anyone these last five years.'

'But ... don't you believe that it is against Islam to grow it?'

This, for some reason, prompted uproarious laughter.

'Allah sees into our hearts,' they said eventually. 'He knows that we are not evil, and that we do this only so that our families can eat.'

'But you do know what opium addiction does to people, don't you?'

They knew all right. Lurking at the back of the crowd was a teenager dressed in dirty brown with a Kalashnikov over his shoulder. The spokesman farmer reached back and pulled him towards me.

'This boy is from Sangin. He used to be an addict. When I found him he was a crazy man,' he said. 'He couldn't talk. He didn't eat. He was going to die, so I rescued him and brought him here. He's fine now.'

I smiled at the teenager, who stared back with eyes as brown and dull as his clothes. I suspected he was a bit simple, or that the drug had caused some permanent damage to his brain.

'We're sorry if opium causes sadness for people, but we don't make them eat it or smoke it,' the farmer said with a final shake of his head. 'Besides, it's not us who turn it into heroin.'

It was hard to make sense of the farmers' words. They could see no contradiction in rescuing an opium addict and bringing him to work on a poppy farm. I had encountered this kind of illogical thinking many times before in Afghanistan, and suddenly I pitied the British Army and their mission to win such hearts and minds. The culture gap was hilariously wide. But the farmers also saddened me, because there really was nothing benign about the poppy business. The rescued junkie teenager was a reminder that opium was harming Afghans as well as Westerners. The old thinking about the drug – that it is a foreign vice and therefore a foreigner's problem, or else a form of Islamic revenge on the decadent West – no longer holds true. According to the UN's Office on Drugs and Crime, some 150,000 Afghans are addicted to opium, with a further 50,000 hooked on heroin, and the numbers are climbing dramatically. Some experts reckon that as much as 5 per cent of the country's total production goes to supply domestic demand. Afghanistan was a narco-state in the making, with all the violent suffering that this was bound to entail.

I was reminded of that by the deputy police chief, who led me away from the field to a mud-walled plot across the track for a closer look at Arghandab's poppy crop. There wasn't much to see: harvest time was months away, and the plants were no more than tiny green shoots, barely out of the ground. We perched ourselves on a slippery furrow, where he recalled how he had been attacked the previous year while overseeing the eradication.

'Look,' he said, opening his shirt to the glacial wind. 'This could happen to me again this year, you see?'

I did see: his stomach and one arm were covered by a livid and barely healed scar caused by shrapnel from a grenade.

'Who did that to you? The Taliban?'

'I don't know.' The deputy shrugged in the Afghan way, without rancour, serenely resigned to his fate. 'In any case, who are the Taliban?'

It was a question asked just as often by the British troops who had to fight them in the summer of 2006.

2

Aya Gurkhali!

Of the many stories I had heard about Herrick 4, the one that intrigued me first and most was what happened at Now Zad, a market town a hundred miles north-west of Kandahar and the most isolated of all the outstations garrisoned by the British. From June to November 2006, a platoon of Gurkhas and then a company of Royal Fusiliers were fiercely besieged in the police compound there, firing tens of thousands of rounds and killing hundreds of their attackers. Unlike the siege at Sangin, the extraordinary fighting at Now Zad went largely unreported. No newspaper journalist or TV crew ever made it to the town, and no gallantry medals were awarded to the men who had held it. When I returned to Britain, therefore, and finally reached an agreement with the MoD under which I could speak to their employees, among the first things I did was to contact Major Dan Rex of the Royal Gurkha Regiment.

It was a warm day, the first of the spring, when I went to see him and his men, six months after their return from Afghanistan and a world away from the din and confusion of battle. Their barracks, named after Sir John Moore, the hero of Wellington's Peninsular campaign, were perched high on a woody cliff above a glittering sea just outside Folkestone in Kent. The regimental band was at practice; the sound of trumpets and even bagpipes spilled from the open windows of rehearsal rooms and was carried away on the salty breeze. The men were just back from Easter leave. I was reminded disconcertingly of an English boarding school, for the Nepalese are a short race, and there was a distinctly headmasterly air about their tall and upright company major as his men clustered about him, fresh and eager to please.

The Gurkhas are still officered by the British, just as they were in the days of Empire – they first fought for the Crown in 1815 – and something of that colonial relationship survives in the respect the men pay to their *washi*, as they called Rex. There is something colonial, too, in the continuing obligation for officers to learn Gurkhali. Each year, a small team of officers travels to Nepal to select new recruits. Joining up remains as highly regarded among the Nepalese as it was in the nineteenth century: in the year that Rex went, a remarkable 57,000 of them applied for 153 places. As he pointed out with pride, his regiment is the only one in the Army that is always fully manned.

Dan Rex was thirty-four. Commissioned in 1993, he had served in Bosnia, Kosovo and Sierra Leone, although nothing, he said, could have prepared him for Now Zad. An NCO from another regiment told me later that the experience had aged Rex, and swore that the grey on his temples was new. His reasons for joining the Gurkhas in the first place were frankly romantic. His father, now in his eighties, had been in the Indian Army. His great-grandfather, Tom Longstaff, was a famous naturalist and mountaineer who in 1907 had taken part in a record-breaking ascent of Trisul, a Himalayan mountain over 7,000 metres high. He made his family's connection to the days of Empire quite explicit; 'Victorian' was an adjective he readily applied not just to his father but to himself, too. At one point he even compared himself to Sir Louis Cavignari, Britain's emissary to Kabul in 1879, whose murder by a mob after a heroic Residency defence was a *casus belli* of the Second Afghan War.

His company, 'D' Coy, was never supposed to be in a real fight. When they began to deploy in April 2006 they were told to expect nothing more arduous than guard duty at Camp Bastion. Within weeks, however, the humdrum mission they had prepared for had turned into the regiment's fiercest action since Borneo in 1965. Military control of Helmand passed from the Americans to the British with the formal launch of Herrick 4 on 1 May. Two weeks later came the fateful decision to occupy the district centres in the north. It was clear to everyone that the 650-strong battle group wasn't nearly large enough to hold down an area that was roughly the size of Wales. The Paras could do it for a while, no doubt, but what would happen when they needed to be relieved? It was an open secret at Bastion that a request for additional troops had been made, but these had yet to arrive, and they would need time to acclimatize and prepare when they did. In the meantime the only reinforcements available were the battle group's supporting units, such as the Gurkhas.

Sure enough, on 2 June a platoon commanded by Lieutenant Paul Hollingshead, a twenty-four-year-old from Merseyside, was ordered forward to help relieve the Para garrison at Now Zad. Two days later, Hollingshead's men took part in Herrick 4's first 'deliberate op', Operation Mutay, an assault on a Taliban arms cache in the woods just to the east of the town. The Paras who dropped on to the target by Chinook met far fiercer resistance than expected. No arms cache was found, no senior enemy commander was captured, and the entire force was obliged to fight all the way back to the safety of the garrison compound. The British had severely underestimated the guerrilla skills, strength and determination of their enemy, and it was a miracle that none of them was killed.

Now Zad lay on a dusty plain between two mountain ranges at the southern end of the Hindu Kush. Its heart was the bazaar, a single tarmac road lined with metal-shuttered shops off which countless narrow alleyways led into a maze of low mud-brick houses and the occasional high-walled compound. The town was the economic centre for a sprawling district of some 150 villages, although it was often hard in rural Afghanistan to know quite how many people called the place home. In 2002, the year of the last UN survey, there were an estimated 50,000 people in the district, with perhaps 7,000 in Now Zad itself, although even the UN treated these figures with caution. A traditionally itinerant people had been forced to move about even more than usual by years of war.

The community was solidly Pashtun and characteristically close-knit. Civic power was wielded, as was customary, by a *shura*, a council of elders drawn from the tribes that dominated the district: the Alokozais, Barakzais, Noorzais, Alizais and Sahagzais. In the weeks to come, the Gurkhas were to learn a great deal about the complex local politics of this place. Here as elsewhere, the traditional power structures were being challenged by the mullahs of the Taliban. The district had been one of their regime's noted strongholds when it was in power in the 1990s, and now they were back. Before the summer was out, the Gurkhas would have an intimate knowledge of the idiosyncrasies of the mullahs, too – their fighting capabilities, their ideological convictions, the loyalties of their troops.

Now Zad means 'New Born' in Persian – a name worthy of the pioneers of the American Wild West, although its inhabitants had little cause for such optimism now. The community had been neglected for years by central government. There was one secondary school, with nineteen untrained teachers and 1,200 pupils, all of them male. There was one hospital, with only twelve beds, and one private health clinic. Malaria and typhoid were common, and the hospital was always short of medicine.

Worst of all was that, from 2000, Helmand had been devastated by drought, the effects of which were compounded by the disrepair of the province's fifty-year-old irrigation system. Around Now Zad, it was estimated, the area of cultivable land had shrunk from over 200,000 acres to 12,000 in only three years. Some 80 per cent of the district's residents were farmers, which naturally intensified the drought's socio-economic impact. Water shortage was the nub of Helmand's troubles, and ultimately the Taliban's best recruiting sergeant. It created strife between rival tribes as they competed for diminishing resources. It exacerbated poverty, and resentment against the politicians in Kabul who did nothing to alleviate it. And it motivated farmers to maximize profits on farms of diminishing size and faltering efficiency by growing valuable poppies instead of the wheat, maize, okra, onions, turnips, pomegranates, almonds, apples, apricots and tomatoes for which the region was once famous.

In 2006, according to the UN, Afghanistan produced 92 per cent of the world's opium; Helmand, where poppy production rose by 169 per cent between 2005 and 2006, was responsible for almost half of it. About 380,000 Helmandis, a third of the province's population, are now dependent on poppies for a living. The province is on the way to becoming the world's biggest drugs supplier, cultivating more drugs than entire countries such as Burma, Morocco and even Colombia. Now Zad was a major cog in the new narco-economy, with all the crime, corruption and human misery that the drug trade brought in its wake.

The British were garrisoned in the town's police headquarters at the southern end of the main bazaar – a square, mud-walled compound, 100 by 120 metres. An office building stood at its centre, with a mosque, a prison and some limited accommodation space ranged around it. There were storerooms and offices in each of the corners whose roofs, now heavily fortified, doubled as sangars. There was a fifth sangar above the main entrance gate to the east, and a sixth in the centre of the wall to the west. The Operations Room was set up in the central office building. During contacts the roof of this building, sandbagged and shaded by camouflage netting, served as a tactical command post, and became known as the Control Tower.

As a static defence position the compound had two distinct disadvantages. The first was that it was part of a town. The civilian buildings surrounding it, even the ones across the street from the compound walls, offered any number of fire points for determined attackers. The second was a 150-metre hill, just 700 metres to the south-west, which overlooked the compound and was obviously a crucial piece of ground. The Gurkha platoon, twenty-seven strong, manned the corner sangars and the Control Tower, with just enough left over to form a small reserve – the Quick Reaction Force, or QRF – to plug any gaps in an emergency. But there weren't enough of them to occupy the hill as well; the Gurkhas had no choice but to let the local ANP, the Afghan National Police, do that. The hill was topped by and named after an old shrine, although now, in order not to offend local sensibilities, it was renamed 'ANP Hill'.

Since Operation Mutay a month earlier, a peculiar calm had returned to the town. By day the bazaar and the weekly market remained busy with people and traffic, but it was different at night, when with increasing frequency shots were fired at the compound. There were short bursts of rifle and machine-gun fire, occasional RPGs, well-aimed sniper rounds. It was just enough to keep the garrison on edge – although that was not the purpose of the attacks. 'With hindsight, it's obvious that they were testing us out,' said Rex. 'They were examining our arcs of fire, our fire-times, our close air support response times. It was quite professionally done.'

The Gurkhas' assailants were seldom seen, even through night vision goggles, while in the daytime they were free to blend in with the populace. In such circumstances, and especially after the close call of Operation Mutay, patrolling into the town in any regular way was out of the question for a garrison so small. 'The Gurkhas are very good at public interface,' Rex told me ruefully. 'They are naturally friendly, and being non-Europeans they are often more easily accepted than we are. They understand the tribal nature of Pashtun society because they come from a tribal society themselves. Many of them speak Urdu, which is widely understood in southern Afghanistan. But in the event, all we got to interface with was bullets.'

Confined to barracks, the platoon spent long hot days manning sangars once again, staring out at a town that seemed studiously to ignore their presence. When not on sentry duty they mostly slept – something that was hard to do now at night. Sometimes they played chess or poker in the shade, or filmed themselves on their digital cameras. A goat was brought in and slaughtered for the curry pot with a kukri, the famous long curved knife that all Gurkhas carry. According to tradition, the goat's head must be severed with a single chop of the blade; anything more is considered inauspicious. There were mixed groans and laughter when the rifleman nominated for the task muffed it.

Dan Rex arrived at the head of a relief platoon for Hollingshead's tired men on 2 July, by which time the mood in the town was deteriorating fast. Shops had begun to close. Entire families were observed driving out of town, packed into battered Toyotas with all their household possessions on the roof. The trickle of departures soon became a flood. It wasn't difficult to read the meaning of the exodus, and it was confirmed by anyone whom the Gurkhas asked: the Taliban, ever-present in the outlying districts of the town, had now infiltrated the centre and were taking control.

'The defining moment was when the Taliban took over the town bakery,' said Rex. 'That was when we knew for sure that we had lost control. Until then the ANP in our compound had bought their bread from there, but that was impossible now. It was a shrewd move psychologically.' Just as ominous was the sabotage of a nearby water-pumping station. The sudden, surprising silencing of the decrepit generators driving the pumps was, the Gurkhas realized, the point of the attack: it allowed the enemy to listen for British helicopters approaching from the south.

The night-time attacks subtly increased in tempo. Watchmen on ANP Hill reported streams of vehicles, sometimes as many as twenty at a time, inching towards the town from both the north and the south-east. Rex went up the hill to see for himself more than once. 'There were times when it was like the M25 down there,' he recalled. 'We knew it was the enemy because no innocent farmer would be moving about like that at night, and most ordinary citizens had already left. The vehicles were all around us, and we were pretty sure that they were preparing an attack, but we couldn't be sure, so we couldn't respond under the Rules of Engagement.'

Finally, one morning in the first week of July, the central bazaar failed to open at all. The normally bustling stretch of tarmac was deserted. Now Zad had become a ghost town.

On 11 July, in a last bid to prevent the inevitable, Rex invited the town's elders to a *shura*. It was far from certain that the elders would agree to come, but in the end about twenty-five of them did so. A spectacular collection of mostly grey-bearded old men shuffled through the compound gates and into the main building's dedicated guest room – a feature of every public building in Afghanistan. They sat on cushions in a rough circle in the usual way, and were served the standard *shura* fare of nuts, dried mulberries and tea. The stratagem was not without risk. Rex had no idea who these people really were or where their true loyalties lay. At a similar *shura* in Kandahar province earlier in the year a Canadian officer had been attacked and seriously injured by the son of an elder who had smuggled in a machete under his clothes. However, it would not do to address the elders while armed or wearing body armour. Rex detailed a couple of his men to keep a close eye on proceedings from the rear, with others posted outside the window with their weapons made ready, and trusted to luck.

The text of his address was no different from the one British officers were disseminating all over Helmand that summer. 'I wanted to look them in the eye. I told them that we had no desire to harm them or their town, but that if we were attacked we would respond with force. I explained that we were there at the invitation of their government – that we were there to provide security, to help. I said that development money was available. I asked them what they wanted.'

The most remarkable feature of the meeting was what was not discussed: the Taliban. 'It was the real elephant in the room. They just refused to talk about it. I don't think the T-word was mentioned even once.'

Most of those attending remained silent throughout the hour-long meeting. Some of them just stared at the foreigner in their midst with an intensity bordering on hostility – 'eyeballing', Rex later called it. He had the strong impression that they were sizing him up. The ANP later confirmed that two of the so-called elders were actually Taliban commanders, for whom the *shura* was an unmissable opportunity to inspect the Gurkhas' defences from the inside.

That they were able to do so without the genuine elders objecting said a great deal about their power and influence in the town. The elders were either intimidated by or colluding with the Taliban, but by this point it made little difference. As a peace-making exercise, the *shura* was almost pointless. Rex knew he was only going through the motions, and that matters had probably already gone too far for a showdown to be avoided. 'About the only thing of any substance that came out of it was a request that the NDS wear uniform when on duty in the town,' Rex said.

This seemed fair enough. The plainclothes men of the National Directorate of Security, a handful of whom had been assigned to the Now Zad mission, were tough, savvy operators who answered to the Minister of Interior in Kabul. Rex took the request as an encouraging sign that at least some of the elders recognized the need for law and order, and were prepared to recognize Kabul's authority. Uniformed men would naturally be more easily identifiable to the suspicious townspeople, and so were more likely to be trusted. An armed NDS patrol was already scheduled for that night. This time, at Rex's insistence, they left the compound in regulation blue.

The request, however, was almost certainly a trick. It was true that uniforms made the NDS men recognizable to the townspeople, but they also marked them out for the Taliban. The six-man patrol headed north up the main bazaar and had covered no more than 150 metres when they were attacked. Whether it was an ambush, or whether they had simply bumped into a Taliban unit infiltrating the town from the other direction, it was impossible to say. Caught in a hail of machine-gun and small-arms fire, one of the NDS men was immediately wounded. The Gurkhas in the sangar overlooking the bazaar stood to, and observed through their night vision goggles as the NDS men rushed back towards them, dragging their injured comrade between them. 'The weight of fire that was going down, it was completely amazing that they made it,' recalled Lieutenant Angus Mathers, Rex's second-in-command. This was the trigger for an attack on the compound that lasted all night. It had evidently been many days in the preparation, and it signalled a sharp change in the Taliban's tactics. It was 12 July, and the battle for Now Zad district centre had begun.

Within ten minutes of the patrol's leaving the compound, all four corner sangars as well as the Control Tower were in action. It began with tracer fire and a pair of RPGs that whizzed past Sangar 4 from a bombed-out building at the far side of some open ground 200 metres to the north-west. Two minutes later, every doorway and window in a wide arc from the north to the east seemed to be crackling with small-arms fire. Sangars 1, 3 and the Control Tower led the response.

The killing power at the Gurkhas' disposal was not in doubt, but the defenders were still required to put their heads above the parapet to fire their weapons. All the positions had been 'fixed' in advance by the enemy, and the two heavy-calibre machine-guns, the so-called '.50 cals' which weighed nearly forty kilos each and were mounted on tripods, were too large to set up behind the cover of sandbags and had been positioned just to one side. The incoming fire was so intense and accurate that the Gurkhas' best weapon now had temporarily to be abandoned. Rex, crouching in the Control Tower and surrounded by maps and radio equipment, saw sparks as rounds ricocheted off the barrel of the .50 cal there.

Sangar 3, the tallest of the corner towers and the location of the platoon's other .50 cal, was even more heavily engaged. The fiercest fire came from the eastern tree line – the target area of Operation Mutay the previous month – and from a conspicuous two-storey building 200 metres to the north-east that the defenders had nick-named the 'Smugglers' House'. Rounds were landing inside the sangar, sending up spurts of dust and pinging off the ammunition boxes. As on the Control Tower, the occupants were quite unable to reach their most effective weapon.

The tide was turned by a twenty-year-old recruit called Nabin Rai who volunteered to go to the reinforcement of Sangar 3. Carrying quantities of heavy ammunition, he sprinted for the base of the tower and made his way up the first and then the second rickety ladder that led to the roof. This in itself was a brave thing to do, for the ladders were desperately exposed, but after a climb that must have felt endless, Rifleman Nabin tumbled breathlessly into the sangar, unscathed. His arrival was followed by a slight lull in the incoming fire. Catching his breath, Nabin moved quickly to the .50 cal and began to fire it at the Smugglers' House.

The response was ferocious. Several rounds glanced off Nabin Rai's gun, until one round, passing through the gun sight, struck him in his right cheek. With blood pouring from the wound he crawled back into cover, although the safety of this position was only relative: another Gurkha, Rifleman Kumar, who was suppressing the area with a GPMG – a general-purpose machine-gun, known as a 'Jimpy' – felt a round strike his weapon's bipod from where it ricocheted into the sangar roof. The sangar commander, Lance Corporal Shree, took one look at Nabin and ordered him down to the medic. Nabin, reaching for a field dressing, flatly refused: his injury, he insisted, was not serious. Fifteen minutes later, when Sangar 1 announced that it had at last identified a precise firing point in the Smugglers' House, he was back in action again, this time armed with the Minimi light machine-gun. He could have peeked over the edge of the sandbags, but Nabin chose instead to stand up. 'I couldn't see properly because of all the smoke and dust,' he explained. Lance Corporal Shree saw three rounds thud into the sandbag immediately in front of Nabin, and then a fourth that passed through the bag and struck him in the helmet. Only then did Nabin drop back into cover, where he grinned at his comrades and smoked a cigarette, before returning to his position once again. It was a further two hours before he could be persuaded to come down from the roof.

Despite such bravery, it was not the Gurkhas but air power that repelled the attack that night. Forty minutes after it began, a pair of American A10s arrived on station along with a Predator drone. For twenty minutes the planes made low passes over the town to attack a heavy machine-gun position and two other targets with rockets and 30mm cannon. For the soldiers watching from the sangars – and especially for Sergeant Charlie Aggrey, the joint tactical air controller (or JTAC, pronounced 'jaytack') on secondment from 7 Para Royal Horse Artillery whose job it was to guide them in – this was an anxious time. Although capable of great accuracy, the slow-flying 'tank-busters' were notorious for their involvement in several friendly-fire tragedies in Iraq. 'Beware the A10', according to Aggrey, remains an unofficial rule of thumb among the British JTAC community. Now Zad, he said, was 'the cheekiest thing I've done in the Army'. In one instance, the only way Aggrey was able to get a decent fix on a particularly troublesome target building set back in the town was to hang off the outside wall of a corner tower by one hand.

Calling in air power could be perilous for other reasons, not least the scandalous inadequacy of some British radios. In June, during Operation Mutay, Paul Hollingshead had risked his life to retrieve a set from a Snatch Land Rover which had been ambushed in a Now Zad suburb and temporarily abandoned beyond the cover of a wall. 'It was a Clansman 351, VHF only – an old one from the 1960s sort of thing,' he recalled. His platoon was badly pinned down by a heavy machine-gun position. He and his men had almost no possibility of extracting themselves without support from the air. At this critical juncture, the radio failed. 'We couldn't get a tone. It was dead. Absolutely nothing. I thought it was broken, but then we noticed this piece of white mine-tape that someone had stuck on the top of it that said "Dodgy, But Workable".' Still under fire, Hollingshead and a colleague spent frantic minutes stripping the radio down, thumping it like an old television set and scratching the terminals with a penknife until, thankfully, it was coaxed into life. 'I won't ever forget the feeling of relief,' he said.

The Americans' marksmanship five weeks later was poor. Two A10 rockets aimed at the Smugglers' House missed by a hundred metres, prompting another defiant blast of machine-gun fire at the compound. In Sangar 1, Corporal Kailash Khebang spotted a gunman flit across a window in the second floor of the building. He stood up out of cover and fired the first of two ILAWs – the interim light anti-armour weapon, a modern version of the shoulder-launched World War Two bazooka. None of the Gurkhas had fired an ILAW before, even in training. Kailash's second shot dropped neatly through a window, but it wasn't enough. In a display of tenacity that astonished the crouching Gurkhas, fire continued to pour from the position. Like so much British equipment, the newly introduced ILAW still used technology developed during the Cold War, designed to penetrate Soviet armour on the plains of Europe. As the Gurkhas had just discovered, it was often ineffective against the thick mud walls of Afghan buildings, which could absorb extraordinary amounts of force.

The Gurkhas again resorted to air power. Following the smoke of the ILAW rocket, one of the A10s dropped a 500lb bomb on the Smugglers' House, destroying its south-west corner, while the other A10 blasted the windows on the eastern side with cannon; yet still the attackers fought back. The A10s were low on fuel and peeled off to base, but were immediately replaced by another two. One of these engaged with rockets, but missed by 150 metres. He tried again with his guns, but missed a second time, by fifty metres on this occasion. The sledgehammer was signally failing to deal with this nut. Finally, using the laser-guidance system on the

Predator, the fourth A10 at last silenced the Smugglers' House with a direct hit by a second 500lb bomb.

That effectively ended the assault. The Taliban tried throughout the night to renew it, but they reckoned without the $3 million worth of technology aboard the Predator. They could only guess at the capabilities of this all-seeing machine, with its infrared cameras that can pick up a human heat signature from thousands of feet up. The Taliban were spotted creeping along walls, moving between buildings, massing in a compound for another attack. (The Taliban later found a way to hide from the Predators by moving about the town through a system of dried-up watercourses that ran beneath the main streets. They also developed a network of tunnels between the earth-walled buildings – 'mouse holes' the Gurkhas called them – which allowed them to approach the compound without once showing themselves. In lulls between gunfire on quieter nights the sinister sound of digging could be heard from all the corner towers.)

The A10s remained on station throughout the night. Finally, at first light, a third 500-pounder was directed on to a large group of fightersas they clustered around two Toyota Corollas – ammunition resupply cars that had been shuttling back and forth all night. The Gurkhas gave a raucous cheer as the cars soared high into the air.

The exhausted Gurkhas were able to rest with the coming of daylight, although the respite did not last long. As dusk began to fall at six p.m., an unusual amount of traffic was observed moving about to the east and north-east. At 6.30, just after the muezzin cried the end of prayers over the loudspeakers posted across the town, three sniper rounds hit the sandbags of Sangar 1. The Gurkhas stood to once again, for the attacks were already starting to take on a pattern. The marksman, they were sure, had gone straight from the mosque to his firing point, filled with renewed

Islamic zeal. Their hunch paid off when Corporal Kailash spotted a group of six men leopard-crawling across a T-junction at the end of an adjacent alleyway, heading for the north side of the compound. The imam's sermon had evidently been an inspiring one that evening. Kailash instantly shot three of the crawlers dead with the GPMG.

The attack this time came more from the north than the east, and earlier than on the previous night. The Taliban knew now that they had a window of about forty minutes before supporting air power could arrive on station. Their solution was to hit the compound harder and faster than the night before, hoping for a breach. And this time, rather than small-arms fire, they concentrated on using RPGs. 'The attack on the thirteenth is the one most etched on my mind,' said Rex. 'It was probably the nearest we came to being overrun. If we'd taken serious casualties, requiring others to extract them, or if they'd managed to take out a sangar or even get inside the compound ... then I think we could have been in serious trouble.'

Back at Bastion, even after Operation Mutay, there had been much scoffing at the fighting capabilities of the enemy. It was often said that the Taliban's foot soldiers were brave but foolhardy, a disorganized collection of amateurs and have-a-go heroes. In a set-piece fight they were held to be no match for the professionals of the British Army. The assault on the 13th strongly suggested otherwise. In fact the tactics and organization displayed by the enemy were disconcertingly recognizable. 'They were good soldiers,' said Rex. 'They used the cover well and they moved about very fast. They had sections of eight or twelve men, and a pyramid command structure just like ours. They don't wear badges of rank on their shoulders but that doesn't mean they aren't a proper army.'

By eight o'clock a full moon had risen, negating the British advantage of night vision goggles. For ten long minutes the fire directed against the north side of the compound was so intense that it was again impossible to bring the .50 cals to bear. The assault, Rex estimated, was 'akin to a company-sized ambush' – about a hundred men. 'I was sure we'd lost two of our positions, just from the weight of fire. I was staggered they survived.' Two RPGs hit the wall just below Sangar 6, to the north-west; two others smashed into the front and rear of Sangar 1 to the north-east; several more overshot their targets and exploded in the air above the compound. Every one of these represented a disaster narrowly averted, for the warhead even on the standard model, the RPG-7, is capable of penetrating armour plating. A direct hit on any sangar could easily have killed everyone inside. 'It was their bad shooting that saved us,' Rex said. 'Either that, or the Taliban were just plain unlucky.'

Rifleman Gaj, Rifleman Nagen and the other young soldiers lying flat in Sangar 1 thought that it was all over for them. They were steadied by Kailash, their corporal, who had just shot the three leopard-crawlers. The men looked up to Kailash, whom they addressed as *guruji*, or teacher. As a senior corporal, he had exercised his right to choose which sangar to position himself in. I spent an hour with Kailash at Folkestone and found it difficult to imagine him in killer mode. He was twenty-six with a kind, open face beneath neatly parted hair, and he spoke English with an eager, scholarly precision. He had, in fact, been top of all his school classes back in Nepal. He was the only son of a motorcycle dealer from a village so far up the Himalayas that it had a view of Everest.

'They were trying to break into my position,' Kailash recalled. 'The fire was just too much, and so close. We could barely defend ourselves. The boys there said, "Guruji! Guruji! We are all going to die!" I tried to calm them. I knew that such intense shooting couldn't last long, so I gave them tasks for when it slowed and we could shoot back. I also thought we would be killed, but I couldn't say that.'

The Taliban moved up for another close assault under the covering fire. Popping above the parapet for a second, Kailash saw about fifty fighters massing one block to his north. He reported this to the Control Tower but there was little Rex could do about it. The weight of fire was still too great for reinforcements to move to any of the sangars from the centre. Charlie Aggrey had already radioed for air support. Rex now urged him back on to the net to find out when the planes would arrive. The timing was going to be critical for the attackers were now fewer than twenty metres away, blasting Sangar 1 with machine-gun fire from the shop buildings across the street.

It was Kailash, once again, who checked them. He reached for a weapon no Gurkha had used in anger for forty years: a hand-held L109 fragmentation grenade. It was the first of twenty-one grenades the Gurkhas were to throw during their time at Now Zad. He pulled the pins on two of them and lobbed them into the open shop fronts below. The moment of detonation was the signal for two of Kailash's men to get back on the GPMG and start suppressing the street below. The weight of incoming fire immediately subsided, although the Gurkhas were still taking sniper rounds from further out. Kailash requested reinforcements, and two men, one of them armed with an underslung grenade launcher, were now able to join them. A flare was fired to help them spot their targets. The extra firepower was just enough to hold on to the initiative.

Ten minutes later, two A10s at last arrived on station.

Immediately after that, Sangar 6 reported that the Taliban had suddenly withdrawn from all their positions to the north-west. The A10s circled for an hour and a half, dropping a 500-pounder on the bombed-out building that had been hit the night before: it had been the renewed source of five RPGs. The A10s were joined later by two Dutch F16 fighter-bombers, which strafed another fire point in the wood line. But the Taliban, no doubt remembering the previous night, had had enough. It was just as well, for the Gurkhas' ammunition had run dangerously low. In some sangars, four-fifths of it had been spent.

The Taliban's frontal assaults continued off and on for another ten days. Of the Gurkhas I spoke to, only Rex, who dutifully logged each contact in his official war diary, retained any real sense of the period's chronology. For the rest of them the time passed in a hot and sleepless blur, one incident blending nightmarishly into another. The constant enemy pressure, the Gurkhas understood, was itself a tactic designed to demoralize and exhaust them, and perhaps to force a mistake.

Nobody moved about the compound except at a sprint or a crawl, and only when necessary. The men in the sangars were forced to lie down when they needed to urinate, which they did into empty plastic water bottles. They did this a lot, for the heat during the day regularly topped 45°C and they were drinking up to ten litres of water a day. When the bottles were full it was best to toss them over the parapet into the street below. On one occasion, in another sangar in another Helmand town, an officer doing the night round of the watchtowers snatched up a bottle half-seen in the darkness and had taken a swig before the chortling sentry could stop him. The days when goats from the bazaar were slaughtered and turned into curry were gone. Now the Gurkhas subsisted on ration packs, hot if they were lucky, but just as often cold – if cold was the word. In the afternoons, a passable mug of tea could be made just by leaving it out in the sun. The street beneath the sangars began to pile up with foul-smelling rubbish, flyblown heaps of human waste and discarded food packaging, all mixed up with hundreds and hundreds of empty shell casings. It was like the filth that accumulated at the base of the walls of castles in medieval times – the mark of a true siege.

The planned assaults on the compound seldom took the Gurkhas by complete surprise. The enemy tended to communicate with each other on cheap and insecure Motorola-style radios; in the 1990s, in northern Afghanistan, I had seen for myself how, for junior commanders, the possession of a simple Motorola conferred status and authority, which tended to rise in direct proportion to how much they used it. During lulls in the fighting they liked to tune in to their opposition's frequency in order to trade blood-curdling insults and threats. Cat-calling over the airwaves was so common that it had become a kind of battlefield tradition; it served as light entertainment for the troops, who regarded it almost as an art form.

The National Directorate of Security's battle-hardened chief, Hazmat, knew how to play on the locals' fears. When his men succeeded in capturing a Taliban company commander, his idea of interrogation was to fire an empty-ish pistol at him, Russian-roulette style; the Gurkhas hurriedly dispatched this valuable prisoner to Lashkar Gah via Bastion for more orthodox questioning. Hazmat and his NDS men had been impressed by the Gurkhas' goat-slaughtering methods, and especially by the tradition that a kukri, once unsheathed, could not be put away until it had tasted blood. So he described the goat-chopping luridly over the radio net in the hope that the eavesdropping Taliban would pick it up. The trick paid off. Much later, when a wounded Gurkha was brought in to the hospital at Bastion, a Taliban prisoner recuperating in the same ward was heard to jabber, 'Get that yellow man away from me! He'll cut me up!'

The flow of useful intelligence was not all one-way. The gunmen outside often seemed to know what the defenders were doing, where the weak points were, when and in which sangars ammunition was running low. As July progressed it became increasingly obvious that the Taliban were being tipped off from within. Suspicion quickly fell on the local policemen of the ANP, dozens of whom were based at the compound. 'The ANP found all sorts of ways to pass information,' said Rex. 'They'd click on their radios, or find an excuse to wander outside the gates just as a patrol was preparing to leave, where it was an easy thing for them to signal one of the dickers [an enemy spotter – a term coined in Northern Ireland] waiting outside.'

The Gurkhas had distrusted the ANP from the start. Although they answered in theory to the provincial government in Lashkar Gah, their chief, Hajji Muhammadzai, was a swaggering bully of a man who, despite the religious probity implied by his title, regarded extortion as a perk of the job. His undisciplined men, whose loyalty like that of many Afghans was based on tribal patronage, were every bit as venal as their boss. They were supposed to have been the beneficiaries of a Western-funded training programme, yet few of them even owned a full blue uniform. They were armed with ancient AK-47s and the odd sticker-clad machine-gun, but none of them knew anything of gun safety, even when they were not smoking opium, or *chars*, the powerful local marijuana. The qualities looked for in a Western police force –

professionalism, a sense of public duty – meant nothing at all to them. They were evidently worse by far than the ANP I had met in Kandahar. 'The city police were corrupt, duplicitous and universally loathed by the locals,' said Rex. 'It would be hard to imagine a worse ally in a situation like Now Zad.'

Soon after he arrived, Rex noticed a young boy among the ANP's number wandering around the corner of the compound that Muhammadzai's gang called home. 'He carried a gun and wore webbing like the others, but he was too young to be a proper policeman. He was quite effeminate-looking and had no beard. I couldn't work out who he was.' He turned out to be Muhammadzai's teenage catamite. Rex described him as a 'butter-fly', a term he had taken from Khaled Hosseini's best-selling novel *The Kite Runner*. The prevalence in Afghan society of homosexual intercourse, or *liwat*, is well documented – the inevitable result, perhaps, of living in a culture that proscribes all heterosexual activity outside marriage. Pederasty is common too, particularly among the soldiery, for whom a catamite is a status symbol as well as a prized sexual partner – the crudest possible expression of masculine power and domination. But, however common in Afghanistan, *liwat* is also specifically forbidden by Islam. 'When a man mounts another man, the throne of God shakes,' according to one of the Hadiths (the sayings of the earliest interpreters of the Koran that carry almost as much authority among Muslims as the word of the Prophet Muhammad himself).

Hajji Muhammadzai's sleeping arrangements were no secret in Now Zad and naturally outraged many locals. The promotion of virtue over vice was so important to the Taliban that when they were in power they dedicated a whole ministry to it. In those days they occasionally put homosexuals to death by toppling a wall over them. Muhammadzai was thus playing straight into their hands with his immoral behaviour – and it did no good to the British garrison's reputation to be seen to be tolerating it, either. The conclusion was inescapable: Muhammadzai had to go. Rex reported his shortcomings up the chain of command with a recommendation that he be replaced as soon as possible. The request was turned down. For all his failings, Muhammadzai was still the senior representative of the Karzai government in Now Zad and as such was politically crucial to the British, who could not be seen to be occupying the town alone. It was emphatically the Afghan flag, not the British one, that flew in tatters above the compound walls. Rex had no choice but to put up with the ANP.

Even during Operation Mutay, Paul Hollingshead had been ordered to 'fix' the police chief to prevent him from tipping anyone off about the Chinooks approaching with their load bays full of Paras. A single mobile phone call was all it would have taken to put the mission in jeopardy. At other times, Hollingshead ordered his men to pretend to prepare for a sortie to the helicopter landing site with as much noise and bustle as possible. They would gear up, check and re-check their weapons, and line up their vehicles in order of departure, gunning the engines with mock impatience. Then, just as the gates swung open to allow them to leave, they would all roar with laughter and pile back out of their vehicles. The police thought this was funny, too. They didn't care if the Gurkhas suspected them. It was all a great big game. The timings of genuine sorties to the landing site were always kept secret. When Chinooks really were coming in, Rex's men got very good at lounging about with their shirts off, dozing or playing cards, before dropping everything and being ready to leave in two minutes flat.

Rex once caught Muhammadzai making a discreet mobile

phone call in the corner of a room, and crossly demanded to know who he was speaking to.

'To the governor!' Muhammadzai protested.

A few minutes later, when his back was turned, Rex pressed the last-number-dialled button on Muhammadzai's mobile – and was amazed to discover that he really had been speaking to the governor's office.

The game was less amusing now. The ANP's signalling did not stop when the fighting became serious. At the start of one attack, one of the NDS men thought he heard Muhammadzai's second-in-command, a man called Nek Mohammed, whispering into his radio that 'the Gurkha commander [was] moving to the roof'. A sudden blast of gunfire at the Control Tower and then a narrow miss from an RPG confirmed that the NDS man hadn't misheard. The Gurkhas had been grumbling about the ANP for days, but when they heard of their *washi*'s near miss the mood suddenly turned nasty. For Angus Mathers, handling it was one of the worst moments of the entire siege. 'The boys had reached a point where they weren't putting up with this any longer. The Gurkhas are easy-going people, but even they have a temper eventually. It was quite clear that something bad was going to happen in the compound if we didn't act.'

The fig-leaf of the alliance was briefly stripped away. Rex was forced to confiscate Nek Mohammed's radio, and placed him under arrest. He was released again once the Gurkhas had calmed down, however, and was allowed to remain in the compound. Rex reasoned that it was better to have him inside than out. At least Muhammadzai himself was soon no longer a problem. One day, he simply vanished. The garrison later learned that he had absconded to Lashkar Gah along with his policeman son and a hoard of money – 350,000 Afghanis, or about £3,500 – he had stolen from the public he was supposed to protect.

Surprisingly, given that they had helped the Taliban's efforts to kill him, Rex privately sympathized with the ANP's disloyalty. 'They were in a very difficult position. They must have asked themselves, "How long are these foreigners going to stay?" They reckoned, and I'm sure they were right, that they'd still be living in Now Zad long after we'd gone – and who would protect them then? They were hedging their bets, and I can't say I blame them. Under the circumstances it was a perfectly understandable thing to do.'

The ANP might not have shared the Taliban's ideology, but the difference was certainly not something they were prepared to die for. For most Pashtuns, ideology counted for far less than traditional tribal ties and the ancient code of Pashtunwali that governs all social intercourse. One of the pillars of that code is *badal*, the obligation to exact vengeance, which has no temporal limit. To kill a member of another tribe is to invite a vendetta that can last for generations. So the local police saw the dispute between the Taliban and the Karzai government not as a struggle for the soul of the nation but as a blip in history, a little local storm to be ridden out in the usual Afghan way by playing both sides as convincingly as possible.

When Muhammadzai left, Rex charitably worried about the catamite. Abandoned by his patron, the teenager was now fearfully vulnerable. The remaining policemen were disinclined to accept him as one of their own. Disarming and releasing him into the town was not an option: if the Taliban identified him there seemed a good chance that he would be killed. Just before the next helicopter resupply drop, therefore, Rex went looking for the teenager with the intention of putting him aboard. It was his only safe way out of Now Zad. He was nowhere to be found, though, and there wasn't time to mount a more thorough search. The Chinook set off again without him. The boy had in fact disappeared, never to be seen again in the compound or the town.

The Taliban's tactics evolved. They constantly varied the speed, direction and timing of their assaults, and in mid-July there was a new focus on sniping and mortar attacks. These had been going on intermittently for days, but now there was a marked improvement in the accuracy of the incoming rounds. Mortars landed inside the compound on several occasions, sometimes as close as fifteen metres from the Control Tower. The Taliban, it seemed, had brought in some specialists. The snipers were just as dangerous, for no matter how carefully the Gurkhas watched for a tell-tale muzzle flash or a puff of dust or smoke, the marksmen never revealed themselves.

It was some time before the defenders understood why they were so invisible: they were shooting from the interiors of build-ings, sometimes from two rooms back, through small, carefully excavated holes that allowed a good field of fire. The Gurkhas eventually identified three such positions, although there were probably more. The enemy snipers were also adept at moving from one to another, never following a pattern, always retaining the element of surprise. The Gurkhas were already cautious when they moved around the compound; now, all sentry changeovers and other essential work were restricted by Rex's order to the hours of darkness. One of the Land Rovers was reversed up to the front door of the central building to provide extra cover. Plastic sheeting, soon riddled with bullet holes, was spread out along the tops of the compound walls on poles to spoil the snipers' view. Sometimes, the Gurkhas would put a helmet on a stick and bounce it about above a parapet, waiting for the shot while a hidden spotter scanned the town through binoculars.

Eventually the inevitable happened. Lance Corporal Cook of the Signals Squadron had just finished repairing one of the field telephones that connected each of the sangars to the Control Tower, and which had been damaged by sniper fire, when he was shot in the back. The bullet struck his right scapula, entering just below his body armour. It was the garrison's first serious British casualty. The landing site was secured and Cook was evacuated within two hours.

The arrival of snipers and mortar teams from the enemy's rear had important implications for Operation Herrick. The marksmen were evidently not locals, for they had not been present at the start of the siege. The question for the commanders at Bastion and Kandahar, and even for the MoD back in London, was this: from how far back in the rear had these specialists come? Their weapons, the Gurkhas were able to determine, were high-velocity Dragunovs, modern 7.62mm weapons much used in Iraq. In Ramadi in April 2004, an entire twelve-man squad of US Marines was wiped out by a single Dragunov marksman. Had the techniques of that insurgency spread to Afghanistan?

The NDS men had heard no Arabic voices in the town, but there were undoubtedly some foreigners out there, and this was troubling. The Taliban had always been an inward-looking organization, distrustful of foreigners and resistant to their ideas, but here was evidence of change. The NDS men detected Urdu-speaking Pakistanis, even Farsi-speaking Iranians. Pakistan and Iran had hosted huge numbers of Afghan refugees over the last twenty-five years, so it was conceivable that the foreign accents belonged to locals who had come back, but that didn't seem likely. An Iranian-numberplated vehicle briefly glimpsed in the town seemed to be a top-of-the-range 4×4, and brand new. What were these people doing here? Was the garrison now a honey-pot for the bees of an international jihad? The implications were scary. An internationalized insurrection would be far harder and more dangerous to contain, not just at the tactical level but regionally and globally as well.

The Taliban never again came as close to a breakthrough as on the night of 13 July, although there were some other narrow escapes for the Gurkhas. As was the case in every Helmand platoon-house, their salvation was air support. The Royal Air Force alone dropped seventy-one 500lb bombs and launched 1,400 rockets in 2006. Many of the photographs I was shown at Folkestone featured tall columns of smoke rising above the town as another 500-, 1,000- or 2,000-pounder fell into it. On every video clip the troops later posted on YouTube, there is someone off-camera whooping with mixed awe and joy as the bombs detonate and the ground shakes beneath the garrison's feet.

The definition of 'danger close', at least as the JTACs had been trained to understand it, was repeatedly ignored during Herrick 4. In some cases the proximity of the air support was unprecedented. On 16 July a British Apache was called in to clear a building only ten metres from the compound, a hot spot directly beneath Sangar 3 known as the 'clinic'. The Gurkhas had tried to dislodge the enemy with grenades. One of them even went into the compound's fetid latrine block and posted a grenade through the tiny ventilation window there, although to no effect. The Taliban had also lobbed grenades of their own over the compound wall.

'How accurate is your 30 mil?' Charlie Aggrey recalled asking, once the circling Apache had identified the clinic.

'I can put them through the window if you want,' the pilot replied.

The Gurkhas, clutching their helmets and crouching low in their sangars, could hear the helicopter's hot and smoking shell casings clattering down into the street outside. Some, they claimed, had even landed on their helmets. Afterwards, when the pilot radioed for confirmation that he'd hit his target, Aggrey was able to tell him that the incoming fire had been replaced by the sound of screaming. In Sangar 3 they could even smell burning flesh – the 'smell of war', as one of them put it later.*

A turning point for the garrison came that same day, for it was on the evening of the 16th that the reinforcements Rex had constantly been requesting at last arrived.

Reports of the fighting at Now Zad had been circulating in Camp Bastion for over a week. For Paul Hollingshead's platoon, back in the humdrum guard duty role at Bastion for which they had first been deployed, this was an anxious and frustrating time. Hollingshead was a particular friend of Mathers' – they were lieutenants of the same age who had been through Sandhurst together – but he had no means of contacting him himself. Only Task Force HQ really knew what was going on, and the officers in possession of hard information from the front were rightly cautious with it. For this reason the stories doing the rounds of the troops were often greatly exaggerated. Rex's men, it was whispered, had at times run out completely of food, water, ammunition; the defenders had had to fix bayonets; they had played 'hot potato' with

---

* For the pilot's account of this incident, see chapter 6, page 224.

the enemy, scooping live grenades from the sangar floors where they had landed and hurling them back over the compound wall; there was even a gruesome rumour that the Taliban had flung body parts at the Gurkhas. None of these things was true, although the hot potato story in particular is still widely believed within the Army, a piece of Herrick 4 mythology that refuses to go away.

The trigger for the decision to send reinforcements was the news of another casualty, Rifleman Baren Limbu, who was hit in the thigh by a ricocheting rifle bullet in the Control Tower and now required evacuation. The relief force, appropriately, was headed by Hollingshead's platoon together with a small mortar and machine-gun team of Royal Fusiliers – the first of the long-awaited reinforcements to arrive from Europe. Hollingshead had been hanging around the Ops Room and asking to be sent back for days. His men, he said, were 'itching for it'. A strong sense of *esprit de corps* had developed among the men of 'D' Company in the few short weeks that they had been in Afghanistan together. Hollingshead was given half an hour to get his men together.

'I didn't know what to expect,' he told me. 'All I knew was that Dan and Gus [Rex and Mathers] were having a hard time. I thought we might have to fight house to house, so we took as much as we could carry, a GPMG for every four men with ammo all over us. Normally there's only one GPMG for the whole platoon. We looked like bloody Rambos. It felt like a rescue mission.'

As the four-tonner left to take them to the landing site, the Gurkhas in the back started cheering.

'That was another moment I'll not forget, a proper Gurkha moment. The driver asked me what the boys were cheering about. I just looked at him and said, "We're off for a fight."'

When they arrived, Rex immediately ordered them to occupy

ANP Hill – a move that ended his reliance on Muhammadzai's men to hold that crucial piece of ground. 'It was just the greatest relief to have my own boys up there,' Rex confessed. 'I never felt tactically secure with the ANP watching my back. Losing the hill was not an option.'

The hill was promptly attacked with mortars, and more heavily than at any time previously, which itself suggested that the ANP had had some kind of arrangement with the Taliban. It was another wild night.

'Dusk was coming on and there was tracer coming from all the corner towers,' said Hollingshead. 'We got up the hill, set up the SF [supporting fire] guns and were straight into it.' Hollingshead remembered seeing the barrel of the .50 cal on the hill glowing red in the darkness. At the height of the fighting he led his men in an impromptu chant of 'Aya Gurkhali!' ('The Gurkhas are upon you!'), a battle cry that he guessed hadn't been heard for half a century. 'I know it was corny,' he said, 'but we were pumped up. It just felt the right thing to do.'

Relief for the Gurkhas finally came on 30 July when they were replaced by more Royal Fusiliers. The attempt to garrison a town with a single British Army platoon was an experiment that Task Force HQ did not repeat. The Fusilier relief force eventually amounted to most of a company. Rex's men were supposed to have been supported in their defence by a detachment of the Afghan National Army, the ANA. In practice, the ANA were of little use. There were just fifteen of them at Now Zad, supervised by Captain Dougie Bartholomew of the Operational Mentoring and Liaison Team (OMLT), which had been attached to the battle group from the earliest planning stages. Small units of supervised ANA were now scattered across the province.

Like the Coalition's alliance with the ANP, the main purpose of the OMLT (or 'Omelette' as it was inevitably nicknamed) was political: a way of demonstrating that the British were not foreign occupiers but an assisting ally, operating in Helmand at the invitation of the government in Kabul. In the long term the OMLT was even more significant, for it represented an eventual exit strategy for Britain and her Coalition allies. The idea was to build up a national army capable of maintaining security and holding back the Taliban on its own – an 'Afghan solution for an Afghan problem', as the official mantra went – and the best and quickest way of achieving that was to train the ANA in the field.

The ANA/OMLT project had got off to a shaky start, however. Despite the years that had passed since Karzai's election, the ANA training programme was still hopelessly under-funded. According to some officers involved, little priority was given to the OMLT at Brigade Headquarters in Colchester when Herrick 4 was being planned. Few had anticipated that the ANA would be involved in such hard-core fighting so soon; the OMLT focus, it was thought, would be on further training. For this reason, vital equipment such as night vision goggles, radios and even vehicles were reassigned to British combat units who, it was judged, would have greater need of them. Thus it was that when the OMLT officers arrived in the spring to meet their new charges, they found a rag-tag, under-equipped force that was far from being what the British Army would consider 'operational'.

The OMLT was headquartered at Camp Tombstone, just next door to Camp Bastion, a location intended to enhance Anglo-Afghan cooperation. But while that looked good on planning schedules, the camps were separated by their own gates and perimeter fences, so that in practice there was little contact between them. Morale at Tombstone was never high. When pep-talking political dignitaries visited Bastion – Des Browne, say, or David Cameron as Leader of the Opposition – the liaison officers were careful to include a quick visit to Tombstone on their itineraries. But there was no disguising the fact that the OMLT camp was an adjunct to the main event across the road. The ANA units housed there looked, and felt, dispiritingly like a forgotten army.

The recruits, most of them drawn from poor, non-Pashtun areas to the north of the country, were badly paid and sometimes of very questionable quality. On one occasion, a group of ANA turned up for target practice on the nearby rifle-range without any of the ammunition recently assigned to them. On enquiry, the OMLT officer in charge learned that they had sold it all in the local market. Their spokesman was genuinely astonished when the officer remonstrated with them. 'But we got a very good price for it!' he said. Another OMLT officer, Captain Will Libby of the Royal Green Jackets, later explained to me how most of his men could not drive. 'My ANA company arrived in a convoy from Kandahar in early May. When they caught sight of Tombstone, two kilometres out, they broke formation and made a charge for the gates. Four of their vehicles crashed.' They tended not to wear watches. Few could read or write. Many of them were short-sighted and wore no glasses; others were in poor health, with disorders as serious as tuberculosis, for which they had never been screened. It was not uncommon, when an inspection or parade was called and the head-count did not tally, for an OMLT officer to be informed quite matter-of-factly that the missing man had died in the night.

The worst problem, however – at least in Libby's view – was their almost total lack of *esprit de corps*. 'It wasn't their fault. Their initial training was done up in Kabul under ISAF supervision. The officers were trained by the French, but the junior NCOs and all the rest were trained separately, by the Canadians, so they didn't know their officers from Adam. And that's reckoned to be an essential part of training in most Western armies . . . At Bastion we focused on the importance of bonding, teaching NCOs to teach their blokes. But the officers got selected on nepotistic lines . . . there was a huge disparity between the best and worst of them in terms of experience and quality. The lack of kit and preparation led to units being hastily bolted together, which led to lack of trust between men and NCOs and officers.'

For whatever reason, of the 1,100-strong ANA *kandak*, or battalion, deployed with the British on Herrick 4, 360 had deserted by July. Fixtures and fittings at Camp Tombstone, which had been built specifically for them by the Americans at a cost of £68 million, were reportedly stripped out and stolen; even some washroom taps and sinks went missing.

Most worrying of all was evidence that, like the ANP, certain members of the ANA were guilty of freelance banditry on the roads – an allegation apparently confirmed when a BBC correspondent, David Loyn, covertly filmed an unofficial ANA checkpoint in action. Loyn was succinct in his criticism when he asked, 'What is the point of sending our young men to die in support of a regime that cannot begin to police itself?' Some of the ANA highwaymen, no doubt, were deserters who had held on to their useful uniforms, but as far as their victims were concerned this made no difference. Who could tell which was which? It meant that public confidence in the new Afghan Army was being eroded long before it was even fully formed.

Despite all that, the picture Libby painted of the ANA was not entirely negative.

'They were asked to fight alongside people they didn't know. They didn't know where they were going, or why, sometimes. They were far from their homes, with minimal training, on a salary of four dollars a day – about a third of what the Taliban paid their fighters. Given those circumstances I reckon we might desert, too.' The deserters were always in the minority, he insisted, and many of those who stayed behind were 'ballsy ... They had different motives for joining up. Some hated the Talibs, some believed in the state, some were just plain bored with their lives and were looking for adventure. But there was a growing sense of pride in their new units ... Given time, they'll be fine. The honour system and the pride that all soldiers need are built-in with Afghans. They were much rubbished, but at least they were there.'

According to Angus Mathers, the Now Zad contingent performed well, under the circumstances. They got on well with the Gurkhas, who taught them a lot about how to man a sangar properly, and he confirmed Libby's view that they didn't want for courage. 'They were really quite poorly trained when they turned up, by Chinook, no night vision, just Dougie Bartholomew on his own in charge ... It was daunting for anyone, let alone at night-time.'

Nevertheless, they 'had their moments', most of them related to the complete breakdown of their supply chain, which was kept strictly separate from the British one. 'They didn't have enough food or water or ammo. Dougie kept asking but nothing ever came up. I don't know why – it was a matter for their high command – but they were never even paid at Now Zad. It wasn't easy to keep them motivated.'

Their fire control discipline was poor, too. Accidents from NDs – negligent discharges – were commonplace. On patrols in the town they could be a liability, as was proved when one of them accidentally killed a civilian interpreter. They were not ready for the intensity of fighting in Helmand in the summer of 2006, and certainly nowhere near ready to garrison outstations such as Now Zad on their own. Rex ordered the ANA to man the compound's two least strategically critical sangars – the one overlooking the main gate and the other on the prison roof in the centre of the west wall – and hoped for the best. Unsurprisingly, when the attacks on the compound grew serious it was the Gurkhas who did 'ninety-nine per cent of the work'.

In the course of July, Rex's platoon repulsed over two dozen attempts to overrun the compound, firing over 30,000 rifle rounds, 17,000 GPMG rounds and 2,000 of .50 cal, and killing an estimated one hundred of their attackers. Yet the return to Bastion was a strange anti-climax. After twenty-four hours' rest they were put back on guard duty almost as if Now Zad had never happened. In December, when the Queen's New Year honours list was gazetted, their achievements again seemed forgotten in the flurry of Military Crosses awarded to 3 Para, and the media hoopla surrounding Bryan Budd, the posthumous recipient of a Victoria Cross – only the second VC to be awarded since the Falklands. There were no medals for the Gurkhas. Five of them, including Hollingshead, Kailash and Nabin, were Mentioned in Dispatches for their bravery, but that was all. They were, perhaps, the victims of their own luck. At Folkestone there was a whisper that the medal tally might have been higher if one or more of their number had been killed.

They didn't much mind. The Gurkhas were used to being slighted by the establishment. The regiment has been squeezed and sidelined over the years, reduced from eight battalions in 1995 (and forty-three of them during World War Two) to just two today. In 2007, after a long legal battle, the Gurkha veterans' pension was finally increased to the same level as the British one. But this victory was spoiled by the Home Office, which continued to resist an effort by forty-four veterans to gain British residency rights, arguing that the men, who had 170 medals between them, did not have 'sufficiently strong ties' to the country.

Still, for the officers who fought at Now Zad there was immense professional pride in a job well done. 'I think I'm one of the luckiest people of my generation,' said Hollingshead. 'I'm twenty-four, I've only been in the Army for three years. But there I was, at the cutting edge of British foreign policy. No other lieutenant that I know of got to command an entire platoon-house.'

For the Riflemen, with their singular reverence for the British Army, there was the promise of honour and glory back in Nepal, and, in a culture that venerates its ancestors, genuine satisfaction at becoming a part of a long military tradition. 'This was our first time in combat,' wrote Rifleman Yam Roka Pun in a contribution to the regimental newsletter, 'and it was hard not to let one's thoughts recall the memories of our ancestors fighting in the World Wars.' Uppermost in 'D' Company's minds was the campaign against the Japanese in Burma, where seven of the twenty-six VCs ever awarded to the Gurkhas were won. Their company battle honour name, Tamandu, recalled the Burmese battlefield where Rifleman Havildar Bhanbhagta Gurung, twenty-four, single-handedly killed a tree-sniper and cleared four foxholes with grenades and his bayonet, before storming a machine-gun bunker from the front and killing its three occupants with his kukri. '*Kaphar hunnu bhanda marnu ramro*', as the Gurkhali motto goes: 'It is better to die than to live as a coward'.

For the Gurkhas' parents, meanwhile, there was a mixture of relief, fear and pride – a response no different from that of the parents being interviewed by their local newspapers all across Britain in 2006. Kailash confided, 'My mum and dad, when they heard about Now Zad, said, "Please don't do this job any more. Everything you need is here." But I told them, "No, I want to be a soldier. It's my hobby."'

The lack of public acknowledgement of what his men had done predictably bothered Dan Rex the most. He was that kind of officer: solicitous, thoughtful, attached to the men he commanded, and with a deep appreciation of Gurkha culture. The lack of recognition for him personally mattered not at all. 'I took a hundred and ten men in there. I brought them all back out alive. That's reward enough for me.'

He smiled. He clearly meant it.

3

The Dragon's Lair

The company of Royal Fusiliers who spearheaded the reinforcements for Helmand announced on 6 July were based at Dhekelia in
Cyprus – a post-Empire anomaly just as strange, in its way, as the
continued existence of the Gurkhas. Dhekelia was one of two
Army bases on the island that amounted to almost a hundred
square miles of sovereign British territory, retained by the Crown
when Cyprus gained independence in 1960.

I was picked up at Larnaka airport by 'A' Company's
commander, Major Jon Swift, who drove me almost immediately
to a drinks party being thrown by his Commanding Officer,
Lieutenant Colonel Peter Merriman. Traces of Empire were
evident even in the dress code. We joined the battalion's officers
wearing 'Planters', which – though no one quite seemed to know
why – turned out to mean light-coloured cotton trousers and a
smart shirt without jacket or tie. We stood about drinking gin
slings in a garden where bougainvillea rioted and a military band
played gentle jazz below a blue and white marquee. I wondered

whether there was something wilful – pathological, even – about this dreamy outpost of British civilization. Such institutional resistance to modernization may have been ludicrous, but I recognized that it was also precious, for the party was precisely the kind of thing that made the Army unique.

Swift, thirty-three, my host for the next two days, spoke in fast, efficient bursts that added to the sense of competence and ambition he exuded. His favourite word was 'gleaming', although others used it too. Like the acronyms that peppered the Fusiliers' sentences, it was a part of the private language of this close-knit community. In his office I watched Swift communicate orders with a look and a word or two that were incomprehensible to me but were always immediately understood by his NCOs, and found myself almost envying the professionalism and pride in their organization that this secret code implied.

Dhekelia was never an easy posting for company commanders. The resort of Napa, with its bars and nightclubs full of sun-burned lovelies from home, was off limits to the troops. But it was also fewer than fifteen minutes from the base, and on both mornings I spent at the barracks I was woken by the bark of a sergeant major as a miscreant or two from the night before was quick-marched around the parade ground, their hangovers pounding in time to their feet. I recognized this cliché of military life from, for instance, George MacDonald Fraser's McAuslan novels, but I still thought I detected a discontent in the air that wasn't normal, a sense of boredom, disillusionment – mild rebellion, even. Swift and his officers seemed powerless to prevent the boys from going off boozing in the town, no matter how much leave they cancelled or promotion they withheld. Even on the way from the airport, Swift had been speaking sharply on his phone to a Fusilier who had found an excuse for delaying his return to base from England, and was effectively AWOL. There was a lot of talk among the troops I later spoke to about leaving the Army, of taking a permanent rest. Futures were being reappraised, alternative careers mooted. 'A' Company, it seemed to me, were having some difficulty in recovering from the shock of Helmand and readjusting to their peacetime role. The Fusiliers presented the perfect snapshot of an Army that, in General Sir Richard Dannatt's words, was 'coping, just'.

Many units were sent into action faster than was normal during Herrick 4, but none so fast as this one. They expected to be deployed at short notice: for eight months the battalion had been the Army's designated Theatre Reserve Battalion, or TRB, and as such lived from day to day at twenty-four hours' 'notice to move'. This was why they were headquartered in Cyprus. The Mediterranean location meant, at least in theory, that the men were pre-acclimatized to the heat of the nearby Middle East, the world's most reliable cockpit of war. All the same, the speed of the deployment to Helmand was exceptional. Swift was completing a staff course at the military college at Camberley in Surrey when he received a text message 'warning him off'. Staff College is a period in an officer's career that is traditionally treated as sacrosanct; only the direst emergency is ever allowed to interrupt it, even in wartime. Swift had therefore been expecting to finish his studies before moving, with his wife, into a new house at Dhekelia. His head was full of military theory and preliminary arrangements for moving furniture, not preparations for combat. Within a day, however, he was on a plane to Cyprus, and twenty-four hours later he was at Bastion, where he found himself in charge of a company he barely knew.

If the move was disorienting for Swift, it was probably more so for some of the men under his command. The sixteen-strong Fire Support Group, with their two mortar barrels and two GPMGs, had been in Bastion for two days when they were flown up to man ANP Hill for the Gurkhas on 16 July – the first of the Fusiliers sent to Now Zad. At Bastion this advance party was in the middle of a training session when the order came through. They were given precisely fifty-nine minutes to board a Chinook. 'We were running around like mad things trying to get ready,' said Sergeant Martyn Gibbons, a mortar fire controller. 'They showed us a map in the JOC [Joint Operations Centre] and said we were going to have to tab up this hill about five grids away. I said, "What, with all our kit? It's a good job we're packing light." I thought it was a normal 1:50,000 map. We didn't have any maps of our own ... It wasn't until we got to Now Zad that I realized the map I'd seen was 1:5,000 scale, and that the hill was next door, just about.'

On the landing site at Bastion, with six minutes to go until darkness set in when the Chinook would be forbidden to fly, although the squad was all aboard with the rotors turning there was still no sign of any mortar ammunition. A forklift truck came hurtling round the corner at the last minute. It was left to Swift and his NCOs, who had come to see the men off, to burst open the packaging and pile as many shells into their laps as they could manage in the time remaining. 'Their faces were a picture,' Swift recalled. 'Blokes had been dying on operations in the district centres. They knew why they were going to Now Zad at such short notice: it could only be because the shit was hitting the fan there. What really worried me was that I didn't even know some of these guys. I thought, "What if one of them doesn't come back? How am I going to write to a mother when I don't even know who the son is?"'

Gibbons and the others were told that their mission would last for two days; they didn't come down off ANP Hill again for 107 days. In their time at Now Zad the Fusiliers fired 1,500 mortars, 10,000 light machine-gun and rifle rounds and 89,000 GPMG rounds. They called in over thirty air strikes in the course of 149 separate contacts, during which they were attacked with every-thing from small-arms and sniper fire to mortars, RPGs and 107mm Chinese rockets. One of the Fire Support Group, Dean Fisher from Nuneaton, personally fired 40,000 rounds through his GPMG. He returned to Cyprus soon after his twenty-first birthday to find himself the subject of a two-page spread in the *Sun*, com-plete with photographs. 'Hero Dean', it said, beneath the banner headline, 'As Tories play politics,* THIS is what our boys face'.

And they hadn't even packed a clean pair of socks.

Their arrival represented another turning point in the struggle for Now Zad. Until then the Gurkhas had been the only garrison without mortars at their disposal. The accuracy and firepower of the mortars now provided by the Fire Support Group made further frontal assaults on the compound almost impossible. The gunners were trained to man, fire and hit their targets within seconds, and the mortars were no less effective. In theory, the minimum distance a mortar round can be dropped from friendly forces is 250 metres; anything less is categorized as 'danger close'. At Now Zad, the mortar crews regularly put rounds down just fifty metres from the compound walls. Since an 81mm mortar is usually only accurate to within forty metres, this was close enough to whiten the hair of any range instructor. It was a peculiarity of Helmand, however,

---

* In the autumn of 2006 the Conservatives supported a Scots and Welsh Nationalist motion for an inquiry into the Iraq War.

that the mortar's 'beaten zone' was much smaller than at home. Gibbons, who had a professional's passion for mortars, explained that a combination of altitude and heat caused the shells to fly so accurately that adjustments to target were typically as little as five metres, allowing 'danger close' ranges to become the norm.

The Taliban responded in the only way they could: for the next three months, the main focus of their attacks switched from the compound to ANP Hill. The Fusiliers were in action almost from the moment they arrived. The first thing the mortar crews did was to set up the barrels and fire two or three rounds in order to bed in the base plates. The usual procedure is to shoot into a convenient empty space, but Gibbons found himself zeroing his weapon on a real target. He had barely caught his breath from the climb up the hill when his second round killed a group of four Taliban in the town.

By Afghan standards, ANP Hill is a hillock, with flanks that rise evenly for 150 metres to a rounded summit about twenty metres across. But it commanded a good view of the compound, 600 metres to the east, and of the town beyond, as well as the main road to the south-east which connected Now Zad to Lashkar Gah and the rest of the world. The British were not the first to recognize its strategic importance. The remains of an artillery piece, upside-down and twisted among rubble, provided an ominous reminder that the Soviets had also kept watch here in the 1980s. The gun's concrete emplacement was still intact and provided some cover for Gibbons, who appropriated it as the mortar fire controller. The shrine on the summit was a simple hollowing in a rock into which two or three men could squeeze. Apart from that there was no real cover for anyone. There was a trench on the side of the hill facing the town into which about ten people could fit, but it was dug out only to knee height. Later – much later – sappers were able to deepen the trench to waist height with a mechanical digger, and to build up the parapets with sandbags. The Fusiliers, however, had no diggers and no engineers.

When Jon Swift and his men arrived to take over fully from the Gurkhas on 31 July, they were equipped with a single shovel – an Afghan one of uncertain sturdiness – and a pick with one spare head. The soldiers did what they could, yet 'the hill', as the Fusiliers called the position, remained woefully exposed through-out their stay there. 'We tried digging down but it was just solid rock. We were digging every night for at least a week, but only got down another inch or two. So we decided to try and build up. At night we were getting rocks from the bottom of the hill, dragging them up again one at a time . . . Big rocks were best. We didn't even have bags to carry them. There wasn't much – it probably gave us another five or six inches or something. You couldn't do it in the day – not a chance, you wouldn't move during the day – but at night we were straight down there, because it was for your own protection in the end.' Eventually a few bundles of empty sandbags started to come in on each helicopter resupply run, but these were nothing like enough. 'What we needed was twenty to thirty thousand of them.'

The Fire Support Group's arrival seemed to take the enemy commanders by surprise. It was not until the end of the first week that the Taliban attempted a concerted attack on ANP Hill, creep-ing as close as they dared to launch RPGs as well as firing mortars and machine-guns. The Fusiliers christened that night 'Suicide Saturday'. The attackers generally made easy targets and never repeated the mistake. The RPGs were inaccurate over such a long distance, particularly as their target was elevated and relatively small. Four RPGs exploded in the air above the Fusiliers, too high to do any damage. One lucky shot hit the wall in front of the mortars but failed to go off properly – which was even luckier for the soldiers sheltering there.

The defenders were astonished by the enemy's bravery. 'They've got bigger balls than what I have,' said Dean Fisher. 'The amount of firepower we put down, we completely blitzed on them, but they still kept coming.' Others thought their courage was simply stupid – or else suspected that the fighters were being duped. 'We were told they always removed dead bodies as quickly as possible so nobody could see them,' said Fisher's co-gunner, Stewart Spensley, from Bury in Greater Manchester, 'so maybe they were just being misled. A commander could say, "Well, he attacked last night, but now he's fucked off to Sangin", or something. He wouldn't tell a fighter that his mate had died, just to get him to attack again. That's what I put it down to, anyway. Mad. Stupid.' Whatever the enemy's motivation, the Fusiliers had to admit they had under-estimated their abilities as soldiers. 'I heard they'd be just crap, but they weren't at all,' said Fisher. 'They were a lot better trained than I thought they'd be.'

Mortars represented the greatest danger. One lucky shot into a trench could bring disaster, and they stood a far greater chance of finding a target than any RPG. There were several mortar crews operating in and around the town, and now they became busier than ever, signalling the start of a campaign that turned into an extraordinary duel with the Fire Support Group.

The goal for the defenders was to locate the enemy's firing position and send a mortar back along the incoming trajectory. This had to be done quickly, before the enemy had a chance to cease firing and move off. The firing points were always hidden, usually set well back in the town. The Fusiliers would hear the tell-tale pop of a shell being launched, and scan through binoculars for anything that might betray the enemy's position: a smudge of smoke, a glint of metal, a puff of dust thrown up by the base plate impacting the ground. Their world became ruled by the vicious geometry of the mortar's rise and fall. Timing was critical, for it wasn't a good idea to be standing up as a shell landed. Even a not-particularly-near miss had enough force to blow a man out of his trench. Closer blasts could burst eardrums, causing ears and even eye sockets to bleed.

There were, on average, sixteen seconds between the pop of the launch and the shell's arrival, depending slightly on the firing angle. The last four seconds before the drop were naturally the worst. The observers, gunners and everyone else would dive for whatever cover they could find, knowing that a direct hit would obliterate them. The dive-to-cover drill became second nature to the garrison, both on the hill and in the compound below. The Fusiliers discovered that the sound of a shell launching was un-cannily like the noise of a Land Rover door slamming. They soon learned to close their vehicle doors quietly, or else to shout 'door closing' as they did so. There were many among the company who, six months afterwards, were still unable to hear that sound without tensing up.

'Mortars are the scariest because you know they're coming,' said Jon 'Jackie' Allen, a twenty-six-year-old captain who was put in charge of the Fire Support Group for a ten-day spell. 'With most ordnance, if you hear it you know it's already gone past, but not these things. You hear them fire, and then a whistle in the descent. You'd curl up in a ball, literally with your head between your legs, just waiting for the bang. That helplessness was the most striking thing for me.' Spensley recalled pulling his sleeping bag up over his head and praying for protection from his 'ballistic dust bag'. There was really nothing else that he could do.

The incoming fire was mercifully inaccurate to begin with. A shell would occasionally land near the summit, but many more sailed over or dropped hundreds of metres short. It takes considerable skill to fire a mortar accurately, and a conical hilltop is difficult to hit even for experts. The enemy crews, furthermore, were often amateur in their launching procedures. Tell-tale dust clouds, in particular, gave their positions away. In the early days, Gibbons and the others were able to strike back with an efficiency that even the enemy acknowledged. 'Ah well,' one fighter in the town was heard to remark, with that curiously British sense of fair play that Afghan fighters often seem to have, 'we've been hitting them hard enough. It's only fair they hit us back now.'

In mid-September, however, the enemy tactics changed. First, the tell-tale dust plumes disappeared. The attackers had learned to water the ground around the base plate, or else to place the barrel in the middle of a wet blanket or carpet to suppress the dirt. Second, the number of firing points in the town was greatly multiplied. Instead of staying in one place and launching as many as eight shells at a time, the enemy now fired a quick salvo of three before collapsing the mortar and scurrying off to another firing point. These were pre-prepared and scattered all over the town, allowing a crew to visit several different firing points in the course of a single attack. The Fusiliers now found themselves hunting a very dangerous will-o'-the-wisp. 'It was very frustrating not being able to see them,' said Gibbons. 'We only got one or two minutes to respond when they fired. You could tell the rough direction the mortars were coming from, but two minutes wasn't usually enough to pinpoint them. They were very clever.'

The normal response would be to shell the general area and hope to catch the enemy as they moved to the next firing point, but the risk to innocent civilians was great in this urban battlefield, and the Fusiliers were constrained by their rules of engagement. 'Once,' Gibbons told me, 'on the wood line, I wanted to push out my mortars a hundred metres either way, to blitz the area. We knew where they were roughly and could have got them that way, but [the officers] wouldn't let me because we couldn't positively ID them.'

Along with the enemy's new elusiveness came a far more sinister development: a marked improvement in the accuracy of the incoming shells. There was a point to firing salvoes of three: the enemy had begun to use a standard mortar technique called 'bracketing'. 'The first mortar would land a hundred metres short,' Allen explained. 'They'd adjust their aim, and the second mortar would land a hundred metres long. So you just knew that the third one was coming straight down the chimney. And we had no OHP [overhead protection]. We'd count from the pop. The last four seconds before the drop of the third were the worst.'

The attackers had not raised their game without outside help. From foreign accents overheard in the town, and certain other clues, it was clear that a group of highly skilled mortar instructors had arrived from Pakistan. There was much speculation about where these people had learned their craft. The technique of bracketing could have come from the British Army's own training manuals – and there were some on the hill who muttered darkly that it probably had. The true identity of the instructors was never discovered. They might have learned their techniques in an al-Qaida training camp. They might equally have been rogue ISI operatives,* or simply ex-Mujahidin Pakistani Pashtuns who had mastered the mortar against the Russians twenty years earlier.

Wherever the instructors came from, they were bad news for the Fusiliers. It was two long weeks before the British regained the upper hand. 'There were some hugely lucky escapes,' Lieutenant Nick Groves told me. 'When the mortars landed you stuck your head up and the first thought was, "Has it landed next to me?" But somehow they always landed in empty parts of the trenches, or literally right on top of the sandbags . . . a foot the other way and four blokes would have been taken out. That happened a lot.'

Groves was from south London. As a teenager he had once worked as a ball-boy at Wimbledon. One day he fielded balls for the teenage prodigy Anna Kournikova. Needing to adjust her skirt during a packed Centre Court match, the bombshell from Moscow summoned her coach to hold up a towel to protect her modesty. Groves, standing on station at the back of the court, was treated to an unforgettable private view. Ten years on, the projectiles being lobbed at him and his men were a lot more dangerous than tennis balls. More than fifty mortar rounds landed fewer than twenty metres from someone on ANP Hill – easily within killing range. On five occasions, shells landed within five metres. One shell even dropped directly down one of the mortar barrels and burst it open like a peeled banana. Fusilier Jim Allan had been crouching next to it. His life was saved by Lance Corporal Chris Freeman, who had

* Pakistan's Inter-Services Intelligence directorate is the equivalent of Britain's MI6, with responsibility for covert operations abroad. There have long been suspicions that the ISI, or at least elements of it, are sympathetic to Islamic fundamentalism. After 9/11, Pakistan's military leader, General Pervez Musharraf, tried to rein in the ISI by purging Islamic hardliners from senior positions, including the head of the organization, Lieutenant General Mahmood Ahmed, in October 2001.

a sixth sense about this particular incoming round, and yanked him down into a trench by the scruff of his body armour a second or two before the shell hit.

Jackie Allen described the panic that ensued when a mortar was launched during a section changeover, when there were briefly as many as seventy-five men on the hill and the garrison was at its most vulnerable. 'A mortar popped. Everyone looked at each other. Was that a Land Rover door slamming? There was another pop. It was mortars. Suddenly, everyone was running . . .' At such times the Fusiliers could resemble a mob of meerkats bolting for their burrows. 'I was sitting at the wheel of the wagon, about to go back down the hill. I just scarpered in it. Was that the right thing to do? I don't know. Maybe not. But there wasn't much space up there.' The company sergeant major, 'Jimmy' Greaves, was in a truck bringing up water and rations. 'He was arriving at the top when the signaller who was riding top-cover just got out and ran . . . he didn't mention any mortars to the CSM. Jimmy was just left there looking at all these people running about, going, "What's going on?" That mortar missed, luckily. An hour later, though, the Taliban switched targets from the hill to the compound. They followed me down! And everyone was, like, "Right, get back up the hill, you!"'

Most at risk were the machine-gunners, whose positions at the front of the hill were particularly exposed. 'I think the worst one that I seen was when we was in the trench,' said Dean Fisher, the hero of the *Sun*. 'It hit the front edge and then just rolled down away from us. It was a blind.'

'I was out spotting one day cos we had incoming,' said Spensley. 'One of the rocks we'd dragged there was pretty big. And normally when I was looking out I'd lean against it – we had the binos on – and it landed fifty metres off. We didn't hear any more incoming.

And then one landed three or four metres in front of me, the other side of the rock. And [fellow gunner] Frankie Canham went, "Are you all right?" and I just went, "Uh-huh."'

The machine-gunners were good friends who had been brought closer together by their shared experience on the hill. Spensley's girlfriend, whom he'd met on leave in Bury two months earlier, was pregnant with his first child; Fisher and another gunner, Duncan Grice, had already been designated as godfathers.

As machine-gun specialists these three were called Drummers rather than Fusiliers. The title was no anachronism. In common with the supporting-fire platoons of other regiments, they were all required to play a musical instrument and to take part in public ceremonies. Grice really was a drummer; Spensley and Fisher were both flautists. It was hard to equate delicate musicianship with their combat role. I'd already seen footage of the Drummers in action on the hill, pouring murderous torrents of tracer fire at an enemy position below, as someone off-camera, probably Fisher, commented, 'Night night, Mr Taliban!' Almost every unit in Afghanistan had filmed themselves at one time or another, and spliced the best bits on to a souvenir DVD, usually to a heavy metal soundtrack. 'A' Company's DVD, entitled *Apocalypse Now Zad*, was set to Iron Maiden's 'Out of the Silent Planet', a pseudo-religious number about death and destruction on a cosmic scale. Given how far the Fusiliers had diverged from the hearts and minds mission, this was apt enough. In one contact, Fisher and Spensley fired over 9,000 rounds between them, punishing who knew how many Afghans with death. 'Remember that contact with the two RPG men in the woods?' said Spensley. 'We must have hit them just as they were about to fire. They fell back and fired them straight up, phwoom! And someone went,

"Mortars, incoming!" And I went, "No, that's RPGs, we just shot 'em!"'

Gallows humour was an important coping mechanism for all of them. 'There were times in contacts when we were just looking at each other and laughing – it was that mad,' Spensley recalled. 'We got incoming, and Fish stayed in his trench, which was the other side of the bit of OHP we'd tried to build. And it landed about two or three metres from that, and all we saw was a cloud of dust – we thought it had landed in the trench – and when the dust cleared we ran in to see him and he said, "Halloahh . . ."'

'There was that time when me and you was over the back of the hill and I had flip-flops on, because I'd been airing my feet,' said Fisher.

'Cos of the heat,' explained Spensley. 'We only had, like, one pair of socks each, for a lot of it. So you'd wash your socks and let them dry, and you didn't want to put your sweaty boots on . . . My combats had no knees, no arse or anything, all just worn away.'

'We were sat over the back with the mortars, just for a chat, you know, cos we're sat with the same people every day. And we'd start arguing between ourselves . . . And we got contacted, and I'm running back over the position in flip-flops with tracer going everywhere.'

'He's just in front of me. I'm going, "Come on, Fish, hurry up, hurry up, keep going," and there's rounds pinging off everywhere. And then we got in the trench and just looked at each other and went "phhh" – started laughing.'

Nick Groves also spoke of a strange, stoical hilarity that infected the hill's defenders. 'It got to the stage where the whole thing became a bit of a joke, it was so constant,' he said. 'I think this is the

British Army way – what people cringingly describe as laughing in the face of adversity. There's no point in worrying or crying about it. You're here, it's happening, and it's happening so much that it becomes quite amusing . . . the surreal becomes quite normal. I remember an RPG came in close once, and we had this massive debate about whether it was an RPG-7 or an RPG-9 . . . it became that every day.'

Sniper attacks were common, too. No Fusilier was ever shot by a sniper's bullet, but they often came close. 'We had one of our lads, Frankie [Canham], who stood up and a round pinged off a rock not far from him,' said Spensley, 'and he looked round at us and said, "Was that at me?" And we all went, "Yeah!" Then he got fired at again and he just run off. I don't think he realized; they weren't too far off. There was one sniper who was close all the time – a metre or so.'

There was no let-up in the counter-sniper battle begun by the Gurkhas. The enemy gunmen, according to Jon Swift, were 'very sharp. Over a week they'd build up a little position for themselves, brick by brick. That's very difficult to spot over a distance of five or six hundred metres.' Fortunately for the garrison their two trained snipers, Corporal Matt Foster and Lance Corporal 'Sully' O'Sullivan, were 'just outstanding at saying, "Sir, it's been built up, there was one less brick on there last night . . ." They used to spend hours just scanning the ground, learning it inch by inch. That was one of the benefits of being there for so long.' Foster and O'Sullivan eventually recorded one confirmed kill each.

Remarkably, only one Fusilier on the hill ever cracked under the psychological pressure. 'He got scared,' said Allen, 'and there's nothing wrong with that. Everyone was scared. He just reacted slightly differently. He had to be brought off the hill . . . once he was out of that environment and we put him in a sangar in the compound, he was fine.'

Although the compound felt safer than the hill, its walls and sangars hardly offered more security against mortars. During one such attack Greaves, who was in charge of the company's light-calibre 51mm mortar section, was about to dash from the cover of the Control Tower to oversee the response. He was clearing the doorway when Swift suddenly ordered him to 'Wait! Wait!' Seconds later a mortar detonated just where he would have been running. A soldier's sixth sense had saved a comrade's life once again.

The compound was also more vulnerable to attack from RPGs than the hill. Mortars may have been more frightening, but it was an RPG that eventually found a target. It was ten a.m. on 6 October, a Friday, when the sangar on the south-west corner took a direct hit. Until then the sangar had been regarded as the least dangerous in the compound because the majority of attacks were directed at the other side. Unlike the area to the east, however, the streets overlooked by this sangar were still partly inhabited, which allowed the RPG men to pass themselves off as civilians as they moved to within 120 metres of the walls.

The RPG burst through the front left corner of the sangar where it struck two ammunition tins, setting off about twenty rounds (Swift brought the shredded remains of the tins back to Cyprus as souvenirs). The detonated rounds miraculously hit no one, but shards of tin blew everywhere, along with shrapnel from the grenade. 'There was a split second of total silence after the explosion,' recalled Captain Lee Phillips, 'and then there was this deep, terrible screaming.'

The garrison had drilled for this event, and those nearest the sangar reacted with the efficiency of automatons. Training, as they all said, took over. This allowed them to blot out the horror of the blood and the screams of pain and pleading from the two victims, Fusiliers Clive Spencer and Phil Fanthome, so loud they were audible on the hill. Spencer, who had been about to replace Fanthome in the sangar and was at the top of the ladder at the time of the strike, had a broken jaw and lost five of his front teeth. Fanthome was in a much worse condition.

The pair were quickly brought down from the smashed sangar and injected with morphine. As mortar and machine-gun fire began to pour on to the suspected fire point from the hill, the doctor, a Navy surgeon on attachment, checked Fanthome's backside for internal shrapnel wounds. Fanthome, reassuringly, had the wherewithal to shout, 'Fucking hell, doc, you Navy hom!'

Just over an hour after the strike a Chinook touched down to take the injured men to the hospital at Bastion. Swift, who went with them to the helicopter landing site, recalled pulling a poncho over Spencer's face to protect his wounds from the swirling dust; Spencer, morphine-addled and terrified that he had been written off for dead, was deaf to all his OC's assurances and kept snatching the poncho away again.

Throughout the crisis the garrison also had to look to their defences. Some of them, Swift noticed, seemed almost paralysed by the sight, even more so by the shocking sound of two of their own getting injured. Even worse, the section manning Sangar 6 had instinctively dived into cover. Swift, touring the compound with reassurances that the injured would live and that screaming was 'not a bad thing, particularly with head injuries', rushed forward and ordered them all to 'Stand up! Stand up!' It was crucial that they did so, he later explained, if the enemy were not to press home their advantage. Sangar 6 stood and almost immediately spotted a suspect threesome, one of whom was pulling something from a motorbike bag, and opened fire with the GPMG, injuring one of them. Then, just as the rescue helicopter touched down, several vehicles and motorbikes were seen in a compound to the north, gathering for an attack. The enemy compound was mortared and then rocketed by a passing US jet.

Swift prided himself in doing the simple things well. In the officers' mess in Cyprus it was firmly believed that tight discipline and quiet professionalism were an important reason why so few of them were injured and no one was killed. According to Allen, the company 'was a special outfit. There was no bullshit.' Despite the heat, Swift insisted that his men always wore helmets, body armour and uniform when on duty – in contrast to certain other units who were photographed manning machine-guns in little more than swimming trunks. The compound was kept scrupulously clean – 'gleaming', indeed. They only moved about in pairs, and only then when necessary. And despite the need to conserve water – a need, admittedly, that was not as urgent as it might have been because Now Zad was blessed with its own well, albeit with a pump that frequently broke down – the men were ordered to wash regularly, and (again, unlike certain other units) to shave. Beards, Swift reasoned, might be necessary for British troops interacting with the locals, but not for those engaged only in fighting them. Some garrisons in Helmand were later dangerously depleted by out-breaks of diarrhoea and vomiting, but thanks to good basic hygiene Swift's company suffered only one serious case of the dreaded 'D&V' in more than three months.

Time passed quickly for the garrison when they were under attack. Then, and for about three hours afterwards, according to

Groves, 'there was this huge buzz . . . everyone was on an adrenalin high. Looking back on that time, it went really fast.' There were, however, long periods when the men were not in contact, and in some ways these times were the most trying of all, especially on ANP Hill. 'I thought the hardest thing was not having nothing to do,' said Spensley. 'It was really really boring. There was five of us overlooking the town. I'd say after about a month we'd run out of much to say to each other. When you're living with each other that long you start snapping at each other. We exhausted each other's conversation.' What conversation there was tended to centre on when they were going to get out of there, and what they were going to do when they did. Napa, the out-of-bounds nightclub strip in Cyprus, featured often in their talk – 'a brilliant place when you're on the piss', Fisher said.

A handful of paperbacks did the rounds: Bernard Cornwell's *Sharpe* novels, a thriller by Stephen King, several Sven Hassel books with titles like *The Legion of the Damned* and *The Bloody Road to Death*. They had a pack of cards, bought from one of the outgoing Gurkhas, a clever entrepreneur who demanded and received $20 for it. Someone made a chess board, with pieces fashioned from spent ammunition. They erected a makeshift wooden sign, a photograph of which later appeared in the *Sun*, that read 'Welcome to the Dragon's Lair – Home of Fire Support Group Second Fusiliers'. They also played pranks on one another – particularly, for some reason, on Spensley. Someone tried to set his helmet on fire; someone else urinated in his water bottle.

'In the ration packs you get the orange screech, you know?' said Spensley. 'I had a bottle and drank three-quarters of it, and went in Fish's trench, and we were sat there when something happened. I was looking out the front of the trench over his gun, and as I was looking out he must have swapped me bottle. And one of them had pissed in it, and I reached down to take a swig. He started laughing, and I sniffed it and went, "You dirty bastard."'

'It was little things like that that put your morale up,' Fisher said with a grin.

Meal times provided another important distraction. 'The ANP used to bring bags of potatoes up,' said Fisher. 'Just to waste time, me and Spenny used to go and rough the spuds so we could make chips. That used to be the highlight of our day, didn't it?'

'We used to give the locals money to go and get us stuff as well,' Spensley added. 'They used to rob us blind, but we couldn't go anywhere. So he was charging, like, fifty dollars for some oil and potatoes and that.'

'Pakio, his name was. One of the ANP blokes. We used to feed him every day, give him, like, chocolate and sweets and everything. He couldn't speak much English but we taught him some, didn't we?'

'His name was Hajji, but when we got up there he was walking round the hill going "PA-KIO!" So that's what we named him. He was a good one, the best one there. He used to make you chips – try and sell you a mess tin of potatoes for, like, ten dollars, so you'd go, "No, you cook 'em. You cook 'em and we'll give you ten dollars." He was all right.'

Despite the occasional supplement, the Fusiliers' diet was dreary. The ration pack menu was supposed to vary, but often didn't. 'The worst one I had was eighteen days of getting the curry,' said Spensley. 'I don't eat curry anyway. In the end I broke. I just threw it.'

More seriously, the garrison began to suffer muscle wastage and to lose a lot of weight. This was partly because it was so difficult to keep fit. The men tried at first to do sit-ups and press-ups in their trenches, but after a month their enthusiasm for exercise dried up in the stupefying summer heat. The other reason was that the standard issue ORP – operational ration pack, or 'rat pack' – was never designed for continuous use. Although in theory it contained the right amount of calories and vitamins to sustain a man, the Army's own guidelines stated that a soldier's every tenth meal should be a fresh one. The Fusiliers didn't see a proper fresh meal for over three months. And not all of the rat pack's contents were always eaten. The heat made cooking easy – the soldiers simply left their food out in the sun for a bit – but it also turned a chocolate bar into an unappetizing mush. The Fusiliers didn't know it, but the chocolate in an ORP is heavily vitaminized; all of the ration pack has to be eaten if men surviving on it are to remain properly nourished. After their tour was over, Swift was contacted by scientists from QinetiQ, the privatized arm of the MoD's former Defence Evaluation and Research Agency. No unit, Swift was told, had ever lived exclusively on rat packs for so long; the Fusiliers' experience was therefore of considerable scientific interest. It was even grounds, Swift understood, for a rethink of how the long-established ORP was physically constituted.

Swift did his best for his boys. In a quiet moment he wrote to Twinings, the upmarket tea manufacturer, and appealed to their sense of patriotism in the most sentencious terms. Much to his surprise, four huge boxes of teabags arrived at Now Zad a fortnight later. 'Guaranteed to make you feel at home,' it said on the packaging. The men were suspicious at first – they were more used to drinking Tetley's – but in the end the tea was a great success. 'Sir,' said one of them, 'this English Breakfast Tea is really quite good.' Much encouraged, Swift fired off equally beseeching letters to Gillette, Kenco, Batchelor's Supernoodles and Lambert & Butler ('about the only fags that squaddies smoke,' said Swift), but never received a reply from any of them. Twinings' generosity – or perhaps their marketing department's eye for a good opportunity – turned out to be a glorious one-off.

There were times when the wider mission in Helmand – to help the Afghans help themselves against the Taliban – seemed futile. There was no clearer illustration of what the British were up against than the Fusiliers' relationship with their supposed allies, the ANP. There were generally three or four policemen on the hill, although the Fusiliers never quite knew how many or even who they were because they came and went as they pleased. They were friendly to the British, and taught them some Afghan survival tricks such as how to keep a water bottle cool by wrapping it top and bottom in an Army issue sock. But, as the Gurkhas had found, they were also friendly with the enemy. 'We knew from the way they talked to each other on the radios that they knew each other,' said Spensley. 'We heard one of them say, we'll have youse tonight. And one of the coppers said, all right, come on then . . . They were just having chit-chat with each other about who was going to die first. It was very weird.'

Despite the departure earlier in the summer of their corrupt chief, Hajji Muhammadzai, and the warning inherent in Dan Rex's arrest of his radio-clicking deputy, Nek Mohammed, it soon became obvious that at least some of the ANP were still working for both sides. 'None of them could be trusted,' said Fusilier Matt Seal. 'They used to go round and count the mortar bombs, and tell the Taliban how much we had up there. You could see the change in the attacks.'

The defenders put up with it at first. The ANP's duplicity could even be helpful. The sight, for instance, of a policeman scurrying down the hill served as what Martyn Gibbons called a 'useful combat indicator'. Not all of them were so treacherous. Nick Groves thought quite highly of one policeman who helped distribute ammunition and who spoke movingly of his hatred of the Taliban. This man was older than the others, an ex-Mujahidin who told good stories about fighting the Russians, and who owned a house in the town. He spoke quite openly about how he and his colleagues made a living by extorting money from travellers at illicit vehicle checkpoints. Like Dan Rex before him, Groves was not wholly unsympathetic. 'They're not being clothed or paid by the government,' he said. 'What else can they do?'

There seemed at least a chance that such men's loyalty, if not their morality, could be swayed. 'There was one ANP guy we were told was proper dodgy when we first got there,' said Seal, 'but towards the end I think he realized the Taliban were fighting a losing battle – that these foreigners are up for it, not going anywhere. He became one of the best sources we had. He completely turned.'

Others, however, seemed beyond redemption. One ANP man became so brazen that he was arrested and, the following day, frog-marched down to the compound. 'He was clearly marking our positions,' said Spensley. 'He came up in front of my gun first, stood up and down a few times – I was round the back of the hill at the time. Then he walked in front of Fish's gun and did exactly the same. Then he walked into the mud building on top of the hill, and as soon as he went in there we got attacked – dead accurate small-arms fire on both positions, smashing in front of the sangar.'

The tenuousness of the alliance with the local lawmen was exposed again when someone in the compound quietly replaced the tattered Afghan flag that flew there with the Fusilier's regimental one, which is based on the Union Jack. Swift quickly ordered the Afghan flag to be put back up again, but it was obvious to him who the Fusiliers thought they were fighting for, and that some of them at least didn't think the Afghans were worth it.

Swift had to put up with a lot from his Afghan allies. On one occasion a fight broke out in the compound between two ANA soldiers when one called the other 'gay'. The ANA sergeant who took it upon himself to break them up did so by firing his pistol over their heads. He did not fire very far over their heads, however, and succeeded in winging Hazmat, the senior NDS man. It was incidents like this that led Swift to write, in a situation report to a senior officer at regimental headquarters in London in late September, that 'the current strategy is following political rather than military imperatives'. ('Talk about the bleeding obvious,' he commented.)

Unfortunately for Swift, the officer at headquarters posted his report as a regimental newsletter on the Fusilier website. The description of life at Now Zad seemed uncontroversial to him, and the garrison's friends and family were clamouring for news. It was a bad mistake. Prime Minister Blair had repeatedly stated that strategy was the exclusive preserve of his generals; yet here was an officer in the field apparently insisting that it was politically driven. Swift's report, which also stated, truthfully, that 'casualty rates are very significant and show no signs of reducing', was leapt upon by the media. The newsletter was hurriedly removed from the website, but too late. 'The *Mail* went huge on it,' said Swift.

'Everyone did. There was even some talking head on CNN or Sky who said, "Whistle-blowers are normally forced out of the Army in a matter of weeks." I thought I was in serious trouble.'

He wasn't the only one. The following day one of 3 Para's commanders, Jamie Loden, was quoted as describing the RAF as 'utterly, utterly useless' after a 'female pilot' in a Harrier mis-identified a target and narrowly missed the compound at Sangin with a pair of phosphorus rockets. Swift was full of sympathy for Loden, who like him had been pulled at short notice from Staff College for deployment in Helmand. It was hardly Loden's fault, for his remark was made in a private email that was multi-forwarded and eventually leaked to Sky News.

Taken together, the stories amounted to a powerful new stick with which to beat the politicians for a war that was clearly not going according to plan. Swift was quickly exonerated by his superiors. From their point of view, the potential damage to relations between the Army and the RAF was much more serious, so it was the unfortunate Loden who ended up taking most of the heat. 'Irresponsible comments, based on a snapshot, are regrettable,' the Chief of the General Staff said. The charge against the RAF was in any case untrue. Although bombs and rockets could and often did go astray, every one of the company com-manders I talked to spoke highly of the RAF, the Harriers included. 'It was a lesson for me,' said Swift. 'It shows you've got to be bloody careful what you say to anyone when you're in theatre.'

For the NCOs and officers responsible for maintaining troop morale, the greatest challenge was the acute sense of isolation on the hill, and the uncertainty they all felt about when or indeed if they would ever get out of Now Zad. The Fire Support Group had packed for a two-day mission. After two days they were told they would have to stay for five. After four days they learned that they would be staying until the end of the month. When two weeks became five weeks the Fusiliers realized that they would be going nowhere else for the rest of their tour. Fisher began to mark off the days on a four-month 'chuff-chart' that he constructed out of a cardboard box, like a prisoner in a cell, although, as he commented, 'I've been in prison and at least you get electricity. And no one's shooting at you ... There were times when you'd just be lying in your trench and you'd be thinking to yourself, "What am I doing here?"'

Several Fusiliers spoke of a suspicion that they had been abandoned to their fate. 'It seems to me like we were just left there, nobody really knowing what was going on,' said Spensley. He and the others still resented the fact that there was no relief, 'even if it was just for a couple of days or something ... It would have been nice to be able to relax for a bit, because you're on edge all the time. You're like, when's it going to happen next? Sometimes you wouldn't even get up in the morning. All you'd hear is "Incoming!". You'd try and get out of your sleeping bag – if you had one – and get your body armour and helmet on in thirty seconds, morning after morning.'

They understood that the battle group commander, 3 Para's CO Lieutenant Colonel Stuart Tootal, had his hands full. Other units were 'fixed' in places just as dangerous as ANP Hill. By the beginning of August, British troops were dying in significant numbers at Sangin and elsewhere, and the Task Force was stretched to its limits. But that didn't stop the Fusiliers feeling that more should have been done to support them. Some of them even used the phrase 'left to rot'. And they tended to place the blame for that squarely on the Paras.

'I'm not too keen on 'em,' said Spensley. 'They seem to be more interested in looking after their blokes than anybody else. That's the view – well, it's my view. The Paras were in there for two weeks, then put the Gurkhas in for five weeks, then we were there for fifteen ... They put us in, didn't they? And just left us there and didn't relieve us. All the Paras were getting switched round everywhere, getting time in Bastion and coming back out, and we just got left there until the end of our tour. It didn't seem quite right to me.'

It certainly did not help that, during the operation to insert the company at the end of July, a month's worth of fresh rations intended for the Fusiliers were apparently scoffed by the Paras in only two days.

'We hate them,' said Seal. 'It'll be quite something to see, the next time this battalion gets put anywhere with 3 Para. I don't think they ever will, to be honest.' He had bumped into some of them in Qatar in early 2007, in transit on another mission to Afghanistan. 'I met a Para sergeant major. He said, "Ah, Fusiliers – I worked with you last year. Yeah yeah, they came in to Now Zad under contact, it was really funny." I looked at him and said, "I weren't fucking laughing, mate." One of the platoon sergeants was stood there and thought I was going to have a go at the guy – which I wanted to. But I know better than that; I know better than to have a go at a sergeant major. And he said, "Oh, you was there, was yer?" I said, "Yeah, I was there for a hundred and seven days. Because you left us there." And I thought, I made me point. I walked off before he could come back with anything ... I was in civvies; he didn't know what rank I was or anything.'

Not only the lower ranks felt disgruntled, nor even only the Fusiliers. A Household Cavalry officer later confided that they too felt they had sometimes been treated as 'ginger cousins' by the core of the battle group.

'The Paras have a different ethos,' said a Fusilier officer. 'We got two phone calls from them in all our time at Now Zad, and one of those was to say goodbye at the end of their tour. They were a manoeuvrist group, while we weren't allowed to leave the district centre. Our orders were to hold ... we were having some intensive fire-fights and some big contacts, but they were saying it can't be that bad because we had no casualties. But there was a picket on the sangars riddled with 7.62 ... half a metre to the right, and you're dead.'

No one from headquarters ever seemed to come and visit the Fusiliers. Each of the 149 contacts they experienced was dutifully reported back to Bastion, yet there never seemed to be anyone more senior than a second lieutenant on the other end of the radio, or else some sleepy watchman whose promises to pass the report up the chain were seldom convincing. And little information came the other way, which only increased their sense of isolation. 'We had no total picture,' said the officer, 'no situational awareness, no update on operations elsewhere in Helmand. In fact we often hadn't a clue what the rest of the battle group was doing.'

On 1 August when a Scimitar light tank was destroyed by an IED at Musa Qala, the Fusiliers found out about it only because someone in the Operations Room happened to be listening in on the net at the time. Yet the incident had potentially crucial tactical implications for the defenders of Now Zad, as well as devastating psychological consequences for those in the garrison who had known the three victims. In fact the deaths mattered so much to the Fusiliers that an impromptu memorial service was held in the compound.

'We posted every incident back,' the officer said. 'Why couldn't they?'

The lack of attention from the Paras was hurtful, but not as serious as the impact it appeared to have on the Fusiliers' requests for equipment and supplies that they repeatedly made in the 'assets required' box of their daily reports back to HQ. Even mortar ammunition ran low. For a four-day period Gibbons' crews were down to only forty shells between them – enough for two heavy contacts. For a while they were forced to fire smoke shells at their targets instead, as markers for close air support. The SF platoon also ran dangerously short of machine-gun ammunition. At one stage they had twenty-one minutes' worth left – enough for a single contact. 'In the end someone got on the radio and wouldn't take no for an answer,' said Seal.

Squaddies always grumble. All the outstations suffered logistical problems that summer, mainly because of the difficulty and danger of getting Chinooks into the district centre drop zones. Yet helicopter troubles did not quite explain the non-appearance of other essential items of equipment at Now Zad. The Fusiliers suspected that the Paras were either directing these items to where the fighting appeared fiercest and casualties were being taken, which was perhaps fair enough, or else they were simply keeping the good stuff for themselves, which felt less so.

The Fusilier wish list was long, and included MSTAR, the latest 'man-portable surveillance and target acquisition radar' system, which might have made a big difference to the men anxiously scanning for mortar dust plumes the old-fashioned way, through binoculars and out of the corners of their eyes. Some of the Paras were equipped with it, yet no MSTAR ever made it to Now Zad during Herrick 4.

There was an unexplained dearth, too, of the latest generation of Osprey body armour, which covered more of the body and offered greater bullet-stopping power than the ECBA system it replaced. Osprey was hotter and heavier to wear than ECBA, a serious drawback for troops involved in patrols and other mobile operations where moving fast was key to survival; for a garrison restricted to manning trenches and sangars, though, it was perfect. Yet there were never more than four sets for the whole of the Now Zad group, despite requests for more.

They also asked for extra sets of SOFIE thermal imaging equipment, which would have helped them to pin-point their attackers in the rat-runs around the compound. None was ever forthcoming. The blame for that, according to Jackie Allen, lay with the planners in London who had failed to provide any of the battle group with enough SOFIE. 'It's usually only supplied to specialist reconnaissance platoons and observers. There was an attitude of, "Conventional British forces – why would they need SOFIE?"' But we were static, in an urban environment ... They didn't anticipate how much it would be needed.'

The biggest complaint, unsurprisingly, was the lack of overhead protection (OHP) on the hill. A small detachment of engineers could have built some up in no time. The necessary materials were not exactly in short supply at headquarters, where the perimeter was protected by thousands of yards of dirt-filled HESCOs.* The

* So many, indeed, that Camp Bastion was named after them. The HESCO 'Concertainer', to give this icon of modern war its proper name, has been manufactured by the Leeds-based company HESCO Bastion Ltd since 1989. HESCOs are squat, typically hexagonal tubes prefabricated from steel mesh and polypropylene. They are light, strong and easily delivered into theatre in flatpack form. Once filled with earth and rocks and pinned together – a quick and simple operation, given enough manpower – they form highly effective bullet- and blast-proof walls. According to its manufacturers, the HESCO is 'one of the UK's most successful defence exports' and has been used in 'every major conflict area since the First Gulf War'.

sappers needed to install such defences were in short supply, however, and the few available had been directed not to Now Zad but to Sangin.

If that was the tactical priority, thought the Fusiliers, then again it was fair enough. Tootal was known to be a brave and inspirational leader, commendably attuned to the risks his men faced.* On one memorable occasion at Sangin he fought alongside his boys, ordering his regimental sergeant major to bring up more underslung grenades so that he could fire them at an RPG man lurking beyond the walls. But as far as the Fusiliers were concerned, Tootal was above all a Para and that meant his first loyalty was probably going to be to the men of his own regiment. The Fusiliers couldn't help wondering whether, had it been Paras rather than Fusiliers besieged at Now Zad, some spare engineers might have been found.

According to the Fusiliers, the Royal Marines who relieved the battle group at the end of October were 'appalled' at the state of the defences on ANP Hill. One of the first things they did was to bring in a section of sappers from 25 Engineer Regiment, complete with mechanical diggers, to dig out the trenches and build up some proper OHP. 'The engineer recce sergeant took one look at the hill and said, "Jesus. *How* long have you been here?"' Swift recalled. 'I told him, "Just under three months now." And he said, "And you've been filling ration boxes with pebbles?"' The sappers later

---

* On 17 November 2007, Tootal made headlines when he resigned from the Army, reportedly in disgust at the 'shoddy' care his injured men had received at the Selly Oak military hospital in Birmingham, as well as their poor pay, standard of equipment and housing. 'My beloved paratroopers are exceptional,' he said in a statement. 'As a nation we are very lucky to have them. I will miss them all dreadfully.'

presented Swift with a group photograph, framed and inscribed with the words 'Now Zad – A Forgotten Town'.

Whatever the truth of the battle group's attitude towards its non-Para elements, the greater and underlying problem was that the Task Force was under-resourced for the job it was now trying to do. The shortage of manpower was largely due to Whitehall's early decision to cap the deployment to Afghanistan at 3,300 personnel – a decision partly provoked by continuing military commitments in Iraq. The shortage of the best equipment available, meanwhile, had its roots in years of Treasury under-funding. Put another way, the government had sent a boy (albeit a very tough one) to do a man's job, and the Paras could hardly be blamed for that.

Peter Merriman, Swift's CO, took a kinder view of them than most of the Now Zad garrison. The headquarters arrangements to which Tootal was working, he said, were 'high maintenance' and 'probably not conducive to good communications and briefing'. The Paras had competing priorities to deal with, so it was 'understandable' that Now Zad was not at the top of their list. 'There were a lot of hard decisions that took a lot of their attention. They put their companies where they thought the most enemy activity was, and Now Zad was not on 3 Para's main effort. This was part of the reason why Gurkhas and Fusiliers were put there, I guess.'

There were times, in fact, when there was more enemy activity at Now Zad than anywhere else. But it was certainly the case that Now Zad was 'not on 3 Para's main effort'. By July it was painfully clear to Tootal how overstretched his force had become. For that reason, at a senior commanders conference in Lashkar Gah on 22 July, he proposed pulling out of Now Zad altogether and leaving the town in the control of the ANA and the ANP. The 'main effort'

Tootal had identified was Sangin, the town that dominated the upper Helmand river valley, which was strategically and economically vital to the life of the province. Sangin also controlled access to the all-important hydro-electric dam at Kajaki, further north. Now Zad, on the other hand, was thirty miles west of the valley and controlled nothing except its own desert district. Tootal's plan was tactically sensible, but he was overruled. Leaving the town to the ANA and the ANP was tantamount to handing it over to the Taliban, and everyone knew it. The message that such a withdrawal would send to Now Zad's residents was something that neither the British nor Kabul felt they could afford – although, before the summer was out, something very like it was to happen anyway, at Musa Qala. No wonder Swift complained that the platoon-house strategy was following 'political rather than military imperatives'.

The burden of decision on whether to open fire or not lay heavily on all the British, and often demanded a degree of judgement and maturity that it was perhaps not always reasonable to expect of them. Gunman or civilian; civilian or gunman? The enemy wore no uniforms in Helmand, and could effectively switch identity simply by putting down or picking up a weapon. For Swift in particular, the responsibility for targeting was awesome. The Army normally tried to account for every bullet fired on operations. Commanders in the field were supposed to fill out forms called a PIP (post-incident pro-forma) or a SIR (shooting incident report) whenever anything happened. But the battle group had deployed so fast and the tempo of fighting was so intense that the standard systems of accountability were somehow forgotten. The regulation paperwork wasn't introduced until 6 October, with the arrival of the Marines. Until then, company commanders often felt accountable to no one but themselves. Even communication with battalion headquarters in Cyprus was difficult. The only means of doing so was by Thuraya satellite phone – the same network used by everyone else in Afghanistan, civilians and the Taliban included. 'The CO phoned us all the time for an update,' said Jackie Allen. 'He couldn't understand why Jon [Swift] kept hanging up on him. Three times in a row! But it was literally because another RPG round was coming in. Jon just had to go.'

The targeting process could also be frustrating, particularly where air strikes were concerned, because it wasn't always easy to persuade air support to attack. On one occasion an Apache pilot declined to fire at two mortar men relocating their weapon under a tarpaulin on the grounds that he couldn't positively identify (or PID) them as enemy fighters. From the air, the pair could have been two farmers shifting a water pump, but to the Fusiliers, who had been mortared from that area of the town for days, and were also in possession of local intelligence about this particular team, the additional visual evidence amounted to a PID. On later inspection of his gun tape back at Bastion, the Apache pilot was forced to admit that the object under the tarpaulin had indeed been a mortar barrel, and ended up apologizing to the Fusiliers.

Arranging a 'pre-fire op' – a planned air or artillery attack on a specific target – could be problematic for other reasons. In one instance the Fusiliers learned through local intelligence the location of a substantial arms cache, but it was out of view of the compound and the only way to destroy it was from the air. Permission for a pre-fire op had to be approved by a body called the Joint Effects Board, which was based in Kandahar or even London. The approval process could take days, and on a battlefield as fast-moving as Now Zad, any time lag could be critical. In this case, much to Swift's frustration, permission to bomb was turned down three times, on the grounds that the suspected cache was too close to a civilian building. Swift then spoke to an operations officer at Kandahar who suggested that he simply ignore the JEB's decision and call in a quick air strike the next time they were contacted. Swift sensibly declined. 'I felt like saying, "So no one at the Joint Effects level wants to carry the can if it goes wrong, but you're ready to let me hang?"'

Eventually, a local source whom Swift trusted informed him that a Pakistani mortar training team had just arrived at the arms cache. Air surveillance revealed a number of suspicious 'pax' [people] milling around the entrance. This was enough for Swift, who called in a 500lb bomb. It was a brave decision, for later that day he was informed by Bastion that the strike was being 'investigated at the highest levels' – by the Brigade Chief of Staff at Kandahar, in fact. As bad luck would have it, this was on the very day that Fanthome and Spencer were hit by the RPG. 'I was going round the sangars, reassuring the guys, thinking, "The next helicopter that comes in will probably be here to take me away . . . given what we'd been through that day I thought it was pretty out of order, to be honest."' He was, perhaps, fortunate that the bomb didn't miss its target: later in the day, an intelligence report confirmed that a Pakistani trainer had been killed. 'At that point I got all sort of bolshie and called Kandahar, and this corporal said, "Oh, don't worry about that, sir, they wrote that off about half an hour ago. LEGAD [the legal adviser from the Army Legal Service] had a look at it and they're fine about it." And I thought to myself,

"Thanks a lot – when were they bloody well going to tell me?"
That was my darkest day. I was pretty knackered by the end of it.'

Another difficulty for Swift was that the British were not in sole
control of the Now Zad area. Herrick 4 was an ISAF operation, but
the Americans had a separate and overlapping mission, Operation
Mountain Thrust, which had begun in June. Mountain Thrust
involved 11,000 troops, and was geared not to winning local hearts
and minds but to the capture of Osama bin Laden and the
destruction of al-Qaida and its Taliban allies. As the garrison sieges
intensified, the difference between the two missions inevitably
became less and less clear. Helmand was still dotted with US
Special Forces units pursuing their own agendas. At the very least,
close coordination between the allies was called for. Instead there
was often an amazing lack of it.

'There was one night in September,' recalled Matt Seal. 'I'd just
come off stag [sentry duty] and there was a boom-boom-boom. I
thought we was getting mortared. It sounded quite close. We
looked out and saw this Spectre gun-ship. You know the way they
lase their targets? The finger of death? It's like an alien abduction,
man. It was just smashing, for about forty minutes, over towards
Saddle Two, five or six k from us, absolutely hammering. We
didn't know what it was. We got told afterwards that it was a US
Special Forces op. That was quite mad that night.'

The American Rules of Engagement were different from the
British ones. Some in the Task Force suspected that proportionality
of response was not always a US priority, and the surprise appear-
ance of one of their gun-ships over Now Zad seemed a case in
point. The Spectre is not exactly a weapon of minimum force. Its
armaments include a howitzer that can fire a 44lb shell every six
seconds, a 40mm cannon that fires a hundred rounds a minute, and

a pair of 20mm Gatlings that fire 7,200 rounds a minute each. It can carry ten tons of ammunition per sortie; at the end of a night's work, its crews were said to use shovels to clear the empty bullet casings from the aircraft floor. It was certainly a weapon to have on your side, but what was it doing over Now Zad? This was supposed to be the Fusiliers' Area of Operations, yet Swift was not consulted about the operation or even informed of it until a few minutes before it began.

It was the kind of incident that caused bad blood between the allies. There was a constant mutter among the British that US Special Forces units, in particular, were sometimes too quick to call in air support when they ran into trouble. The accusation spilled over into the press in the summer of 2007, when a commander at Sangin reportedly requested the withdrawal of US Special Forces from the district, so damaging was their effect on the British campaign for hearts and minds. Most locals, of course, made no distinction between the US and the UK, Mountain Thrust and Herrick 4; the foreign soldiers, and especially their air bombs, were all one to them. The British complaint was not academic. Garrisons like Swift's really did have to deal with the consequences.

'This car comes driving down the main bazaar one day, and I was on stag right at the front,' Seal recalled. 'It looked a bit dicey – a geezer in the front, with two people in the back at either side. It looked like there was something in between them. The boot was open – it was an estate car. I said, "There's something dodgy about this." It could have been a suicide bomb. I got my gun up, safety catch off. There was dead bodies in the back. There'd been a bombing raid the night before, six or eight k away, nothing to do with us. We saw it happen but we didn't call it in. They'd bombed some white 4×4 thing – apparently it was Iranian or Taliban or whatever – and these guys said, "You bombed us, we're nothing to do with the Taliban, blah blah blah, and these people are dead." And there's people crying at the front gate and all this sort of caper.'

The situation then turned darker. As the grief-stricken driver and his passengers ranted at the sentries on the main gate, a stray dog appeared and began to drag the body parts out of the back of the car. Seal, looking on from his sangar, laughed. 'It's a bit sick really, but when you're in that situation you've got to laugh or you'd end up crying your eyes out every day,' he said. 'I was in stitches. I'm like, "Jesus Christ, look, check this out!"' A dozen other Fusiliers crowded to the front of the compound for their own look at this surreal black comedy.

Then things suddenly threatened to run out of control. 'I looked right and there's, like, a football crowd walking up the road! And we'd never seen that many people before, you know what I mean? About forty, forty-five people, all blokes, walking towards us. And I said, "Here, gunner, check this out." This was developing into a potential riot at the front gate. So the QRF [Quick Reaction Force] are crashed out – that's only about twelve blokes – and we didn't have a proper front gate then, it would have been a bit mad. And I'm thinking, "Shit me, man, this is gonna go tits up."

'Next thing, bang bang bang, there's rounds hitting the sandbags in front of me, rounds, like, winging through the sangar from X-ray 58. I saw movement – a gap in the wall that went into the wood line. So I started firing back, but then I realized it wasn't X-ray 58 because rounds were still hitting us. We couldn't tell where they were coming from. Anyway, I looked right and all these people had took cover, turned round going the other way. So the contact helped us really, because it could have been a disaster.'

In truth, the British were probably not as good at exercising 'proportionality of response' as they thought they were. In the heat of battle the logic of that principle sometimes became hopelessly confused – as an experience of Seal's on ANP Hill perhaps illustrated. He had been trained to use the Milan wire-guided anti-tank weapon, but had never actually fired one and was longing to do so. Each Milan missile, he observed with some satisfaction, cost the British taxpayer £16,500 – 'a bit like firing an XR2 down the lane, I suppose'. One night a suitable target presented itself: three gunmen hiding behind a wall, safe from machine-gun bullets and mortars. He had the safety catch off and was about to fire when he was ordered to stop by a Household Cavalry officer, a troop of whose Scimitar light tanks were then on the hill.

'I thought, "Bollocks." I put the safety back on. Five minutes later an F18 comes in and, boom – a 500lb bomb. And I said to this guy after, "I've been gagging to fire that Milan. I've got something in me sights, I can take it out – why, what's the crack?" And he went, "Well, Fusilier Seal, it's all about proportionality and the laws of armed conflict" and all this crap . . . he said it was the wrong weapon system to use against people. And I said, "What a load of bollocks! Five minutes later you dropped a 500-pounder on them! How does that work?" He went, "Yeah, yeah, good point," and just turned round and walked off. I thought, "You absolute wanker. That was my chance!" He was a nice bloke, mind. Good at his job. But that night I thought he was a wanker. Really posh.'

Matt Seal was a regimental classic. At thirty-four he was the oldest private in his company and known as 'the senior Fusilier'. He was a big man from Birmingham whose middle name was Busby (his father, he explained, had been a die-hard Manchester United fan), although he himself supported Aston Villa. That much was clear from the tattoos that coated his meaty arms and shoulders – the work, he said, of an ex-Fusilier mate who lived in Preston. There was also a fierce-looking British bulldog, a large star with the words 'Strength and Honour' around it, a Samurai warrior attended by a pair of dragons, and the names of his children picked out in Gothic lettering on his forearms.

His Brummie background was typical of the old units from which his Royal Fusilier 'super-regiment' was amalgamated. Fusilier recruits have been drawn from the Midlands and the north-east for well over 300 years. The 'fusil' was a seventeenth-century word for the flintlock musket with which they were once armed, an elite weapon at a time when most European armies were still using matchlocks. The red and white hackle on his beret supposedly gained its colour when it was dipped in French blood at St Lucia in 1778. Fusiliers fought at Badajoz, Inkerman, Lucknow, Khartoum, Alma, Sebastopol, and at Kandahar, too, in 1880. As the *Sun* liked to point out, it was Fusiliers who famously won six VCs 'before breakfast' at the Gallipoli landings in 1915.

Seal was suitably proud of all this. Like many others who took part in Herrick 4 he compared the siege of Now Zad to Rorke's Drift in 1879, when 139 Redcoats held off a Zulu force of between 4,000 and 5,000, winning eleven Victoria Crosses in the process. The difference was that he claimed Rorke's Drift was also among the battle honours won by his regimental forebears. 'Everyone thinks it was the Welsh because of the Michael Caine film,' he said, 'but it wasn't, it was us. There were a few Welshmen, and some of the officers, so that's how it ended up. But most of them were from Birmingham and stuff.' I checked later and found that he was broadly correct. Rorke's Drift was defended by a company of the 24th Regiment, the Second Warwickshires, only nineteen of whom were actually Welsh. The regimental march of the 2/24th, tellingly, was not 'Men of Harlech' but 'The Warwickshire Lad'.

Seal had thought about what the British were doing in Helmand, and come to the conclusion that the deployment was quite justified. 'Iraq is an absolute joke, man, and the sooner we're out of there the better. But, Afghan ... these people cannot be allowed to just cut about doing what they want – and they do do what they want, don't they? In these places like Now Zad, there's no law. But the normal civvies, they just want to get on with their lives.'

On his latest tour in Kabul he'd had more chances to talk to ordinary Afghans, and what he heard had solidified his view that the Taliban were a menace. 'Some of the horror stories that came out ... There was one lad and his mum in Kabul. We were chatting to him; he spoke quite good English. He came from somewhere in Helmand. The dad had been killed, shot in the face, by the Taliban because they wanted his land. They were living in a shit hole but it was better than Helmand ... we started realizing how these people were getting shit on from everywhere, and the government aren't doing anything about it, are they?'

His experiences at Now Zad had clearly changed him. 'I had nightmares when we got back. Quite a few, around Christmas. I kept hearing Phil Fanthome screaming. It was horrible to hear. I was under the sangar when it happened. As we drove out [to the helicopter landing site for the casualty evacuation, or casevac] there was a lad lying outside, one of the locals, with a gunshot wound, and an old geezer with him. He was about sixteen. He'd been dicking us for weeks. After the RPG hit he pops out of the alleyway where it was fired from, so one of the lads shot him. He got taken to Bastion. He survived, shot in the leg. I still remember his face. He was there, right next to me. I said, "That's the dicker." I reported him four or five times; he was pacing out the alleyways. I reckon he pulled the trigger too. There's no one else come out of that alleyway. He ended up lying in the same hospital as the blokes he'd RPG'd. It's surreal, but there you go.'

Despite the rough exterior and, one suspected, a Saturday-night-fighting nature, there was a moral, even sensitive soul within. 'I felt quite sorry for the locals to be honest – what little contact we had with them,' he said. 'It's just like stepping back two hundred years. They've got nothing, have they? Absolutely nothing. I was gobsmacked, me. I used to give the kids sweets – throw them out the sangars and that. We didn't have a lot to go round ourselves, like, but they had jack shit.'

The British occupation of Now Zad, he agreed, had brought a great deal of death and destruction. More than 18,000lb of explosives had been dropped on the town by 10 October alone. But he also thought the hearts and minds process was far from being a lost cause. The fact that the Fusiliers could, and often did, offer medical assistance to the locals gave him particular cause for hope.

'No one would come anywhere near us to start with,' he said, 'but one day this guy turned up with two young children, a boy and girl, and they'd been really badly burned ... it was nothing to do with us. They were carried down from some village. They'd been playing with something phosphorus. When they came in, the guy was shitting himself. Absolutely shitting himself. You could see pure fear in his face. We calmed him down, and the kids got casevaced. One of them died later. And we said to the guy, "What's wrong?" And he said the Taliban had been telling everyone that we were all white infidels, eating babies, shagging women and getting pissed. And they believed it, because something like ninety-six per cent of Now Zad can't read or write ... And this guy saw that wasn't correct, and that we'd helped him out, and he went back to his village a couple of k down the road and spread the word.'

From then on a steady flow of injured appeared at the gates of the district centre. In many cases it was their only hope of survival, for there was no other medical facility functioning in the region. People often turned up with a gunshot wound ten minutes after a contact, angrily claiming that the British had just shot them. The medics would examine them, only to find that the wound was any-thing up to a week old. But they never turned anyone away, even when they suspected that the injured had just been trying to kill them. This was the British Army at its most humane.

'Towards the end I felt we were actually doing some good in Now Zad – like we'd actually achieved something. At the beginning, nothing moved in No Man's Land [the urban area to the east of the district centre], but by the end people were coming back to their homes there, to collect their belongings or whatever. There was even one bloke who moved back into his house, right under Sangar 6. The Taliban had used that house to attack the compound when the Gurkhas were there, but he still wanted to move back in. We said, "Crack on, mate!" Very brave.'

Such moments of optimism were rare, however. By the middle of September the pressure of the siege was beginning to tell on Seal. His stint on ANP Hill, although terrifying, had at least passed quickly. The fear and tension of the seemingly endless nights of sangars duty in the compound was of a different order, even on quiet nights, and the stress was cumulative.

'On stag, at night, three in the morning, pitch black, everyone's asleep, there's me and that bloke over there in that sangar, and you'd start flapping. You could hear your heart beating, and you'd start thinking, "Jesus Christ, man, there could be a geezer stood a hundred metres down that alleyway and I wouldn't be able to see him." So you get your night vision up and you'd have it fixed to your eye for, like, two hours. You'd make yourself panic. Then you'd hear something and it would be a dog going through rubbish – every time. There were thousands of dogs. You knew it was a dog, you just knew, but you'd still have to stick your head out and have a look. What if it's a bloke with an AK-47? You'd lean out, and out a bit more, and then bow-wow-wow, and you'd jump across the sangar – Jesus, shit yourself . . .'

It wasn't easy, being the senior Fusilier. The younger men looked up to him, and nicknamed him 'the Gerber' after the American-made multi-tool (a reflection of his long-standing position in the company's transport section), but that didn't help him now. The only person he felt he could really talk to was his mate Stewart Spensley; but he was out of reach, up on the hill with the Fire Support Group.

'I was feeling the pressure quite a lot, mid-September. I'd come off stag, and me being the senior Fusilier, supposed to be cutting about, looking after the younger blokes, cos there's a lot of young lads out there . . . and I'd be absolutely fucked. You'd be up there for twenty-four hours and in contact for three of them. You'd come down, physically and mentally drained, you're not in the best of moods, you just want to get into bed. And Jackie Allen would say, "What's up, Gerber? You all right?" I'd say, "Not really, no." And he'd say, "You've got to keep your chin up, man, you're the senior Fusilier" . . . I had a few blokes come to me, saying, "I'm struggling a bit here, I'm getting a bit scared." And I think, "Who do I go and chat to? I can't always be the joker." '

It didn't help that his marriage was in crisis. 'The wife said she wanted a divorce, but when we got posted I said, "Wait until I get back, maybe we can work something out." But she wouldn't wait, and posted the papers out. It was horrible, because you look forward to the postbag, you know? And it was my divorce papers. I don't think she had any idea what we were going through out there. And I lost it – I shouted my head off. I think the Taliban must have heard me from the wood line . . . I proper struggled in the week after that.'

Now Zad forced Seal to face himself in other ways. According to local estimates, about 170 fighters were killed during the Fusiliers' time there. Many of these were accounted for by mortars and close air support, but shooting a man was different. The act of killing was more personal, the responsibility more direct. Few if any of the Fusiliers had been called upon to kill a man before, and the first time was difficult for all of them – even for Dean Fisher, the machine-gunner who fired more rounds at the Taliban than anyone. In a contact on the day that Spencer and Fanthome were hit, Fisher shot up a speeding car. 'The body fell out of the passenger door,' he recalled, 'and you've actually seen it and you've done it yourself and the body was just lying there at the side of the car. I was watching through the binos for any more movement, and I was shaking. Shit, I've just killed someone.'

It was no different for Seal. It was his first time, too, despite his twelve years in the Army. As he pointed out, no amount of training can prepare a soldier for the real thing. 'It's not a nice experience. I shot two blokes. The first one . . . I was looking out into No Man's Land from Sangar 3. There are only a couple of points where you can see straight into the wood line. There was this one point, just above the blue garage door – 578 metres, it was a good shot. I was on the sandbags when this geezer just popped up. He had a rifle. He just walked into me sight picture, and I just thought, "Fucking hell." I hit him. He went down, then he got back up again – you know, nearly six hundred metres with an SA80, it's not going to do that much. I went to pull the trigger again, and I had a massive stoppage. Jammed solid. And I thought, "Shit." So I shouted at me mate, Sony, "There he is, blue garage door, just above the razor, one finger left, he's there in the wood line." He said, "Oh yeah, I can see him!" So I said, "Well shoot him then!" Thirty rounds off an LMG, and he missed him. And the geezer dragged himself back into the wood line. Afterwards I sat there and I thought, "Hang on. I just shot someone." I had a brew and that. And I don't think I spoke for the rest of that stag. Not a word to anyone. I just sat at the back. I didn't get to sleep that night. I just lay there all night thinking, "Fucking hell, man, I shot someone." It's something strange. A really strange feeling.'

Introspection was followed by a range of emotions, including guilt. 'You feel like, you know, a bit happy with yourself – I've done me job, it's what I've come here for, know what I mean? He's Taliban and I've got one of them. You feel quite chuffed about it. Then you're feeling, like, you know . . . well, you know, sad. You're thinking . . . well, you know . . . you know . . . the, the geezer's another human being at the end of the day, like. Then you get the feeling, well, you know, bollocks to him, it's either him or me. And then you're thinking . . . I think people get, like, you know, religious then as well. You're thinking, well, in the bigger picture, if there is like a Geezer up there and a Geezer downstairs, what does that mean to me now I've just fucking shot someone? Is that me bollocksed? Am I going to hell or what? And all of that went through me mind that night, for hour after hour after hour. I think I did fall asleep for a couple of hours towards the end. But really strange.'

Garrisoning Now Zad was a lonely business, and as Seal hinted, religion stepped into the void for many of them. A padre who arrived towards the end of their tour – 'a Marine padre, with a big round head, red-faced' – was in heavy demand. Indeed, the first impromptu service he held at the compound was so packed that Seal was unable to get in. I had had my doubts about General Dannatt's contention that the Judaic-Christian tradition underpins the Army, but wondered now if I had been wrong.

'I spoke to the padre,' said Seal, 'and he said, "How are you getting on?" And I said, "I'm finding it quite hard, to be honest, sir. I need to get out of here. It's grinding me down now." I said to him, "To be honest, I'm struggling, mentally, in me conscience-wise, with what we've been doing out here." He said, "Do many blokes feel like that?" I said, "I think there's a few, yeah. There's quite a few who said they couldn't get into that church service today." He said, "I'll have another one if you want." So he did, in the room at the top of the central building. There was about ten of us in there. And he said a few prayers and that, and touched on killing people. He was nice. He said, "I know you've done things out here that you may find trouble with God for what you've done. But God under-stands, and you're here doing a job, and you're here for the greater . . . you've got to look at the bigger picture." It helped a little bit, but not a lot.'

However tough they were, or however tough they thought they were, men engaged in state-approved homicide for the first time needed sensitive handling. At the very least they craved some kind of outside acknowledgement of the 'strangeness' of their experi-ence. Many of the Fusiliers spoke of the impossibility of describing what it was like to their friends and family, whether during or after the tour. 'You can explain it to 'em but they can never understand it properly cos they've never been in that situation,' said Fisher. 'You can only explain it so much.'

There was nothing new about this. I was reminded of a song from the satirical 1960s film and stage musical *Oh! What a Lovely War*, the lyrics of which were based on a ditty actually sung by British troops in World War One: 'And when they ask us how dangerous it was, / Oh, we'll never tell them, / No, we'll never tell them.'

'You'd have these strange phone conversations,' said Seal. 'They just didn't get it. I phoned my brother once and I'd go, "We got RPG'd twice today," and he'd go, "Didja? Did you watch the footy?" And my Dad sent a tenner once. And I got offered a PlayStation. What were we supposed to do with that when we had no electricity, no batteries? It was the same with the videos, showing them to people back home. They always go, "Are those real planes?" Or the tracers: "Are those real bullets?" And you'd have to explain what tracer is, that only one in five is lit up and there are four more invisible ones for every one you can see. And then they just look at you.'

Some of the Fusiliers who had been redeployed in Helmand at the beginning of 2007 had plainly tired of the novelty of combat. 'I'd be happy now just to stay here [in Cyprus] and go through my Army career without doing it again, you know?' said Dean Fisher. The waning of his enthusiasm was particularly striking. This, after all, was the man dubbed a hero by the *Sun* in November 2006. His photograph had appeared in the local newspaper in Nuneaton, prompting the mayor to phone his father with a request for Fisher to lead the Remembrance Day parade – although he couldn't go because he was too busy preparing for redeployment to Sangin. That district centre, he said, 'was more or less the same as Now

Zad, but you had all the new lads there that had never been in a contact before, running upstairs, like, really excited, wanting to get on the guns. I just sat downstairs without a gun, going, "Go on then. Go and do it. I'm all right down here."' Fisher's experience hadn't made him want to leave the Army – yet. 'I wouldn't say that, but it's made me think, like, do I actually want a permanent job here? Because I'm pushing my luck now. Do I want to settle down with a family and that?'

The blooding of his generation had consequences, and one of them was a realization that soldiering was nowadays actually very dangerous. Fisher understood that a career in the Army was a different proposition from what it used to be, and saw straight through the *Sun*'s shallow jingoism. Lee Phillips, a forty-one-year-old captain with a twenty-two-year Army career behind him, told me that before Helmand he had fired precisely eleven shots in anger, all of them in Northern Ireland. He fired more than that in the first hour of his arrival at Now Zad. 'I can't remember who said the business of a soldier is not to kill but to be killed,' said Peter Merriman, the battalion commander, 'but what's happening now is fundamentally different. Last year we had five wounded, two severely, and two killed in Iraq on Telic 6. And we've been very lucky. There are some battalions who have had over seventy killed and wounded on their tour of Basra. These are quite big figures.'

The potential impact on retaining trained men was clear, and so was the threat to recruitment figures in the future. 'I think the CGS [General Sir Richard Dannatt] was spot on when he said the problems for the Army would come later, in five or ten years' time,' Swift said. 'We're in OK shape now, but he's right when he says the present tempo isn't sustainable.'

The official psychological effect of so much combat was looking pricey for his company. Eight of the 128 men who went to Helmand had reported to the medics with symptoms of suspected post-traumatic stress disorder (PTSD), and Swift worried privately that there were more to come. Captain David Baxter, a doctor, worried about this too. He explained that PTSD was still poorly defined medically. The symptoms, which include depression, alcohol and drug abuse, flashbacks and nightmares, take an average of thirteen years to present themselves and there is no predicting who is going to suffer from them.

The battalion was acutely conscious of the dangers and worked hard to foster what they called 'a supportive environment' for the troops returning home. First the men underwent a period of 'decompression' in the form of an obligatory holiday in Kuwait. (Fisher didn't think much of this, mainly because the beer on sale there had been alcohol-free.) Then they were subjected to two days of lectures designed to teach them to spot the symptoms of PTSD in themselves and in their mates. For the first few days back at barracks they were also ordered to keep on the combat kit they had been wearing abroad. 'I thought it was rubbish, but it works,' said Baxter. 'It makes the transition to home more gradual.' Drinking too much was something the medics watched particularly carefully for. 'It's fine if they go on the piss with their mates for a bit, but if they're still at it after four weeks, alarm bells start to ring.'

The twenty-fifth anniversary of the Falklands campaign was marked in June 2007, and among the slew of newspaper articles accompanying it was one claiming that 300 veterans had since 1982 committed suicide – fifty more than were killed in the conflict itself. Baxter questioned its accuracy – 'people commit suicide for all sorts of reasons', he said – but acknowledged that it was disturbing all the same. According to Robert Marsh, a spokesman for

Combat Stress, the ex-Services mental welfare charity, the fighting in Helmand represented an even greater mental health time-bomb than the Falklands.

The fact that the combat in Afghanistan was the most intense in a generation played its part in this, Marsh explained; so did the fact that the MoD's 'Harmony Guidelines' – according to which there should be a twenty-four-month interval between six-month operational tours abroad – were being routinely ignored. But the main reason was the nature of the war the troops were fighting. The conflict in Helmand was 'asymmetrical'. In the phrase coined by retired general Rupert Smith, the author of the influential book *The Utility of Force*, it was 'war amongst the people' – an environment that brought special psychological pressures that were absent in the conventional wars of the past.

'Lots of people join the Army to have a fight, but they've got that now; they've done it,' said Baxter. 'They tell me, "I'm out now. I've killed someone, and now I'm off to become a good family dad." I've heard that ten times in the past year, all from infantry guys and across regiments. It will be interesting to see how the Army copes medically in the future with all those suddenly leaving.'

'You don't think it affects you that badly, but it does,' said Fisher. 'I was sat down with one of my mates in a pub in Coventry and I was thinking, "Why am I feeling like this? I should be enjoying myself." But you just feel really down in the dumps. Just sat there, thinking to myself.'

'I didn't know how to fill me days when I was on leave,' said Stewart Spensley. 'It was, like, what shall I do? All your friends and family are still going out to work, and, like, you go home and ... I wasn't too bad, cos one of the lads who lost his leg out there [Fusilier Barlow, in a mine incident near Kajaki] lives just down the road from me in Bury, and we used to go out on the piss together. But other times he was down in London, at Headley Court [military hospital, in Surrey], and I just sat there wondering, "What can I do?"'

'I couldn't sit down for more than fifteen minutes,' said Duncan Grice.

'I fell out with my missus on leave,' said Fisher. 'You get used to having a phone call – that phone call relationship – but as soon as you spend more than a week with them, that's it, you're at each other's throats, cos you're not used to doing it.'

'Me ex-missus, when I got back, wanted to try and spend all the time in the world with me,' said Spensley, 'but I just weren't interested. I said I'd rather be out with me mates or have a bit of time on me own . . . I suppose that's life, isn't it?'

Martyn Gibbons, the mortar fire controller on ANP Hill, was not in Cyprus when I met him, shortly before the Dhekelia trip, but at Headley Court hospital. He was in a wheelchair, recovering from an SPG-9 recoilless rifle strike at Sangin. He was lucky to have survived it with just his legs smashed; if the missile had struck a few inches higher he would certainly be dead. The recoilless rifle is a misnomer, for it is neither a rifle nor recoilless. A Russian-invented, tripod-mounted weapon designed to penetrate tank armour, it fires an 82mm missile at 700 metres per second – more than twice the velocity of an RPG. The missile certainly penetrated Gibbons. It exploded against the sandbags in front of him, but ten inches of tail fin carried through and came to rest in his left thigh, the hot and smoking metal poking out on both sides like an arrow in a cowboy hat in a Lucky Luke cartoon. 'I was ecstatic when I saw him,' said Baxter, who attended him in his sangar, 'because he was screaming so much. It proved his airways were clear.' Part of

Gibbons' stomach muscle was later taken out to patch up the gaping wound. He had kept the tail fin as a souvenir. When he was better, he said, he planned to tip it with silver and mount it on a stand at home.

His wife Kim was visiting at the same time. They were older than the average patient, he thirty-two, she thirty-one, and I found them good company as we sat chatting on a roof terrace where the sun shone. They were from Rochdale in Greater Manchester, and spoke with an uncompromising Lancastrian accent that exuded maturity and common sense. The accent fitted the man. Gibbons was the epitome of the experienced sergeant: courageous, uncomplaining and unshakably philosophical, a steadying influence at Headley Court among the injured teenagers and twenty-somethings even from other regiments.

He had escaped from Now Zad unharmed, only to be sent almost immediately on a second Afghan tour, this time in support of the Royal Marines. 'I had a bad feeling about this one from the start,' said Kim. 'He's been in Bosnia, Kosovo, Ireland – but this was the worst. I was sure something was going to happen to him.'

The most stressful thing, she said, was the endless waiting for news. The troops in Helmand were permitted only twenty minutes of phone calls home each week – a cause of much bitterness among the troops, who pointed out that even British prison inmates were allowed thirty minutes. In response, early on in Herrick 4, the phone time allowance was duly raised to half an hour. At Now Zad there were three satellite phones available, but there was only one charger, and one or two of the batteries were usually flat. Phone calls were often interrupted by incoming fire. Sometimes, thanks to a communication lockdown across the battle group, they couldn't be made at all. This was to ensure that the first to hear the news of a death or serious injury was the next of kin, and that they heard it through official channels rather than on television – a humane policy that was nevertheless tough on everybody else connected to the deployment. 'You'd hear that someone had been hit but I never knew if it was him or not, or even if it was one of the Fusiliers. You'd wait for twenty-four hours sometimes before hearing he was OK. That happened quite often, actually.'

Marooned on the base in Cyprus with their three young daughters, Kim found it hard to carry on with life as though nothing was happening. There wasn't much support from the other Army wives, since only five members of her husband's company were married, and these women weren't particular friends of hers. The problem, in the end, was loneliness – a common complaint among Army wives and partners, but particularly acute for this battalion. A posting to Cyprus used to be seen as a cushy number – 'the tour in the sun', as it was known – but there was little time for sun-bathing at Dhekelia for this over-committed Army. In 2006 the Theatre Reserve Battalion was on deployment almost all the time. 'In the last fifteen months I've seen my kids for a total of three,' Gibbons said.

To the Fusiliers, the MoD's 'Harmony Guidelines' were a bit of a bad joke. Not everyone's relationship was as strong as the Gibbonses'. In 2006, according to Jon Swift, there were six divorces and ten separations within the battalion. Matt Seal's was obviously one of them. There had been talk recently in senior military circles of altering the length of the standard six-month tour, but that didn't impress Kim. 'It won't make any difference,' she said. 'The TRB will still be out there all the time. What we really need is a bigger army.'

Peter Merriman was as upbeat about all this as one might expect a lieutenant colonel to be. He acknowledged the high level of divorces and separations over the previous year, but argued that these might have happened even without the operational deployments. 'In September, annually, after a long hot summer in Cyprus, there are usually a number of people who have had their fill,' he said. He agreed that 2006 had been 'a big ask for an infantry battalion' and that they had had to 'dig pretty deep' while insisting that it had been professionally satisfying and that they had all 'come out the other end stronger – and I include the wives and all that as well'. He played down the notion of 'overstretch' – 'one of those great words that has been around since the 1980s at least' – but even he admitted that the battalion couldn't have done more in the year without setting themselves up for some serious problems. Apart from two Afghan tours, in the course of 2006 his battalion helped evacuate British citizens from Lebanon, trained the special forces in Jordan and deployed to Iraq twice. In Helmand, when the bulk of Swift's men were at Now Zad, other members of 'A' Company were in action at Gereshk, Kajaki and Musa Qala. At one stage there were Fusiliers simultaneously manning a dozen locations in six different countries. 'It's been finely judged, or lucky, whichever way you want to look at it.'

At Headley Court I was discussing the vagaries of the military honours system with Martyn Gibbons when Phil Fanthome briefly appeared, sallow and underweight, like so many of the patients there. His legs and right arm had been raked by shrapnel. He was still able to walk, even to run, just about, but his right hand was swollen and clenched in an immobile claw as he listened in silence to our conversation. 'There weren't many medals for us,' said Gibbons with a shake of his head. Then he turned to Fanthome and winked. 'But you might get one for the loudest scream, eh, Phil?'

Although Jon Swift was eventually Mentioned in Dispatches for his commander's role, and two others received Joint Commanders' Commendations, the steady nerve it took to defend Now Zad generally went as unrecognized in the end-of-year honours list as the courage displayed by the Gurkhas who preceded them. This was in marked contrast to the Paras, who won a dozen medals for bravery and were Mentioned in Dispatches eleven times. Lieutenant Colonel Tootal, who was himself awarded the DSO, seemed to me to be defensive about the disparity when, much later, I interviewed him at his Colchester headquarters. 'I think they performed superbly,' he said. 'I take nothing away from them.'

Tootal confirmed the Fusiliers' suspicion that the absence of fatalities among them was a factor in the lack of formal recognition. 'But,' he added, 'it was also a measure of intensity . . . There is a difference between doing it for three months and six months. And when you look at due recognition . . . part of that is reflected on people's endurance. It's one thing to do something once or for a very brief period of time; it's an entirely different thing to keep on doing it, day in day out, for a six-month period. That is partly and probably the main reason why there is a difference in emphasis in terms of reflection.'

Yet the Fusiliers on ANP Hill, the Army all agreed when they got back to Cyprus, had just completed the longest defence of a static trench position in British military history, and even Tootal conceded that it was largely a matter of extreme good luck that none of them was killed.

4

The Joint UK Plan for Helmand

When Captain Jim Phillipson died on 11 June 2006, shot in the face when his patrol was ambushed near Sangin, Leo Docherty was wearing the combat holster that he'd borrowed from him. Phillipson, twenty-nine, from St Albans in Hertfordshire, was the first British soldier to be killed on Herrick 4. He was a gunner from 7 Para Royal Horse Artillery who, like Captain Docherty, had been attached to the Afghan National Army as part of the OMLT, the British-run Operational Mentoring and Liaison Team. Docherty had shared a bunk room with Phillipson at Camp Tombstone, the ANA base adjacent to Camp Bastion, and indeed was sitting on the bed next to his friend's empty one when the terrible news came through, watching *Wild Geese* on Phillipson's DVD player. The news filled him with despair. But it also made him angry – so angry that he quit the Army soon afterwards. He was convinced that his friend's sacrifice was futile, and even before his commission was served out he was explaining why he thought so to the press. Not content with that, he went on to write a damning memoir of his experiences called *Desert of Death*. As Herrick 4's first credible whistle-blower his remarks were taken seriously by the media, and they got him into very deep trouble with his Commanding Officer.

I met Docherty, by now an ex-Scots Guardsman, over tea and crumpets in the kitchen of a north Oxford flat belonging to his aunt. He had two Flashmanesque pencils of hair sculpted along the tops of his cheekbones – all that now remained of the full beard visible in a photograph on the refrigerator door, a group shot of him and half a dozen other young men in desert fatigues, squinting in the sunshine as they posed with weapons in front of a pair of machine-gun-festooned Land Rovers. The whiskers were both a memento of his tour and a symbol of his new freedom, for they certainly wouldn't have complied with modern Queen's regulations.

The Victorian look was no accident. A linguist who spoke Urdu as well as some Pashto, Docherty consciously saw himself as a modern-day Great Game adventurer. Indeed he was only temporarily in England, having taken time off from a 3,000-mile journey by horseback through central Asia – an attempt to repeat the solo exploit of his hero Frederick Burnaby, whose epic *Ride to Khiva* became a best-seller in 1876. Burnaby, who was also six feet four inches tall and a Guardsman, was said to have once carried two Shetland ponies, one under each arm, and was reputed to be the strongest man in the Army.

Docherty hadn't changed his mind about Herrick 4, and had no regrets about abandoning his Army career. The Helmand campaign, he said, was 'ignorant, clumsy and destructive – a vainglorious folly'. As an officer attached to the ANA he had been among the first British troops to arrive in Sangin, in May 2006. The town, it had been reported, was 'overrun' with Taliban. His group's orders amounted to just five words: 'Seize Sangin and re-establish governance.' The ANA were included in this early foray because the need to put an Afghan face to the counter-insurgency was still considered paramount – although in the event there were very few ANA available, and the job was largely left to the British.

The Taliban threat had been exaggerated. Docherty found himself patrolling a town peaceful enough to allow him to stop and buy mangos in the bazaar. The troops wore no helmets and removed their sunglasses in a bid to appear less intimidating. The locals were wary of their intentions, though. One day a friendly petrol pump attendant asked him if the British intended to ban the growing of poppies.

'Well, we will offer an alternative – something for the people to grow.'

'What?' he asks, still smiling.

'Well, it's not certain, but there will be other benefits, like improvements in the town ... that is, development,' I reply, disappointed at the hollowness of my words.

Sensing my unease, he does not question me further.

The British had entered Sangin with little preparation, and so little intelligence on the town that when they first arrived they couldn't even find the governor's office. Much worse, in Docherty's view, was that they had nothing concrete to offer the locals once they were there. They had certainly not been briefed on how to answer the all-important question about poppies – partly, of course, because there was no answer. The British and Americans were still arguing about counter-narcotics strategy a year later. Docherty regarded this early period in Sangin as an opportunity disastrously wasted, the moment when a 'quick-impact project'(or QIP, pronounced 'quip') like sinking a well or re-paving a road could have demonstrated the Army's peaceful intent and perhaps forestalled the violence that followed. But no QIPs were launched. Instead, as Docherty understood, the British antagonized the suspicious locals by their mere presence. That distrust, he reckoned, led in turn to the killing of Jim Phillipson, an incident that brought a swift end to the days of soft-hat patrolling and altered the dynamics of the town for ever.

Docherty, wondering what the British were going to do now that calamity had struck, went to see the OMLT officer at Bastion HQ.

'What's the form?' I ask, approaching his desk. 'Are we pulling out of Sangin or what?'

'Mmm, no. One of the Para companies is going to stay on at the district centre. Other than that the plan's not really changed, Leo.'

'What plan?' I retort, flashing with anger. 'There is no plan . . . We fucking well made it up as we went along going into Sangin, you know that.'

'Easy, mucker, it's not my fault this has happened,' he says plaintively.

'This is fucking nonsense. We've blundered into that town not even knowing what our objective was, and we've sat there like a bloody great target doing fuck-all.'

'Mate, chill,' he says, standing and raising his palms.

'Don't tell me to fucking chill!' I want to grab his pasty white face and smash it on the desk between us. 'This is a fucking disgrace! More blokes'll die up there, for no reason, and we're doing fuck-all about it!'

Docherty was not the only one in the summer of 2006 who feared that the British were making it up as they went along in Sangin. He was right: they were. But the inference that there was no plan for Helmand was false. The British had in fact spent months in 2005 working out how to proceed, and had come up with a plan that was very detailed. The problem, rather, was that the occupation of the northern district centres was never part of it, and that the Task Force had departed from the script.

The 'Joint UK Plan for Helmand' was finalized in December 2005. Because it was commonly accepted that there could be no purely military solution to the region's problems, the planners were determined to pursue what was known as a 'comprehensive approach' under which the military would work hand in hand with the government's main civilian agencies, the Department for International Development (DfID) and the Foreign Office. The brain-storming was mostly done over an intensive six-week period at the military airbase at Kandahar in November and December 2005. Representatives of DfID, the Foreign Office and PJHQ, the Armed Forces' Permanent Joint Headquarters at Northwood in Middlesex, were all present. According to one official who took part, 'hundreds' of people were involved. The unenviable task of coordinating these disparate bodies, and of making sure that the plan they produced really was 'joint', fell to a small but dedicated team from the interdepartmental Post Conflict Reconstruction Unit, the PCRU.

The unit was headed by Mark Etherington, who had been in the post-conflict business since Bosnia. As the senior international representative in Kut in Iraq in 2004, his compound was besieged by armed followers of the Shi'ite leader Moqtada al-Sadr. Etherington – who, by strange coincidence, was a former Para company commander – helped to organize the compound's sixteen-hour defence. He was supported in Kandahar by Minna Jarvenpaa, a Finn who was hardly less experienced. She was a former adviser to the Finnish president Martti Ahtisaari, and had administered Mitrovica, a particularly turbulent town in Kosovo, on behalf of the UN.

The British plan was ambitious, perhaps overly so. The planning committee was encouraged to 'think big' in Afghanistan. Tony Blair, whose interventions in Kosovo and Sierra Leone had been such a success, was on the way out as Prime Minister. Helmand was his likely swan-song, and he took a personal interest in it – had done so, indeed, ever since Britain agreed to lead the G8 on counter-narcotics in Afghanistan. The PCRU advised a more measured approach, but the sense of purpose emanating from the Cabinet Office was impossible to ignore or resist. Britain was led by a man who had said on many public occasions that he *believed* in the doctrine of intervention.

'London gave us the headline ideas – the strategic aims and objectives,' recalled Jarvenpaa. 'We then discussed them and jointly agreed that they were probably not achievable, and that we needed to moderate our ambitions . . . All of us on the ground had a pretty good idea of what could and couldn't be done. We tried to signal some of that to London, although not all that successfully.' Still, the finished plan was a good one in so far as all the contributors appeared to agree on it. There was a consensus that the 'comprehensive approach' was the right one to take. The difficulty would be putting theory into practice.

The counter-insurgency theories developed in Malaya half a century ago haunted British thinking on Helmand to a surprising degree. 'We had study days at Colchester,' Docherty recalled. 'We did problem-solving practice, and talked about inkspots. The Malaya model wasn't an official strategy – it was more of a history lesson – but "inkspots" certainly became a term of reference among ourselves when we were out there.' A preliminary reconnaissance mission in southern Afghanistan was code-named 'Operation Malaya'. The very phrase 'hearts and minds' was coined by Field Marshal Sir Gerald Templer, Malaya's ex-military High Commissioner. The legacy of the 1950s was even concealed in the Household Cavalry's Scimitar light tanks, the unusually narrow gauge of which was originally designed to allow manoeuvres between the long lines of trees on the peninsula's rubber plantations.

Some of the similarities between the Malay and Taliban insurgencies were also striking. For instance, like Mullah Omar and many of the other ex-Mujahidin who filled the Taliban's senior ranks – and, indeed, Osama bin Laden – the Malay guerrilla leader Chin Peng had once been our ally. While the Mujahidin fought a proxy war against the Soviets, the Malay Communists fought the Japanese alongside British commandos in 1942. Chin was twice Mentioned in Dispatches, and even awarded the OBE (an honour that was later rescinded). Like the ex-Mujahidin, therefore, Chin came to the battlefield with an insider's knowledge of his friend-turned-enemy's mindset.

But however useful the Malaya precedent might have been, and however successful that counter-insurgency, there were certain caveats. First, the strategy did not offer a quick fix. The Malaya Emergency lasted for twelve years, from 1948 to 1960. Yet it was not until June 2007 that the Army, in the shape of another speech by General Dannatt, acknowledged that British engagement in southern Afghanistan was likely to last as long, and even then it did so at a meeting closed to the public. Dannatt predicted 'a generation of conflict' for the British Army. Whether the necessary political will can be sustained for so long remains a very moot point.

Second, the effectiveness of the counter-insurgency in Malaya depended on a strong and unified chain of command. As a senior Army figure in a civilian role, Templer provided the perfect bridge between the country's colonial and military administrations, and was able to control both. The Afghan counter-insurgency still has no such supremo, despite repeated calls for the appointment of a 'Paddy Ashdown-type figure' to coordinate the competing priorities inherent in the international approach.* Instead, and partly as a result of the lack of unified international leadership, the military chain of command was a mess at the start of Herrick 4. ISAF was controlled by Nato, some of whose member nations had no intention of fighting anyone, which was bad enough. Brigadier Ed Butler, commander of 16 Air Assault Brigade from which the 3 Para battle group was drawn, and the officer ultimately in charge of the Helmand Task Force's operations, should logically have come under the command of ISAF's southern headquarters, Regional Command South, based in Kandahar. However, the Task Force was initially deployed under the auspices of the American Operation Enduring Freedom, and it did not come under formal ISAF command until 31 July.

* In January 2008, a US-backed attempt to appoint not just a Paddy Ashdown-type figure but Paddy Ashdown himself as a United Nations 'super envoy' to Kabul foundered at the last minute after President Karzai objected. He was reportedly worried by Ashdown's previous role as the international community's High Representative in Bosnia, where he wielded viceroy-like powers including the ability to overrule the Bosnian government. See, e.g., Julian Borger in the *Guardian*, 28 January 2008.

To make matters worse, in February 2006 command of RC South had passed to a Canadian, Brigadier David Frazer (leadership of RC South rotated between the British, the Canadians and the Dutch, who controlled Helmand, Kandahar and Oruzgan provinces respectively). But because Frazer was a brigadier, the same rank as Butler, it was thought prudent to headquarter Butler in Kabul rather than Kandahar. Having two brigadiers in the same theatre, it was felt, was a recipe for confusion and had to be avoided. This arrangement obliged Butler to begin operations through an intermediary, Colonel Charlie Knaggs, the designated British Task Force commander in Helmand. Knaggs, an Irish Guardsman and not even a member of Butler's brigade, was headquartered not at Kandahar or Camp Bastion but in Lashkar Gah alongside the Provincial Reconstruction Team, the PRT, which was part of a national civil-military outreach project that had been run by ISAF since 2002. This made sense for a mission focused on winning local hearts and minds in a development triangle, but none at all for the gloves-off battle with the Taliban that developed. Knaggs could not even communicate with Kabul at times because of the absence of a secure phone line. All this meant that Butler, an officer with a strong hands-on reputation, was left frustrated in the capital, second-guessing the commanders on the ground and, at least until 31 July, effectively falling outside anyone's chain of command except PJHQ's.

The third lesson of Malaya, and the ultimate key to that campaign's success, lay in an early realization that there could be no purely military solution to the insurgency. It was Sir Henry Gurney, Templer's predecessor, who first appreciated that winning the war would depend not on the ability to pour in more and more troops but on gaining the support of the people. This is standard counter-insurgency strategy today, but it was far from orthodox in 1948. The military, under Major General Sir Charles Boucher, a veteran of Monte Cassino in 1944, was all for taking on Chin Peng's jungle-based guerrillas by conventional means – 'running the military show', as he called it. His attitude was one of 'give us the tools and we'll finish the job'. But Gurney understood that such escalation would not necessarily 'finish the job'. Indeed, it risked making the job much harder. As one of his advisers, Bob Thompson, pointed out, in this kind of war a stray bomb that killed one innocent child could make a thousand enemies – an observation that is often made these days in relation to Helmand. 'It's all very well having bombers, masses of helicopters, tremendous fire power,' Thompson said, 'but none of these will eliminate a Communist cell in a high school which is producing fifty recruits a year for the insurgency.' Exchange the words 'Communist' for 'Taliban' and 'high school' for 'madrasah' and that remark, too, could apply to modern Afghanistan.

In Helmand, the civil-military wrangling that characterized the early stages of the Malaya campaign was supposed to be forestalled by the adoption of the 'comprehensive approach'. Butler understood the fundamental importance of carrying the civilian agencies along with the military effort. His battle group commander, Stuart Tootal, agreed wholeheartedly that there could be 'no purely military solution' to the Taliban problem. Yet the alternative laid out by the British plan was never given a chance to work. Instead of concentrating on securing the development triangle and the 'soft' mobile operations that had been envisaged, most of the battle group was rapidly deployed to the northern district centres which were cut off from the centre by miles of desert. As a consequence the civilian development agencies, nervous of the security implications in the troop-denuded triangle, could not or did not arrive. Brigadier Butler was to argue later, convincingly, that their nervousness was misplaced; but meanwhile, far from winning hearts and minds in the northern towns, his forces became fixed in fort-like compounds from where they called in astonishing amounts of airborne ordnance, alienating the locals by destroying their homes and, sometimes, accidentally killing their children. As Herrick 4 progressed, it looked more and more as though the British had indeed chosen to pursue a purely military solution. The development triangle towns, Gereshk and Lashkar Gah, began to fill not with itinerant job-seekers but with refugees traumatized by the fighting. It was precisely what Bob Thompson had feared would happen in Malaya if General Boucher's approach were taken.

The key figure in Butler's decision to move his forces north beyond the development triangle was the Governor of Helmand, Engineer Mohammed Daoud, a technocrat with a background in distributing food aid, closely connected to President Hamid Karzai, and effectively Britain's placeman in the province. His predecessor, Sher Mohammed Akhunzada, was alleged to have pocketed at least $32 million in protection money from the heroin trade, an accusation he denies. He was once caught by anti-narcotics agents with nine tons of opium stored in his office. He said that his men had recently confiscated it, and he was on the point of handing it in. The British felt they couldn't work with such a man, and at the end of 2005 they successfully lobbied Karzai to replace him. Daoud was regarded as the cleanest governor in the country, but he had a serious disadvantage: he was not from Helmand. For all his faults, Akhunzada was also an influential tribal leader who in his three years as governor had kept

Helmand remarkably stable. The unconnected Daoud had no chance of exerting such influence. 'Helmand might have been full of druggies, but the Taliban were not dominant,' said General David Richards, who took command of ISAF on 31 July. 'They were there – they were in a lot of those southern provinces – but there was a marriage of convenience between them and the drug lords and Akhunzada, and there was very little violence.'

Daoud's lack of local influence soon caused him problems. By April 2006 it was clear that the Taliban were on the march. First, an American PRT clinic in the village of Bashling, just north of Kajaki dam, was burned to the ground. Then came news that the Taliban had taken over a village in the district of Baghran, further to the north. This was more than an affront to the governor's authority; in Daoud's estimation it was a threat to government control of the province. The risk to Kajaki, a hydro-electric dam that, once repaired, had the capacity to provide power for the entire region, was particularly serious. 'You know, Kajaki is our national treasury,' he told me. 'It's very, very important for the whole country. We had to protect that dam.'

I spoke to Daoud by telephone in his home in Kabul in the summer of 2007. He had been sacked by Karzai the previous December, eleven months after his appointment to the governorship, and was still out of a job – another victim of the revolving-door world of Kabul politics. Daoud's first line of defence against the insurgents, he explained, had been his police force. But as the British troops who fought alongside them found, the ANP were mostly useless. 'Officially we had seventeen hundred policemen in Helmand, but actually we had only two hundred and fifty,' he said. 'The rest answered to warlords.'

His second line of defence was the Afghan National Army; but the ANA, too, were significantly under strength. Of the quota of soldiers promised him by Kabul, 'seventy per cent were still not in the area', either because they were deployed elsewhere or because they had not yet been trained. It was probably unrealistic to expect even a full quota of this fledgling force to deal with the Taliban – although that did not prevent Karzai from pushing for it. A functioning national army was an important yardstick of progress, and the President was under constant pressure to demonstrate that the billions already spent by the US and other foreign backers had not been for nothing. Karzai also hoped to start eradicating poppies in the region – an ambition that General Richards thought was the purest wishful thinking. 'Karzai said to me, "You're responsible for security. What do you think?" I said, "You aren't ready to handle the second- and third-order consequences of eradication. You haven't got your police force ready. You haven't got your army trained. Half your governors are up to their eyes in it" . . . It just wasn't thought through.'

Governor Daoud, closer to what was going on in Helmand, understood the limitations of his country's paper army. In an armed struggle with the Taliban, foreign troops were really the only option available to him.

Daoud's initial requests for help were not answered. 'I asked the American PRT commander to go back to Bashling and start some operations there. I thought that if the enemy saw there was no re-action from the government side, they would increase their activities. But I received a message that the US were leaving Helmand and that this was now a British responsibility.' With Karzai's support, he began to put pressure on the British. A weekly meeting with Colonel Knaggs had been instituted in Lashkar Gah, and he used these to press his case for Task Force intervention. Leo

Docherty, who was then Knaggs's aide-de-camp, remembered very clearly the first occasion he raised the matter. 'It was just after the incident in Now Zad, when a Pathfinder patrol got into a fire-fight with some ANP.* Knaggs was summoned to the Governor's office for an explanation. He apologized, and the apologies were accepted, but then the Governor asked us if we'd send troops to Baghran. That was the real point of the meeting. Apparently the Talibs had occupied a school there. Knaggs said he would see what he could do; he told me to make a note and promised to pass the request up the chain of command. That set the tone of our relationship.'

The British, however, were not yet in much of a position to help. Daoud had expected the British Task Force to be in place by February; in reality, they were still arriving in theatre three months later. 'The Brits only arrived gradually,' said Daoud, with some bitterness. 'They had no knowledge of the area, and their logistics came very slowly ... the exchange took five or six months. There was a vacuum of command, and because of this the exchange plan was not properly designed or scheduled. During that time the Brits had no possibility of controlling Helmand on their own.'

The power vacuum created by the handover from Operation Enduring Freedom to ISAF was evidently critical. Could it have been avoided? Brigadier Butler later referred to the episode as the 'misalignment of the strategic levers of power'. The decision to delay the deployment of British troops was linked to Dutch

---

* The reasons for this unpromising start to Herrick 4 remain murky. It is clear that the ANP fired on the Pathfinders first; they later claimed that they thought the British were Taliban. The British, for their part, suspected that the ANP were engaged in some form of criminal activity, probably related to narcotics. They were certainly in a location where they were not supposed to be.

prevarication over sending their soldiers to Oruzgan province. Responsibility for that decision ultimately lay with the then British Defence Secretary, John Reid.

Meanwhile, in Butler's view, Daoud's expectations of British capabilities were badly mismanaged. The Governor apparently could not understand why, even when it was fully deployed, a Task Force numbering 3,300 people could muster no more than 650 fighting men. The rest, of course, were involved in logistics, communications, technical support, engineering (especially for air and aviation), administration and all the other jobs that kept the British in the field 7,000 miles from home. Afghans did these things differently. To Daoud, a force of 3,300 meant exactly that: 3,300 gun-carrying fighters. To be fair, the proportion of support-ing personnel was very high – high enough to make even some of the British wonder at it. 'What are the rest of our people up to?' wrote Tom Burne in an email home on 7 July. 'A common question asked by those of us on the front line.'

Minna Jarvenpaa of Whitehall's PCRU, who spent many weeks in Kandahar and Lashkar Gah working on the British plan, remembered calling a meeting with Daoud to try to ascertain if he really understood what the British were and were not capable of. As a veteran of the reconstruction missions in Bosnia and Kosovo, she knew all about the tendency of local actors to treat foreign forces as a kind of magic wand. She was not alone in suspecting that Daoud had also been dazzled by all the air power and technology at the Task Force's disposal, and she tried to inject some realism into Daoud's expectations. As Daoud saw things, however, his options were severely limited; and even if the Task Force was too small for the job in hand, he not unnaturally assumed that ISAF would pro-vide reinforcements. He could not have foreseen the unwillingness of Britain's Nato partners to do so. The lack of cooperation among the Coalition members evidently astonished him. 'Helmand is not a different country,' he said. 'I am talking about Coalition forces. It was up to the British to ask Kabul for more help.'

Brigadier Butler faced a difficult dilemma. He knew that his Task Force was neither ready nor sufficiently manned or equipped to deviate from the development zone plan, and at first he politely refused Daoud's increasingly strident requests for help against the Taliban, who were showing no sign of stopping their southward progress towards them. After Baghran came news that the Taliban had taken control of the district centre of Musa Qala: a detachment of British Pathfinders had observed civilians streaming out of that town. Trouble was brewing in Sangin and Now Zad as well. The pressure on Butler to act was immense. He and Daoud argued about it constantly, sometimes long into the night. On one occasion the Governor stormed out of a meeting at four o'clock in the morning, threatening to resign if the British didn't help. 'His line was, if you're not prepared to defend northern Helmand, then we will lose central Helmand – and you might as well all go home now,' Butler said. 'It may go against military logic, experience and tactical wisdom, but this was a GOA [Government of Afghanistan] strategic imperative. You've got to put it in context. We'd been invited in to a sovereign state, with a UN and Nato mandate. We agreed we'd work for Karzai, and he asked us in. So there were two options, which I put to ISAF, to the GOA, and to Whitehall: do we (a) do as requested, or (b) walk away, and refuse to acknowledge and follow HMG's declared policy of supporting President Karzai, and delivering on the UN- and Nato-backed mandate?'

Governor Daoud had powerful allies in Kabul. He enjoyed President Karzai's full support, and spoke to him on his mobile phone on a regular basis – 'the bungee-jumping approach' to policy-making, as Butler called it. 'Daoud would ring him and say, "The British, Ed and the boys, are not supporting me." Karzai would then talk to the Americans – General Eikenberry, at that stage [Lieutenant General Karl Eikenberry, the Combined Forces Commander in Afghanistan]. So then there was a GOA–American alliance against the Brits, who were not doing what they were told. Then Karzai gets on the phone and he says, "No, you will do something. If Daoud is in trouble you have to help him." I've got what he said jotted down in my notebook. He said, "If the black flag of Mullah Omar flies over the district centres then our credibility and ability to govern is directly threatened." So we were being directly accused of threatening the GOA by not protecting the governorship. It meant that we were already failing on the first and principal reason we were in Helmand, which was to provide security to protect and enable proper governance. In my shoes, what would you do?'

Whitehall played its part in pressurizing Butler too. 'London visitors came over,' Butler recalled. 'The Secretary of State made it very clear. John Reid and then Des Browne both got it from Karzai, and from Daoud when they were bounced down through Helmand ... so did Hilary Benn [Secretary of State for International Development], and Adam Ingram [the Armed Forces minister], and the Chief of the Defence Staff, and the vice-chiefs, and everyone else.'

Butler's position was impossible. He was being second-guessed in London and countermanded by Kabul. Unlike Gerald Templer, who enjoyed 'both the responsibility *and* the authority' to run the counter-insurgency in Malaya, Butler had only been granted the responsibility – 'and it still took Templer twelve years'. Through no fault of his own he was usually stuck in Kabul at the end of a much-attenuated chain of command, obliged to make complex calculations over a battlefield that was distant, dangerous and fluid; and time was not on his side. In the end he was forced to agree to Daoud's demands. Yet there were plenty of senior figures, both civilian and military, who muttered after the event that he should have resisted the Governor and stuck within the parameters of the British plan.

I later corresponded with General Richards on a different matter. I was arguing that had Bill Clinton negotiated with the Taliban rather than bombing al-Qaida's Afghan training camps in August 1998, then 9/11 might never have happened. He replied with a point about the challenges of high military command that humbled me. 'We are where we are today and I do/did not have the luxury of wishing things were different, however tempting and interesting. I am sure you accept this but, especially given the inadequacies and failings of our fellow man, it is much harder to be an active practitioner than to be an analyst/historian/academic/journalist etc, especially when they have the benefit of hindsight and no pressure of time and events – i.e. to do, rather than criticise others who do.'

In July, by which time the fighting in the northern areas had intensified to Korea levels, Butler became aware that he was being briefed against in London. It was his fault, the whisperers implied, that the 'comprehensive approach' had gone off track. He and his Paras, it was alleged, had effectively scuppered the British plan by being too keen for a fight. Butler bitterly rejected the charge, and still does. 'The philosophy behind the comprehensive approach was right, and I absolutely agree with it, but it's about time and timing – and there was always going to be a reaction, a fight, when we deployed to Helmand . . . people don't understand this. We didn't want a fight. Civvies always say that about the Paras, and it irritated Stuart [Tootal] and me more than anything. We're all human beings . . . No one likes taking another man's life.'

Part of the explanation for the accusation may have lain in Butler's personality. At forty-four he was among the youngest of the Army's sixty or so combat brigadiers, and regarded as one of the brightest blades they had. 'Brigadier Ed Butler has it all – piercing eyes, an Eton education and features that are determined, tough but charming,' gushed one newspaper profile. 'He is a man ready-made to lead.' The grandson of the Tory statesman Rab Butler, a Royal Green Jacket and a former member of the SAS, he was multiply decorated for actions that included a celebrated assault on a suspected al-Qaida camp near Spin Boldak in eastern Afghanistan in 2002. In curious contrast, perhaps, to his famous grandfather (a non-military man who supported the appeasement of Hitler in 1938 and privately opposed the Suez adventure of 1956), he was clearly not a man to shirk an opportunity for a fight. When British ammunition ran out during the attack near Spin Boldak, hand-to-hand fighting ensued.

There were those who accused him of over-confidence, even arrogance. On 17 October 2006, when he was fresh back from Afghanistan, I watched him give a press conference at the Ministry of Defence in Whitehall, where the way he handled his questioners was certainly businesslike. 'The trouble with him,' one experienced defence correspondent muttered as we filed for the exit, 'is that he's another bloody old Etonian.' Butler subsequently felt some of his words had been misreported by a correspondent from the *Independent*, to whom he sent an angry letter of correction. 'Your front-page story paints a misleading and mischievous picture of what I said,' he wrote. 'It omits some of my comments, and

extrapolates meaning and intention from others which is completely false. I did not say the operation in Iraq had cost "years of
progress" in Afghanistan; I did not say it had left "a dangerous
vacuum"; and I did not say that British soldiers faced a tougher
task now because of it.'

Butler, his detractors said, was the kind of commander who felt
more comfortable in the field than manning a desk at HQ, a man
who instinctively preferred action to words and theory, and pro-
activity to caution. In his pre-deployment message to his
commanders he paraphrased Rupert Smith, the retired general and
author regarded by many as a guru on asymmetric warfare. The
Smithism he chose was revealing: 'Command and leadership on
operations (even more so in the multinational arena) is about "come
on" and "go on",' he wrote. 'Wise words.'

But was he gung-ho? Butler found the allegation insulting.
'To people who say that I just like to get in a scrap, I say, but I've
done all that. I've been in a number of contacts; I've experienced
close-quarter combat and proved myself at the tactical level. And
once you've done that, and risen through the ranks, and
experienced all the pressures and adrenalin moments, you do break
through a ceiling, in terms of responsibility and leadership requirements, [into a place] where you're in a completely different
business.'

He was not surprised by the hunt for a scapegoat in Whitehall.
A lot of people, he noted, had hung their reputations on the
comprehensive approach working in Helmand. 'We had the same
thing in Iraq, when the civilian development mission began to fail
in Basra because of the increase in violence. The OGD [other
government departments] said it wasn't their fault, and blamed the
military commanders for failing to provide security.'

With an MA in international relations from St John's College, Cambridge, and another in war studies from King's College, London, Lieutenant Colonel Stuart Tootal understood the principles of counter-insurgency better than most. Mobility and the element of surprise, he knew, were critical to its success. His battle group, he was also very aware, had been trained, manned and equipped for mobile operations, not an occupation. He fretted that his operations were too 'reactive' – which was inevitable, given his obligation to accede to Governor Daoud's ever-increasing requests for help – and that in reacting to crises, his forces were too stretched to focus on the work of reconstruction which was supposed to go hand in hand with military operations.

Tootal sometimes suspected that the battle group's services were being abused. On 21 June, for instance, Governor Daoud told Colonel Knaggs that the son of a friend and ally, the District Chief in Sangin, had been critically injured in a fight with the Taliban, and urged the British to rescue him. Tootal didn't want to do it. Intelligence reports said the Taliban were strong in the area. A successful rescue would require a company-sized operation at least, and he feared the political consequences of sending such a force into the febrile environment of Sangin. He passed his concerns up the chain to Kabul, but was overruled. Supporting Governor Daoud was paramount, and a company of Paras was duly dispatched. Yet when they reached the chief's son, the Para medical officer found his condition wasn't critical at all, but actually 'very, very stable'. He had already been operated on and needed nothing more than another shot of antibiotics and some pain-killers. The rescue operation was supposed to last a few hours, but it ended up marking the beginning of an occupation of Sangin town which was to last until the end of the Paras' tour, and on into Herrick 5.

Did Daoud deliberately exaggerate the medical condition of the District Chief's son? Or was it a genuine case of miscommunication – or else panic? Some of those who dealt with the Governor suspected that he was prone to 'flap'. Was Knaggs, who had spent many weeks building a close friendship with Daoud, too quick to acquiesce? If Butler had been located in Lashkar Gah instead of Kabul, might he have read the Governor differently? The only certainty was that the locus of the battle group's activity shifted incrementally northwards. By the end of June, Tootal's troops were strung out across the province in half a dozen locations and un-comfortably dependent on vulnerable helicopters for survival. His battle group had become irrevocably 'fixed', and the mobile operations necessary to make the comprehensive approach work had become a distant dream.

Despite the pressure they put on Butler to support Daoud militarily, the Americans were not best pleased by the con-sequences. Bitter experience of the region had taught them the importance of staying mobile; getting stuck meant losing the ability to take on the Taliban on the Coalition's own terms. Operation Medusa, in early September, was a case in point. Although British forces did take part in that battle – notably the fourteen killed when an ageing Nimrod reconnaissance plane exploded in mid-air following an avoidable fuel leak – the operation was Canadian-led, and effectively won by American air power. Perhaps as many as a thousand Taliban fighters were wiped out there – a devastating set-back for them and the single biggest Coalition victory in years. Yet Britain was unable to contribute more than a handful of troops because they were all tied up in platoon-houses in Helmand.

US Major General Ben Freakley, the commander of Task Force 76 under whose control Regional Command South fell, was furious with Butler for allowing this to happen, and complained to his superior, Lieutenant General Karl Eikenberry, the Combined Forces Commander in Afghanistan. A veteran of both Gulf Wars, Freakley was reportedly so irritated at the manner of this upstart British brigadier – a one-star general whom he outranked but, because of the tangled chain of command, was unable to control – that he 'came close to causing a diplomatic incident', according to one source.

'You nearly had to send me to Leavenworth,' Freakley told Eikenberry, referring to the US military penitentiary in Kansas.

'Why?' said Eikenberry.

'Because I nearly knocked that Limey's lamps out.'

Butler, for his part, was well aware of Freakley's feelings, but was surprised at quite how 'tactical' a perspective he took. Butler felt that Freakley's conviction that the military should always act independently of their political masters was 'rather naive', although it didn't particularly surprise him. In his experience, American two-star generals had 'neither the benefit of higher-level training, nor the exposure, in places such as Northern Ireland or the Balkans, to the pol-mil [political-military] level of command'. Freakley, in Butler's view, had no appreciation of the role a British national contingent commander was expected to play. Nor did he seem to understand the pressures under which Prime Minister Tony Blair was labouring at the time – either domestic ones, such as the cash-for-honours scandal then breaking over the House of Commons, or foreign policy ones, such as Iraq. Their disagreement was neither the first nor last time that the allies clashed over strategy in Helmand. The problem was partly cultural – a re-run, perhaps, of the falling out between Eisenhower and Montgomery during World War Two.

Was the choice of northern Helmand as a battle ground – whoever's choice it was, and whatever the tactics used – the right one?
Not everyone thought so. Among its sternest critics was Sarah
Chayes, an American author and former National Public Radio
journalist who covered the US-led invasion of Afghanistan in 2001.
After the overthrow of the Taliban she decided to stay on, although
not as a journalist: for the last seven years she has lived alone in
Kandahar running a women's soap-making collective. Clever, on
friendly terms with the Afghan President, a fluent Pashto speaker
and protected by affiliation with powerful tribes in Kandahar, she
remains the only Westerner now living 'amongst the people' in the
city, and as such knew better than almost anyone what was going
on in the region at the time of Herrick 4.

The Taliban's ultimate goal, she told me, had always been
control of Kandahar – the movement's birthplace and the Pashtun
spiritual home. Everything the enemy did had to be seen in this
light. There were many lines of approach to the city. Helmand was
only one of them, and not necessarily the most obvious, which
was from the north through the valley of Arghandab rather than
from the west. It was significant that the critical battle against the
Taliban in 2006, Operation Medusa, was fought not in Helmand
but at Panjwayi, barely twenty miles from Kandahar.

Chayes's point was that even before the British conceived the
development triangle, they were guilty of 'Helmandcentricity'.
The reason, she thought, was the way the south was divided up
among the Coalition's willing nations. As a Western military
organization, Nato naturally liked to use maps in its planning, and
so assigned each of its member armies a neatly delineated province
to control. The Taliban, however, neither thought nor fought in
such basic cartographical terms – which was perhaps unsurprising,

Harvest-time in Helmand: a Chinook helicopter flies over fields of pink-flowering opium poppies, the economic mainstay of the Taliban (*right*).

Defence Secretary John Reid (with Brigadie[r] Ed Butler, *centre right*) hoped the Helman[d] mission could be carried out without a shot being fired. But in May 2006, with the insurgency accelerating (fuel trucks sabotaged outside Kandahar, *top left*) and the fledgling police force (*centre left*, with Kandahar police chief, Ismatullah Alizai, *bottom left*) powerless to halt it, Helmand Governor Mohammed Daoud (*above far right*) requested help.

A British battle group was deployed northwards under Lieutenant Colonel Stu[art] Tootal (*above right*) but the peace (Captain Leo Docherty patrolling in Sangin withou[t] helmet, *right*) did not last long.

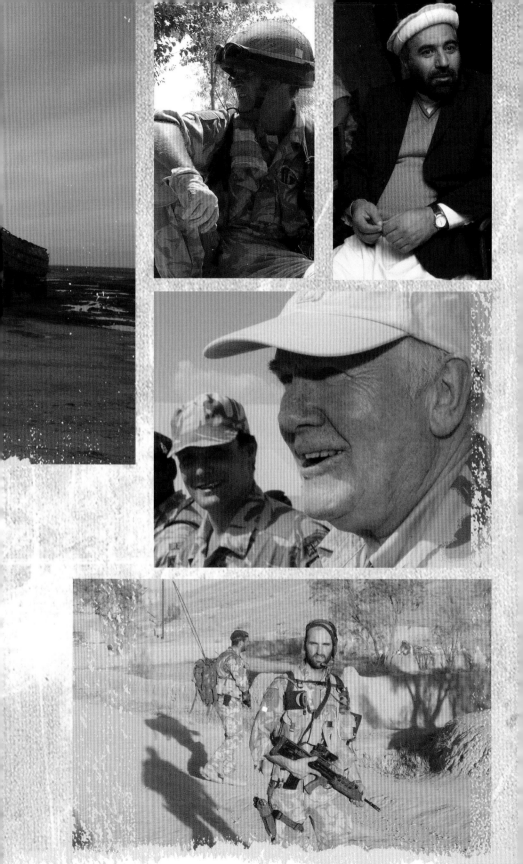

Taliban resistance at Now Zad (seen from ANP Hill with an army fixer whose identity has been obscured, *below*) was stiffer than expected (Operation Mutay, *top left*).

The platoon of Gurkhas sent to garrison the town (*centre left*) came close to being overrun (Major Dan Rex in the 'control tower', *below left*).

There was no let-up for the Fusiliers under Major Jon Swift (ordering a raid on a firing point in the town, *below far right*).

he Fire Support Group
on the helipad at Bastion,
bove; on ANP Hill,
elow; and in the *Sun,
ght*) duelled with their
tackers for 107 days
the longest static trench
efence in history.

Hero Dean fires 40,000 bullets at the Taliban..

runs
Brian
niper
the
rifles.
with

muni-
before
ed.
d over
their
missed.
shaves
re still

struggling to believe they got out of Nowzad – which is 85 miles from the nearest reinforcements. Two mortar rounds which failed to go off would have killed at least three of the Fusiliers.

One landed in a trench 2ft from a pair manning a machine gun. The other came in 6ft from a soldier as he crouched with his pants down, going to the loo.

On another occasion, shrapnel smashed into two ammunition boxes and set off their bullets. Miraculously no one was hit.

Mortar Fire Controller Sergeant Marty Gibbons, 32, from Manchester, said: "You only have time to think about a close shave after

it's happened. When the rounds are coming in, it's a big adrenaline rush. You just get up again and do your job."

Five citations for bravery medals are going forward.

Company Sergeant Major Jim Greaves, 37, from Newcastle, said: "The teamwork among the lads was second to none. Everyone pulled together and I'm incredibly proud of all of them.

It was another piece of illustrious gallantry to add to the annals of the regiment which famously won six VCs "before breakfast" at the 1915 Gallipoli landings.
t.newtondunn@the-sun.co.uk

Hero 'n villains . . Dean Fisher and, left, Taliban   Picture: A

Mobile operations in the marshland beyond the platoon-house at Sangin (*centre left*) could be deadly.

The garrison, including Lieutenant Tom Burne (*top left*), were supported by the 30mm cannon of the Household Cavalry's Scimitars (*bottom left*) and of the Army Air Corps' Apaches (*bottom centre*).

Air bombs of up to 2,000lb (*far left*) were commonplace.

It was the same for the Royal Irish at Musa Qala (Sergeant 'PJ' Brangan and GPMG, *below*). The 'unacceptable' threat to Chinooks at the drop zone here (*bottom right*) almost forced a British retreat.

ISAF commander Lieutenant General David Richards announcing the 'Musa Qala deal' (*top*); fourteen weeks later the deal collapsed.

Britain's exit strategy still depends on training up an Afghan army capable of replacing the foreigners, but the ANA may be trying to run before it can walk (*centre*). Could it be time to talk to the Taliban (the author in Wardak, *below*)?

given that Afghanistan's provincial and indeed national boundaries had almost all been imposed by nineteenth-century colonialists in the first place, notably the British. From a strategic point of view, Chayes thought, ISAF would have done better from the outset to concentrate its operations along and to the east of the Helmand river valley, an area that crossed the boundaries of three provinces – Dutch Oruzgan, Canadian Kandahar and British Helmand – with the all-important Kajaki reservoir and hydro-electric dam at its centre.

The dam's significance was not missed by the inhabitants of Kandahar city, fifty miles to the south-east; they had depended on it for their power supply for more than thirty years. In early 2007, according to Chayes, a rumour that the workers responsible for maintaining the cable link had been threatened by the Taliban caused panic in the bazaars. Despite this, ISAF seemed, at least to the inhabitants of Kandahar, to give little military priority to protecting the dam. Instead, as reports of the fighting made increasingly clear, the British had committed themselves to fighting the Taliban in district centres further to the west, places of little immediate relevance to the worried inhabitants of the city. In truth, the British did understand the importance of the dam. In mid-June they succeeded in destroying two enemy mortar teams which had been attacking the area; they later established a permanent garrison. In the course of operations in the district, a British soldier was killed and six were seriously injured, several of them in one horrific incident when a patrol strayed into an unmarked minefield. But the fact remained that the battle group was never able to spare more than about forty personnel to protect the dam – the asset that Governor Daoud had called Afghanistan's 'national treasury' – let alone the vast area surrounding it. It was not until January 2007 that the Royal Marines made a concerted effort to control the district, fighting village by village and compound by compound to establish a two-mile security perimeter. By then, of course, the assaults on the other district centres had diminished with the deepening of winter; and the Marines had more troops and resources at their disposal than Stuart Tootal's battle group ever had.

If Britain's early strategists were guilty of 'Helmandcentricity', they were not the only ones. The fighting in the province was eventually so well publicized that the British public, too, tended to forget that it was only one province among many, in a country whose affairs were inextricably linked to those of its neighbours, particularly Pakistan. Helmand's leading role in the opium industry made the province look more important than, strategically, it really was. Back at home, the poppy question was constantly used to justify Britain's military sacrifices in Helmand, the source of up to half of the country's vast output of opium. This was unsurprising, given that the troops on the ground often did the same. 'I go back to England, I live in the city of Birmingham where the heroin problem is outrageous – and ninety per cent of it comes from here,' Fusilier Matt Seal told me. The truth, as General Richards explained, was that counter-narcotics was a highly emotive red herring. 'It was never on the Army's agenda. It isn't even within the Nato O-plan! All the nations signed up to this . . . Counter-narcotics is not a specified [ISAF] task. All it says is, "Within means and resources, as a secondary task, you can help." But in practice, given we're all so stretched, you don't. Now, we tried to do a bit, but . . . it was never even in our remit to do it.'

It was, however, within the Foreign Office's remit, and it was on this issue that the hollowness of the comprehensive approach was

most starkly revealed. Britain was the G8 leader on counter-
narcotics in Afghanistan. Policy was implemented through the
embassy in Kabul by ADIDU, the government's Afghan Drugs
Inter-Departmental Unit, which was set up 'very much in response
to Tony Blair's personal interest in the Afghan drugs issue', according to Minna Jarvenpaa. But despite this prime ministerial
influence, the Coalition partners were never able to agree on a
counter-narcotics policy in Helmand. The US advocated an
aggressive policy of forced eradication, using aerial crop-sprays if
necessary; ADIDU preferred the slower approach of providing
farmers with alternative livelihoods. Compensation schemes of
various types had been tried in the past, though with very mixed
success, and remained another source of controversy. Buzzing on
the sidelines was the mysteriously well-funded NGO Senlis which
wanted, with the public support of General Richards himself, to
convert Afghanistan into the world's premier supplier of licit
opium for the manufacture of medicinal morphine.

Karzai dithered between all these options, understandably
uncertain whom to listen to. Meanwhile, the British military
warned that any assault on the crop that underpinned Helmand's
economy would inevitably set back the campaign for hearts and
minds. The Taliban, adeptly presenting themselves as the doughty
defenders of poor farmers' interests against the treacherous infidel,
were already far ahead of the Coalition in the propaganda race. In
2007 a row developed when it emerged that British troops had
handed out leaflets in Pashto designed to assure the disbelieving
locals (most of whom couldn't read them anyway) that poppy
eradication formed no part of British plans. Confusion ruled.

'During the planning the military were aware that the counter-
narcotics issue would be really difficult to handle, and were trying

to get away from it being one of its mainstream tasks,' said Jarvenpaa. 'What didn't happen, but should have, was a policy discussion at ministerial level at Whitehall, about what it means to be trying to do counter-narcotics and COIN [counter-insurgency] at the same time; and I'm not sure it's good enough for generals to say, "Well, the Foreign Office is doing something" when it was agreed by all ministers that counter-narcotics was part of a *joint* UK strategy.'

'It's tragic, I agree,' Richards said. 'It wasn't joined up at all. What Whitehall doesn't realize is that you can be as joined up at home as you like, but if you're not joined up in theatre, you count for nothing. If you're only playing with yourself, no one's interested.'

'I am not sure we were that joined up at home,' said Mark Etherington, the leader of the PCRU planning team. 'Tensions often exist in any cross-departmental planning process, and not all can be resolved. Things get left out or left over because they don't "fit", don't match departmental tasks. Important questions for Helmand remained. How, exactly, were we to satisfy the twin imperatives of a counter-drug strategy and economic regeneration, when opium was the province's major industry? What was our communications strategy to be? How were we to disseminate our core message in a province half the size of the UK, where seventy per cent of the population is illiterate? These questions were asked at the time, but there was no obvious address for them, no door marked "over-arching UK interests". I am not sure they were ever tackled. Damaging gaps were left where the roof should have been. I have always felt we ought to be able to do better than that. You have to wonder whether we are properly configured for this kind of broad effort. I was concerned at the time that we had fudged some of these issues. It reminded me of that Walpole quote about eighteenth-century public enthusiasm for the war with Spain – "They now ring the bells, but they will soon wring their hands." We just seem to drift into these wars with such insouciance.'

It wasn't only the British who were at fault. The UK Plan for Helmand was only one plan among many that were hatched for the region. The Americans, the Canadians and the Dutch all had their own ideas about how to proceed. As Brigadier Butler pointed out, the real problem was that there was no single, unifying campaign plan that all those involved were prepared to sign up to, 'no unity of command, and little unity of effort', as he put it. 'Most importantly, the Afghans themselves had no plan to resolve their own insurgency . . . Too many stakeholders failed to recognize that this was an Afghan problem that would require an Afghan solution, delivered with an Afghan face and at an Afghan pace.'

Why were the British military assigned Helmand in the first place? The process by which this decision was made was a mystery even to General Richards. Britain's anti-narcotics role within the G8, he said, 'probably' had much to do with it. 'They thought, "What a good idea, we'll deal with the province with the biggest narcotics problem." ' Minna Jarvenpaa thought that 'a lot of British foreign policy was set around domestic consumption: heroin ending up on British streets' – although she wasn't sure, either. 'My sense is that the decision to go to the south wasn't because of drugs and therefore Helmand. It was more to do with Nato's needing to take on the south, and then which nation should do it – and there were only a few nations volunteering.'

Even so, it was never a done deal. In fact, when Richards was ordered to start the military planning for southern Afghanistan in 2005, he secured an agreement – or so he thought – by which the

British would take charge of Kandahar. His rationale was three-fold. First, like Sarah Chayes, he understood the political and symbolic significance of the Pashtun capital. Second, the British already had an armed presence in Kandahar, a squadron of Harriers at the military airfield. Deploying there would ensure 'a strong fulcrum' between him in Kabul and the British command in Kandahar. Third, compared to Canada and the Netherlands – the only other two nations offering to send significant numbers of troops to southern Afghanistan – Britain's Task Force was always going to be the strongest. Canada's armed forces, according to Richards, were geared more to peace-keeping than to war-fighting. 'They're fine, and I've huge respect for them, but they haven't got any helicopters ... at that stage they were still coming to terms with what you need to fight quite an intense conflict and run the region.'

Despite this, it was Canada and not Britain that ended up with Kandahar. 'After a meeting held by MoD officials in Ottawa with their Canadian counterparts, we were told the Canadians had asked to do Kandahar, and that we would go to a place called Helmand. And I thought, "Where's Helmand? That's not very important. Kandahar is what matters." And I've never yet had a good reason given me why that decision was taken.' Richards was convinced that if the Canadians had been assigned Helmand instead of the British, everything could have been different. 'They [the Canadians] would have gone slower at it than the somewhat over-energetic, rather macho approach the British took – partly with little alternative, given their troop numbers – and then you could have had a calmer and perhaps healthier situation. The British, with superior numbers and more development cash available, would have been in the province that mattered the most, and which was not so complicated by the opium issue. And you would have avoided the Maiwand thing.'

His reference was to the Battle of Maiwand of 1880, when a brigade under General George Burrows was driven back from the banks of the Helmand river by a force under Ayub Khan, resulting in almost a thousand British killed. The victory was Pyrrhic, since Khan lost even more dead, although the fact was conveniently forgotten by Afghans. Maiwand was still remembered as a famous win, and remained deeply entrenched in local folklore. According to the journalist Christina Lamb, when the Paras moved into Camp Price outside Gereshk in May 2006 and their commander held his first *shura*, it took the elders only ten minutes to bring up 'the Maiwand thing'.

It was typical of Afghans to talk about 'the time of the British' as though it were yesterday. A strong oral tradition meant that the nation's sense of history was often strangely compacted. Fact was routinely intertwined with myth. Also, the physical legacy of wars long ago had a unique tendency to linger in the Afghan landscape, serving as a constant reminder of past martial glories that could only encourage the story-telling habit. The country is dotted with the wrecks of Russian tanks and the poignant remains of nine-teenth-century British forts. In 1998, in the Panjshir Valley, I once came across a teenager out shooting ducks with a huge muzzle-loading musket. On inspection the gun turned out to be a relic of the First Afghan War. The polished steel side-plate was even engraved with the British royal crest and the legend 'VR 1840'.

The British knew that their deployment to Helmand risked pro-voking the locals. Every Pashtun in the province claimed that his forefather had fought for Ayub Khan. The Task Force even con-tained elements of the same regiments that had fought in the 1880 campaign, such as the Royal Horse Artillery, which was at Maiwand, and the Gurkhas, who marched from Kabul to avenge them. In view of Helmand's history, a task force from almost any other nation in the world would have been a more appropriate choice for a mission intended to conquer hearts and minds. Instead, to the Afghan mind, the return of the Brits looked like an Allah-driven invitation to a punch-up, round four of a conflict between two nations that had been at it intermittently for 170 years. Even some British soldiers were susceptible to the romantic notion of carrying on the business begun by their forefathers – Leo Docherty, for instance, who freely acknowledged that he was re-enacting the spirit of the Raj with his horseback journey to Khiva. ('That's the general idea,' he said. 'That's my thing.') Concerns about the legacy of Maiwand were raised by Richards at the early planning stage, but the decision to send the British to Helmand had already been taken, and it was out of his hands.

Several among the Army felt let down by the civilians who were supposed to be responsible for the reconstruction effort, including General Richards, who repeatedly urged the need for 'more construction and less destruction'. On the ground, Leo Docherty felt that the Department for International Development in particular had failed to capitalize on the opportunity for QIPs (quick-impact projects) that the battle group's move into the north had bought at such a high cost. 'We've had a friendly response from the population so far, and now is the time to show them how their livelihoods might be improved,' he wrote in *Desert of Death* of the brief period when the British were still patrolling Sangin in soft hats. 'I cast my mind back to the glib jargon I heard from the DfID girl in Colchester before deployment. She needs to be here now with us, making it happen.'

As he pointed out, of the £390 million DfID had spent on development projects in Afghanistan since 2001, only £10 million had been spent in Helmand by the end of 2006. 'The whole approach was wrong – is wrong,' he told me. 'You don't win hearts and minds with soldiers; you need engineers, builders, the development people from DfID. We have embedded journalists; they risk their lives to do their jobs. Why can't we have embedded development officials? That's what we need.'

There was some truth in Docherty's criticism. The civilian side, Minna Jarvenpaa admitted, '*was* far too slow to be able to operate on the ground'. And never mind Docherty's complaints about Sangin; in May, Britain's full complement of civilian officialdom hadn't even arrived in Lashkar Gah yet. In October, Governor Daoud complained to the BBC that there had been no DfID representative in Helmand for two months. Part of the problem, according to Jarvenpaa, was the lack of secure accommodation. Lashkar Gah might be acceptable for soldiers, she said, but no British government official was going to be posted there without proper protection from rockets and mortars. The town was only relatively benign. Apart from anything else, their contracts would not allow it. 'There were only ever six hardened pods available in Lash – truck containers with sand and gravel on the roof,' said Jarvenpaa. 'The Foreign Office had outsourced to the military the buildings and infrastructure the civilians would need. But the military had other priorities and sub-contracted to some Afghans, and it all got delayed and delayed.' I had known Minna for a long time, since my own days in the Balkans, and knew she was no coward. Would the threat from the air have caused her to think twice about a posting to Lashkar Gah? 'Rocketing?' she replied. 'Without hard-cover accommodation? In tents? Yes, probably.'

Brigadier Butler, ever the soldier, had little time for such reticence. The lack of security in Lashkar Gah, he complained, was grossly exaggerated. Apart from two suicide bomb attacks on the first two Fridays in April, he insisted, there were no attacks on either Gereshk or Lashkar Gah. There were no mortars, and certainly no rocket attacks. From mid-April on, the security situation in the development triangle was 'more than sufficient' for preliminary development work to begin. 'I could quite happily walk through Lashkar Gah any day of the week, and feel more threatened in somewhere like Lagos, where I'm going to get mugged and robbed of my wallet and laptop ... In terms of a terrorist threat it was a bit like walking through Antrim in the nineties in the Province: actually pretty safe, apart from the risk of meeting a hood, or a bad luck incident.'

Daoud was equally mystified. As he pointed out, from an Afghan perspective, security in the provincial capital was about as good as it ever got.

The problem, Butler realized, was that there were differing perceptions of the violence, which was being falsely portrayed. 'DfID and Foreign Office officials, especially those in Kabul, were reporting back to London saying that Helmand was on fire. But no: it was only on fire in half a dozen northern platoon-houses. The tinder may have been dry, but it wasn't happening! Nine people getting killed inside two weeks – that's a very alarming figure. But they painted that picture across all of Helmandshire.'

Although he accepted that the development agencies operated under different constraints, and that government ministries had a duty of care towards their civilian employees, he was still disappointed and frustrated by it. Those constraints, he pointed out, had certainly not been imposed by *him*. He later came to describe the northern platoon-houses as 'breakwaters' against which the Taliban destroyed themselves, creating a 'window of opportunity' for the civilian agencies to get to work in the province's centre. He admitted this was a *post facto* justification of the move northwards, but insisted that it didn't make it any less true. 'It's something we worried about over many a cup of coffee and a cheroot, but I'm certain that if we hadn't gone to the north, the front line would have been Highway 1. The Taliban were going to come south. There would have been fighting on the doorsteps of Lashkar Gah and Gereshk.' In short, he argued, a large part of the blame for the comprehensive approach going off track lay with the development agencies which failed properly to exploit the window of opportunity created by his troops.

On the other hand, Jarvenpaa thought that it probably wouldn't have made much difference even if development officials had been available when the Army wanted them. QIPs of the sort Docherty was thinking of in May were fine – a new well sunk here or a road patched there could indeed buy local good will – but the effect, in her experience, was usually temporary. If public opinion is genuinely going to change, she explained, development projects have to be sustained; their dispersal had to be logical and fair, and they had to have the consent of the people. There was little point, for instance, in building a school for girls if the Taliban were going to burn it down again. 'Communities are perfectly capable of both accepting your presence and withholding consent. There were instances of the military going into a community to deliver a QIP and then walking out and being ambushed . . . the correlation is not always clear.'

Besides, she added, what Helmandis most wanted was not development projects but proper governance – an end to the corruption, at every level of officialdom, that had so constantly blighted their lives. The British plan encompassed the development of government institutions, the reform of the police, the governor's office, the line ministries. This was the whole point of centring the development zone on Lashkar Gah, the seat of the provincial government; outlying communities such as Sangin were for much later on. The West's entire civilian reconstruction effort was geared, as it routinely is in post-conflict countries, to a long-term solution that would take years, not weeks, to implement. There was, Jarvenpaa thought, a fundamental lack of understanding within the Army about how, and how fast, the development community operated.

'A lot of military people like to talk about the comprehensive approach as though it were a military-led doctrine,' she said, 'but by definition it is not ... if we're saying that counter-insurgency and stabilization should be eighty per cent led by the political and development side – because there *is* no military solution – then, logically, the lead needs to be taken by civilian actors, and the military aspect needs to be de-emphasized.' The Army's expectations of the Foreign Office and DfID were 'totally and wholly unrealistic', and not only because of the danger. 'The point is,' she said, 'I'm not sure that anyone can deliver on the soft end of things if you are in a war-fighting situation. For instance, who are we supposed to talk to in the community? Which elders are going to talk to you while it's unclear if you or the Taliban are going to win? For the work that comprises those non-military, non-kinetic aspects of the comprehensive approach, you do need a relatively benign environment.'

Jarvenpaa's principal assertion was that the Task Force had never properly committed themselves to the British plan, and was too quick to depart from it when conditions changed. Part of the reason, she thought, was that Butler's brigade staff had taken no formal part in the process under which the plan was first drawn up. Well into Herrick 4, it became dispiritingly apparent to her that several brigade officers had never even read it. During the key six-week consultation with the civilian planners in Kandahar in 2005, the Army had been represented by a 'prelim-ops' team from the Permanent Joint Headquarters (PJHQ) in Essex. 'We were quite naive on the civilian side,' she said. 'We thought that the tactical HQ coming into theatre would do what PJHQ had previously agreed – obviously – because they were a lower-order HQ. But that wasn't what happened. The brigade chose instead to do their own planning and their own thinking.'

Mark Etherington, her superior, remembered looking forward to seeing the Paras when they came to Kandahar. As a young officer he had once lived with Ed Butler, and he anticipated a sense of 'kinship' with the battle group staff, even though he did not know Lieutenant Colonel Tootal personally. 'I remember being surprised at the apparent disconnection between our planning HQ and this incoming group. I had thought they had come to be briefed – basically to execute the joint plan, with the necessary adjustments; so I was discomfited to see the Paras gather in a corner of the tent and draw elaborate pincer movements on a whiteboard. We had to request a meeting in the end. I got the early impression that they had arrived with their own plan. Of course no one expected slavish adherence to what we had, but the fact that it was a genuinely joint product was very important. Military operations are designed to have tremendous momentum. They are resource-rich and they just tend to subsume everything else – which is dangerous, because there is very rarely any such thing as a purely military solution to these problems.'

Jarvenpaa was not unsympathetic. 'I very much understand the military. They put a lot of effort into training leaders, and when they see a vacuum of leadership they tend to jump into it. But I'm not sure the military mindset of "going in and getting things done" works in this kind of war. You build up to stabilization. You need years of patience – and that's where development actors with lower timelines might actually be more appropriate. You don't necessarily achieve much in the first six months or even the first year. That's where the thinking is very different. We've got a lot of work to do on the relationship between the military and civilian agencies.'

Few were more impatient with the development officials than the energetic Tootal. It wasn't just that their approach was un-military; there were times when their slowness looked suspiciously like unwillingness. Tootal was in great demand as a lecturer on his return to the UK, and in his talks he was apt to illustrate his complaint with the saga of the Gereshk hospital washing machine. This had been donated months earlier by USAID, the US Agency for International Development, which reckoned there was room for improvement in the cleanliness of the hospital's sheets. The machine was still sitting there when the Paras arrived, swathed in plastic and unconnected – understandably, since there was no water supply to plumb it in to. The Paras thought they had spotted a likely-looking QIP, and informed DfID that they intended to order their engineers to sink a well. But DfID, to their amazement, told them not to – apparently on the grounds that the hospital was part of the national healthcare system and the contract to run it belonged to an Afghan NGO.

To Tootal and his 'Toms', as the Paras are known, a commendable attempt at pro-activity seemed to have been blocked by needless bureaucracy. But to Jarvenpaa the episode illustrated not civilian obstructionism but an irksome example of military short-sightedness. It wasn't just a question of water supply. The hospital, she explained, had no electricity for most of the time. The local NGO running the hospital was worried that accepting help from the British might compromise its neutrality in the eyes of locals. A washing machine, moreover, would put a number of local women out of work who depended on washing the sheets by hand for a living. Hygiene was atrocious by Western standards, but by Afghan ones it was actually pretty good. For all these reasons the NGO had refused USAID's kind offer when it was first made – though evidently too late to halt the machine's delivery. 'Tootal's criticism isn't fair,' Jarvenpaa insisted. 'But that isn't a reflection of my view of the Army. Tootal was a very good and brave field commander, and all his units performed incredibly well at the company level. The question is whether all that bravery and competence is being properly directed.'

Military attempts at peace-making, it was true, had an awful habit of going wrong in Afghanistan. The Americans were particularly bad at it. In 2001, hundreds of bright yellow MRE (meals ready to eat) ration packs were airdropped in a bid to show the people that the US came in peace. Unfortunately the ration packs were the same colour as BLU-97/B cluster bombs that had been dropped in significant numbers a few weeks earlier. According to one worried UN official, hungry children were particularly drawn to the deadly sub-munitions. The US Air Force insisted that no MREs were dropped in the same locations as the cluster bombs, but that hardly mitigated the public relations disaster. In 2007, another attempt to curry favour with children back-fired when an American helicopter bombed villages in Khost with footballs decorated with the flags of nations, including the green one of

Saudi Arabia. As every good Muslim knows, the Saudi flag in-
corporates the words of the *shahada*, the Islamic declaration of
faith. Kicking such a ball was unlikely to amuse the local mullahs,
and there were demonstrations in Khost. 'To have a verse of the
Koran on something you kick with your foot would be an insult in
any Muslim country,' the Afghan MP Mirwais Yasini told the BBC.
Even FIFA, the international football federation, had learned to
avoid this trap during the World Cup in 2002.

The British approach to public relations in theatre is considered
– at least by the British – to be more sensitive. The Task Force
therefore spent a lot of time trying to establish a distinction in local
minds between the allies. The effort was not always worth it. In
early 2006, a number of British reconnaissance units reported that
they had been mistaken for Russians. On Chicken Street in Kabul,
the centre of the capital's tourist trade, carpet-makers have long
profited from a line of rugs depicting blown-up MiGs and BTRs,
the eight-wheeled armoured personnel carriers used during the
Soviet invasion. These diverting souvenirs are still popular,
although the design on the rugs has changed: these days they depict
twin-rotored Chinooks instead of MiGs, and American Humvees
instead of BTRs. One infidel invader looks very much like another
to an Afghan, regardless of the equipment they use or the justification of their presence. Besides, how conversant were the British
troops, actually, in the subtle art of counter-insurgency? Not very,
if the experience of one newly commissioned (and worried) young
officer was anything to go by. The fourteen months he had spent
in officer training included fifteen weeks of field exercises but 'just
one two-week COIN exercise at Sandhurst and, more staggeringly,
a two-hour refresher lecture in COIN on Platoon Commander's
Division'.

Some in the Army also wondered why the MoD had chosen Paras, of all people, to spearhead a mission to win hearts and minds. The Defence Secretary John Reid announced in January 2006 that Britain's engagement was expected to last for three years. It was always known, therefore, that the 3 Para battle group would be the first of at least six six-month troop rotations, and that the first ones in would have the difficult and sensitive job of setting the conditions for all who would follow them. The Paras trained for this crucial role for a month in Oman, where they practised entering mocked-up villages and, according to Captain Martin Taylor, 'establishing relations with the locals and displaying a culturally aware attitude to the people [we] would be dealing with'. Yet however much they trained, this kind of work was never a Para forte. According to one very senior officer who asked not to be named, 'What we're not particularly good at is the information operation needed to set the conditions on the ground for what happens next. Is the best person to sell the message a sergeant from 3 Para? Probably not. It's not what he's trained or equipped or briefed to do.'

Tootal's men – and there were only men in this toughest of British regiments – had generally joined up not to go on soft peace-keeping operations but to 'live the dream' of combat. Whatever he or Butler said, the Toms themselves were hungry, even by ordinary Para standards, for the chance to prove themselves in action. Iraq had been a disappointment for 3 Para in terms of war-fighting experience. The battalion's last real fight had been in the Falklands, twenty-four years earlier. Indeed, the feeling among the Paras that they had been passed over for deployment on previous occasions was probably an influence in the decision to send them on Herrick 4.

Tootal was proud of the 'Para ethos' and the spirit of 'controlled aggression' that underpinned it, and it is true that any skill must be practised if it is to be maintained. But were Paras really what was required on such a sensitive 'condition-setting' mission, in a place Butler himself described in his post-tour press conference as 'an empty canvas' which 'thrived off insecurity' before the British arrived there? 'If you take a battle group of Paratroopers that looks like a hammer, they are inclined to look for a nail,' continued the very senior officer, 'and they found a nail. In fact, lots of them. We got what we wanted on Herrick 4, which was a battle,' he said.

'The Army has been driven by the prospects of action, promotion and decorations for hundreds of years and I doubt much has changed,' said Mark Etherington. 'I think there was an urge among the military to get stuck in to the Taliban; and the lure of deep patrols in the mountains and deserts of Helmand, together with the almost overpowering presence of history, tends to eclipse the rather more mundane requirements of "reconstruction". I do not doubt the military's bravery and commitment in Helmand for a moment. But did we lose sight of our objectives? It is at least arguable.'

Part of the trouble, the very senior officer believed, was that British troops are rotated every six months, far more often than American troops, whose standard tour lasts from twelve to fifteen months. 'When people arrive for their six-month rotation there's a danger that they (a) have their private battle and want to prove to themselves that they can do it, and (b) think that they might actually be able to win it. But you can't win anything in six months – obviously. Nor can you lose it. But you can set back the conditions [necessary for ultimate victory] . . . by a considerable measure.'

A twelve- to fifteen-month tour could play havoc with a GI's home life, and it was politically controversial in the US. But it also gave soldiers a chance to become properly intimate with their Area of Operations, to gain deeper intelligence, to learn about the people and their culture. Soldiers on longer tours also tended to take a slower, more considered approach to their jobs – and on a mission as long and delicate as Operation Herrick, that could be critical.

Tootal, of course, insisted that he and his men had done their best to apply the comprehensive approach. If the campaign had become too 'kinetic', it was not the fault of the Paras. His men had done what should have been expected of them, which was to fight. If the plan had gone awry, it was because the Task Force's hand had been forced. He defended the decision to go north, as so many did, by quoting the dictum of the Prussian Field Marshal Helmuth von Moltke, a disciple of Clausewitz and the most talented strategist of his generation, that 'no battle plan survives first contact with the enemy'. Yet was not von Moltke merely describing the effect of the 'fog of war' that swirls around every battlefield? He did not mean that battle plans were of no use. As his brilliant execution of the Franco-Prussian War of 1870 showed, he was in fact an obsessive planner whose technique was to try to anticipate every-thing that might happen. Contingency planning helped him to see through the battle fog, to keep sight of the wider goals of the war – which in Helmand's case was the conquest of hearts and minds. 'War is a matter of expedients,' as he also said. The strategist's role, he believed, was to prepare, and fight, accordingly.

Von Moltke would have spotted the main drawback of the British plan for Helmand immediately, and it was this: there was no Plan 'B'. 'The prelim-ops team did a fantastic job on how to implement the comprehensive approach,' said Brigadier Butler, 'but what they didn't do was to foresee the tactical realities of [entering Helmand with a foreign military force] that was never going to own the plan, or the risk – which I ended up doing – when we were the only ones executing it.' He frankly doubted whether the plan had ever been workable as originally conceived. He believed that the 'break-in battle', the military part of the comprehensive approach, was 'always going to surge ahead of the reconstruction, development, governance and counter-narcotic lines of operation', and would remain ahead until, eventually, those other lines caught up. He also firmly believed that the battle was inevitable, and that those who argued that the plan could have been executed without violence were guilty of 'naivety of the first order'. 'I've been in this country twice before, and these people fight – they fight very, very hard. I know – I've done it, I've seen it, on surgical ops and on more steady-state, peace-keeping-type ones in 2002.'

Butler's long experience of soldiering, not just in Afghanistan but in places like Northern Ireland, Bosnia, Kosovo and Sierra Leone, had perhaps darkened his opinion of human nature. I struggled especially with his assertion of the need to go through a 'Hobbesian cycle of violence' before the tipping point of popular support for any international peace campaign could be reached. 'I'm not a military historian,' he said, 'but based on my twenty years plus of experience in the operational field, you've got to go through . . . an attritional war to exhaust those physical battles before people start to recognize that there is a political solution which needs to be negotiated.' In other words, he believed that military action was a necessary evil. The imposition of an external foreign force was always going to provoke further peaks and troughs of violence, but over time, given proper management and resources, the violence could be reduced to an acceptable level. 'The Task Force never set out to fight the Taliban,' he insisted. 'But we were entirely realistic in our expectations that by threatening the power bases of all the Helmand stakeholders – the Taliban, the narcos, the warlords – we were always going to provoke a violent reaction . . . What is fundamental to understanding southern Afghanistan is that a minority of the stakeholders only want a failed state, so that their various power bases and finances can prosper. The entrance of the Task Force and Nato forces, with the principal purpose of turning Afghanistan into a non-failed state, threatens their very livelihoods and futures. Hence the fight.'

The only possibility of avoiding a fight in Helmand, he argued, had been lost long before Herrick 4 thanks to the 'Iraq effect' – an opinion in revealing contrast to his riposte to the *Independent* reporter at his post-tour press conference a year earlier. 'I've said this publicly,' he told me. 'A strategic opportunity was missed, by the Americans and ourselves, by maintaining a minimal presence [in Afghanistan] from 2002 onwards. We could have gone where we wanted after all that widespread swing of support to the GOA [after Karzai's election]. The opportunities were all there in 2002. I was there then; you could see it all slipping away. But everything was on the other place [i.e. Iraq], and that's what the Taliban have exploited.'

He spoke of a 'declining glide path of consent' among the civilian population for the foreign presence. As a military man, he said, all he could do was buy space and time for reconstruction and development work to have its effect. But could the British military ever buy enough time? 'That,' said Butler, 'is the six-million-dollar question. How long does it take to start winning and maintaining indigenous popular support? Three years? Five years? It's probably in the two- to five-year bracket.'

He remained optimistic that it could be done. There had been 'significant steps forward' in terms of reconstruction and development since Herrick 4. Sangin had been transformed from a 'narcocentric' town into one of 'relative prosperity' in little more than a year. But he admitted that 'the tide of popular support has yet to jump over the fence' in Helmand as a whole. 'The Afghans all say they hate the Taliban, but they haven't said unequivocally that they support ISAF and the GOA, because they are still not sure that the Coalition is prepared to stay for the long term. If an Afghan sides with ISAF, and we leave, then he is dead. So no matter how much he hates the Taliban, he would prefer to be alive under them than dead if we aren't prepared to invest the necessary time and resources in the campaign, and decide to leave in a couple of years.'

The slow pace of progress in Helmand worried Butler far less, ultimately, than the decline of support for the war within Nato and among the British public at home. 'The Taliban know that domestic Western support for this war could well go the same way as Iraq. Five years to them is nothing, never mind the thirty years some people are talking about. That's what will lose us this campaign in the end.'

5

The Chinooks Push the Envelope

The aviator's phrase 'pushing the envelope', first used by test pilots in World War Two, was decisively back in fashion during Herrick 4. The crews of the Army Air Corps' Apaches were, in effect, test pilots, because it was the first time their machines had flown in combat. The Apache was an American machine with a proven track record – it was first used in Panama in 1989 – but the Air Corps were flying a new British version that, for political procurement reasons, was fitted with engines built by Rolls-Royce rather than General Electric. There was much other clever technology and weaponry on board that had not seen active service before. No one knew for sure how the machines or their newly trained crews would perform. Herrick 4 turned out to be the hottest baptism by fire imaginable for both.

The pressure on the Army Air Corps was intense, although moderate compared to what the RAF's Chinook transport helicopters worked under. It was very quickly clear that the platoon-houses could not rely on road transport for their supplies. Instead, the garrisons had to depend entirely on Flight 1310, as the Chinook contingent was known, for their 'bullets and beans' as well as for troop rotations and the evacuation of casualties. The Task Force's whole strategy would have collapsed without them, and everyone, including the enemy, knew it.

Although agile for its size, the Chinook was still almost a hundred feet long and weighed twenty-two tons fully laden, and it was never more vulnerable to attack than when putting down near a platoon-house to unload. The Taliban nickname for the machine was 'big mosquito'; the Paras called it a 'big bullet magnet'. No matter how much the pilots varied the frequency, time of day, speed, height and direction of their approaches, there were only a certain number of places for a Chinook to land near the district centres, which meant the drop zones were frequently 'hot'. 'It was the flights into the platoon-houses that really put people's hairs up,' Squadron Leader Paul Shepherd confirmed. On troop rotations and 'deliberate ops' there were sometimes more than forty soldiers crammed into the back. Destroying a Chinook, therefore, was naturally the glorious jackpot sought by every gunman. A well-aimed RPG in the right place at the right time, or even a single lucky heavy machine-gun bullet, could cause a catastrophe with what Shepherd called 'Mull of Kintyre ramifications'.

The reference was to the fatal accident in 1994, when a Chinook carrying almost the entire top tier of Northern Ireland's military intelligence officials crashed on the west coast of Scotland in heavy fog. The political implications for John Major's government, which was then struggling against a resurgent IRA, were immense – and the stakes were just as high in Helmand now. Ed Butler and the MoD worried that public opinion could turn decisively against the Afghan mission if a fully laden Chinook were to be brought down. That fear intensified after 2 September 2006, when a Nimrod surveillance craft crashed over Kandahar following a controversial technical fault, killing fourteen. Their bodies were repatriated to the Nimrod's base, RAF Kinloss in Morayshire, where a fraught memorial service for the dead was widely publicized. 'I want to know exactly why these guys had to die,' said the distraught wife of Flight Lieutenant Leigh Mitchelmore. 'Leigh went into Nimrods because he said it was one of the safest jobs he could have. It was meant to be a family man's job. He should be coming home. They should all be coming home, and they are not.'

The chances of a successful Chinook strike looked so high in the eyes of some visiting senior officers that, one day in early September, ISAF commander General David Richards was informed that the British would be unilaterally pulling out of all the platoon-houses in three days' time. Richards overturned the decision, correctly arguing that it would be perceived all over Afghanistan as a defeat for British arms. The Chinooks continued to fly. The risks, however, not only remained but increased. The more the Chinooks used the same drop zones, the better the Taliban were able to prepare for their arrival, and the greater the threat became. 'We were flying into the same unsecured landing sites, in built-up areas, in daylight – everything you shouldn't do in SH [support helicopters],' said Shepherd. 'It was only a matter of time before we lost an aircraft. I prepared the boys for that.'

The enemy's weapons systems were also improving all the time. That summer a suspected SAM-7 – an Iranian-made shoulder-launched heat-seeking surface-to-air missile – was reportedly launched at a Chinook. Another was apparently fired at an American Hercules the following July. Neither missile found its target. In the Chinook's case, the SAM was thrown off by a sophisticated on-board defensive aid suite, said by the RAF to be the finest in the world. The Taliban were not discouraged. In early 2007, intelligence sources suggested that they were considering obtaining more missiles from Iranian agitators keen to stir up trouble for the Great Satan to their east. At first the Iranians had tried to sell the weapons to the Taliban; now they were willing to give them away. This was eerily reminiscent of the campaign against Soviet air power in the 1980s, when the US covertly supplied the Mujahidin with portable Stinger missiles. The results then were devastating; in 1987 alone, 512 Soviet helicopters and aircraft were lost. Flight 1310 responded with traditional British pluck, and even made up some jocular shoulder-patches depicting a missile spiralling past the tail of a Chinook above the legend 'It *is* rocket science!'. They had tremendous confidence in their state-of-the-art defensive aid suites, which were packed with technology unavailable to the Soviets in the 1980s.

Even so, when Brigadier Butler disclosed in October that he had come within thirty-six hours of ordering the abandonment of the platoon-house at Musa Qala, one of the reasons he gave was the 'unacceptable' threat to Chinooks. The missile threat was small compared to the risk of a successful RPG strike. Chinooks had experienced ten near-misses by RPGs in eight weeks. Politically as well as militarily, in other words, the big machines were by far the weakest link in Herrick 4's over-extended chain – and once again it was largely through luck that the chain was never broken.

There was, though, as Butler recognized, some 'phenomenal flying' from the pilots. In contrast to Jamie Loden's first impression that the RAF were 'utterly, utterly useless', the Paras were so pleased with the Chinooks' performance that Stuart Tootal was later moved to initiate a formal 'bond of friendship' between the Paras and the Chinook wing, with the official endorsement of the Prince of Wales. One unit alone, 18 Squadron, was awarded three Distinguished Flying Crosses – the most any RAF squadron had received in one go since World War Two. Four other Chinook crew were Mentioned in Dispatches, and there were also four Joint Commanders' Commendations, or JCCs.

Their job was difficult even when they were not under fire, mainly because of the dust in Helmand, which was as fine as talcum powder and lay eighteen inches deep in places. It was particularly bad at Bastion, where it had been ground and re-ground by the tracks and wheels of hundreds of heavy vehicles. One pilot likened it to Fuller's earth, a super-absorbent, clay-like compound used as a decontaminant in chemical warfare. It got into everything: food, air-conditioning units, tents with all the zips down. Sensitive avionics could be badly affected, but the real danger came from the clouds thrown up by helicopter rotors. Few machines have a greater downdraught than a Chinook. Each of its rotors is sixty feet across, and powered by an engine generating 3,750 horsepower. There were times, over landing sites, when it was impossible to see as high up as a couple of hundred feet. 'Brownouts', as they were called, were the norm. Landings often had to be performed entirely on instruments, even in daytime – a manoeuvre compared by one pilot to 'parallel-parking a car with your eyes closed'. Brownouts had been blamed for numerous fatal Chinook crashes in Iraq, and the conditions in Helmand were worse. 'Iraq is O-level,' said a Chinook crewman who had served in both theatres, 'but Afghanistan is a master's degree.'

One DFC was awarded to Flight Lieutenant Chris Hasler for, among other actions, an extraordinary resupply run to Sangin in

July 2006. The day before, a Para had been killed trying to secure the regular helicopter landing site. It was too dangerous to land there, but the garrison were desperate. Hasler, who was twenty-six, responded by putting his machine down in an area never previously used, and which was surrounded by buildings on three sides. Actually, he did not fully put down: the space was so tight that there wasn't room. Instead he put the aft wheels down and kept his nose in the air, with the forward rotors spinning a few feet above a single-storey building. The margin for error was tiny; to strike the rooftop would have been catastrophic. The resupply was a complete success.

Another DFC went to Major Mark 'Sweetcorn' Hammond, a pilot on exchange from the Royal Marines, who on the night of 6 September was involved in three separate casevac engagements, all of them under fire. Sweetcorn was a big man for a pilot; they tend to have the physiques of fly-halves rather than prop forwards. He had already won a QCVS, the Queen's Commendation for Valuable Service, in Iraq in 2002. On his second call-out, to Musa Qala, the drop zone was so hot that he was forced to abort, weaving off with his crewmen blazing away Vietnam-style on the machine-guns mounted in the rear. The crew of an Apache hovering in support witnessed a pair of RPGs pass only ten metres above and below the fuselage. Back at base, four rounds were found to have hit the machine, one of which had caused 'almost catastrophic damage to a wing blade root', according to his citation – the closest a British Chinook had yet come to being shot down by small-arms fire in Afghanistan. Undaunted, Sweetcorn immediately returned to Musa Qala in another helicopter. He and his crew again came under fire, but this time he was able to land and the casualty was rescued.

The Chinooks were pushed hard in Helmand, and never more so than on Operation Augustus on 14 July. This was the biggest 'deliberate op' the battle group had yet attempted, a classic airborne assault on a much grander scale than Operation Mutay at Now Zad the previous month. The target was a cluster of compounds about three kilometres north of Sangin. The two main compounds, code-named 'Claudius' and 'Tiberius', were thought to be a Taliban stronghold – possibly a training camp – and a key command post in the continuing siege of the district centre further south, where the garrison had been trapped for sixteen days, their ammunition running low. The Paras hoped to neutralize the area before fight-ing southwards into the district centre where they would relieve their besieged colleagues. En route they intended to capture a senior Taliban commander, a designated HVT or high-value target, who was known to be based in one of the compounds. The plan was to take the compounds one by one using combat engineers to blow holes in the inter-connecting walls, while a company of Canadians in eight-wheeled LAVs (light armoured vehicles) pro-tected their flanks.

A successful troop insertion was obviously critical. A suitable landing site was identified in advance – a dry river bed close to the target compounds. With twenty-four hours to go, reconnaissance photographs showed that the target area was all quiet. At two a.m. on 14 July, therefore, five Chinooks took off from Bastion, each one fully packed with Paras, some of them accompanied by a quad bike and trailer – about two hundred men in all. They were protected from above by a Predator drone equipped with Hellfire missiles, a Spectre gun-ship, another plane carrying sophisticated electronics to block Taliban radio traffic, Harriers, A10s, Apaches and an American B1 bomber from Diego Garcia – the full panoply of air cover, operating at the Coalition's impressive maximum strength.

It was not until the flying circus was airborne that there was any indication of trouble. The target area, it seemed, was no longer all quiet. Footage from the Predator showed people moving about on the rooftops overlooking the landing site, and in a ditch that ran alongside it. Tootal, on board an American Black Hawk command and control helicopter, was unable to see the video feed for himself and radioed back to the Joint Operations Centre for clarification. But the Predator could only pick up so much at night. The footage wasn't clear enough to identify the people on the ground positively as enemy, which ruled out a suppressive air or artillery strike. Tootal had to decide whether or not to abort the mission – and time was not on his side. The heavily laden Chinooks were already over the target area and running low on fuel. They had taken a decoy route from Bastion, flying low with their lights out, and had expected to land and unload their human cargoes as soon as they arrived. Instead they were put into a holding pattern in a nearby valley while the intelligence from the Predator drone was weighed up.

'That was when it started to go wrong,' said Flight Lieutenant Adam Thompson. 'We were stacked up for twenty-five minutes, waking up the entire region and losing any element of surprise. And we were fast coming up to our "Bingo" level: the point when you'll run out of fuel if you don't go home immediately.'

Thompson was thirty, a married man from Yorkshire, and relatively new to the Chinook wing. As a member of 27 Squadron, which replaced 18 Squadron midway through Herrick 4, he had only been in Helmand for five days at the time of Augustus. He had begun his piloting career on search-and-rescue Sea Kings based at RAF Boulmer in Northumberland, where he spent four years rescuing fishermen and oil-rig workers in the North Sea, or 'fallers' who had lost their way in fog and snow in the Lake District. He was unaccustomed to combat flying and had never been in a contact before. Tonight he was co-piloting for Chris Hasler, the daredevil resupplier of Sangin, who as a member of 18 Squadron was just a day from the end of his rotation in Helmand. Hasler, suspecting that some spare 'chicken fuel' might be useful in this operation, had loaded an extra 200kg of it before leaving Bastion. The weight was so great that when they took off the rev meter needles briefly surged into the red band of emergency power, more than twelve seconds of which can cause the engines to burn up. Thompson privately thought Hasler's precaution had put their mission in jeopardy, but now he conceded that the younger but more combat-experienced pilot had been absolutely right.

Tootal desperately needed a clearer picture of what was happening on the ground, and ordered an Apache to sweep the area for better clues. The job fell to Major Andy Cash, the OC of 656 Squadron. 'That was the hardest,' Cash told me. 'Time was critical, and I knew it was basically my call. I looked and looked but I couldn't see anyone moving down there. Not a thing.' He reported in, and Tootal gave the order for Augustus to go ahead.

The first Chinook broke from its holding pattern and clattered down on to the wadi, where it was immediately ambushed. The dykes on either sides were filled with hidden gunmen. They had dug themselves in and kept utterly still as Cash's Apache swept over them, and he had missed them. The airwaves were suddenly filled with urgent yells of 'Ice! Ice!' – the code-word for the command to abort – but it was too late: a wave of Paras was already charging down the ramp into a hail of tracer fire.

The fourth and fifth Chinooks, carrying most of the Para 'C'

Company, did in fact hold off, but the second and third ones in the flight had been ordered to land at any cost once the first one was down: without the extra support, the point unit on the ground risked annihilation. In the back of the second Chinook, controlled by Wing Commander Mike Woods, were thirty-seven Paras, a quad bike with a trailer full of Javelin anti-tank missiles, and Sergeant Graham 'Jonah' Jones, the loadmaster.

Jones was thirty-three, from the fishing port of Grimsby, and married with teenage children. He was another ex-search and rescue man who had done ten years on Navy Sea Kings before joining the RAF in 2001. 'I only transferred to get me third tape,' he said in a homely Lincolnshire accent. He had been a Leading Hand in the Navy, the two-stripe equivalent of a corporal. There were only 120 Sea King crewmen in the Navy, he explained. 'They only employ you until you're forty, and promotion is mostly a case of dead man's shoes.'

He had done three tours in Iraq but he had never seen anything like this operation. 'We were straight on behind the first Chinook, a couple of seconds,' he recalled. 'Their crewmen had already opened up with the port and starboard M60s, so our crew did the same.' The Chinooks were normally armed with three swivel-mounted machine-guns for defensive use on hot landing zones, one on each side and another in the centre of the loading ramp to cover the vulnerable rear, although on this occasion the ramp gun had been removed to allow the quad bike and trailer a speedy exit. In any case, there was a limit to what the crew could shoot at once the Chinook had landed, because the elevation of the side guns was restricted to prevent the crews from damaging their own rotors, and the enemy were on higher ground at the tops of the dykes.

With the cargo bay so full, Jones was perched on top of the

loading ramp, and he had nothing to shoot with but his standard issue SA80, stowed in a sling on the wall. As the Chinook landed he pushed the ramp control switch and then the toe ramps off, and ran out with his rifle to make way for the quad bike. In the safety of Bastion the Paras had rehearsed the unloading procedure countless times. The quad was always carefully reversed on board last so that it could be driven off fast and first. In practice sessions the Paras could get all thirty-seven men out in under thirty seconds; but this wasn't a drill. Jones watched in horror as the quad rolled to the bottom of the ramp, and stalled. 'We were taking rounds through the fuselage. There was a guy on the quad, desperately trying to start it, with the rest of the guys all stuck behind him and the trailer, all scrambling over ... there were rounds coming in past the ramp. I've never experienced anything like that before, it was just outrageous.'

Through his night vision goggles, Jones could see gunmen running down a ditch to a firing point fifty metres away, firing as they went. His job was to supervise the unloading. Instead, in an action that later won him a Mention in Dispatches, he crouched behind the starboard wheel and began to return fire with his rifle.

Reconnaissance photographs had suggested that the wadi would be flat and dry, yet the Paras found themselves stumbling in a bog, and had a hard time extricating themselves. The place had become a war zone, the darkness spectacularly latticed by tracer fire, the air filled with flashes and deafening explosions. The Apaches and A10s were blasting the dykes and compound roofs with 30mm cannon; RPGs and heavy machine-gun fire were coming the other way.

The third Chinook, piloted by Hasler and Thompson, had the roughest landing of all. 'There was so much incoming it was like putting down on the set of *Star Wars*,' Thompson recalled. He and Hasler were so distracted by this, as well as blinded by the dust that had plumed up to fifty feet from the first two Chinooks, that they badly misjudged the speed of their approach. They only avoided a crash by 'flaring' violently at the last minute – a manoeuvre that uses the fuselage's belly as an air brake, and very dangerous in a Chinook, because if the angle is too great the rear rotor can hit the ground. As it was, the machine bunny-hopped and then landed with such a thump that the Paras in the back, who were all on their feet in preparation for the charge off the ramp, collapsed in a violently cursing heap of limbs and weaponry. There would be no thirty-second unload from this Chinook, either. The force of the landing was so great that the engineers at Bastion later discovered it had bent the airframe.

Hasler and Thompson were under fire from a machine-gun nest about a hundred yards to port. The side-gunner tried to return fire, but stopped in horror when he realized that there were women and children in his sights. The gunmen had pushed them out in front of their positions for cover – a Taliban tactic the crewmen had heard of but never seen used before. The crew might have obtained a better angle from the ramp machine-gun, but this had been put out of action by a Para who tripped over it in the scramble to disembark. The skin of the Chinook was only lightly armoured, according to Thompson, so on the ground it was a very easy target. A machine-gun round punctured the side, missing a crewman's head by six inches. Jones, still pumping away with his rifle by the aft wheel of the second Chinook, watched amazed as an RPG streaked twenty yards past his ramp and just in front of the nose of Hasler and Thompson's machine.

The crews had been warned beforehand not to remain on the

ground longer than the thirty seconds it was supposed to take to get everybody out from the back, so Hasler, urged on by his crew, began to lift off. But too soon: three men, two of them Para sergeants, were still struggling with a crate of ammunition on the loading ramp. Rather than stay safely aboard, the three of them looked at one another and then leapt into the darkness – a brave thing to do, since it was impossible to gauge how far from the ground they were. In fact it was about fifteen feet. One broke a hand, the other fractured a leg; the third man was unscathed. He was Flight Lieutenant Matt Carter, a thirty-two-year-old from Worthing and a joint tactical air controller with the RAF regiment, a unit whose usual role was airfield defence. Carter had already proved himself at Now Zad during Operation Mutay, when he directed Apache cannon fire on to a position only thirty metres in front of him. Now he did it again, this time with the firepower of a Spectre gun-ship at his disposal. He was later awarded the Military Cross.

Over at the second Chinook, Graham Jones was understandably anxious to be gone. As the first Chinook was taking off, banking sharply to port as soon as it lifted, he saw another RPG streak a few feet below its undercarriage. 'We got the lads off eventually and I said, "Right, troops gone, let's go!" And then I looked forward and saw we'd got a man down. I thought it was the number two crewman, Matt Clarkson. And Woodsy [the captain, Wing Commander Mike Woods] said, "Who is it?" And I said, "Don't worry, let's go, let's go!" And we lifted.'

As soon as they did so, the Chinook surging and weaving away from the trap on the ground, Jones stowed his rifle and scrambled forward to the casualty. 'The man down wasn't Matt. He was actually behind the armour, still firing his M60 as we cleared away.

It was a Para lad, one of the last to get off, who had taken a round through the fuselage. Not down the ramp – he didn't get that far. He was really unlucky because the bullet hole was only an inch above the ballistic protection.' Others might think that Private Steven Jones was actually very lucky. The bullet, almost certainly from a Kalashnikov, had passed straight through his left arm. 'He'd got his weapon off himself; we took his body armour off. He was all right, he was with it. He turned down his morphine. So we put a field dressing on, and my old tourniquet. It was an amazingly clean wound – because I've seen casualties out there since who have taken 7.62mm rounds, and they do a lot more damage.' His name-sake's courage greatly impressed the ex-winchman from Grimsby. 'I've got massive respect for the Paras. As I was patching him up he said, "Is there any chance of getting me back on the ground?" And I laughed and said, "No, no chance, mate, you're going back to Bastion. You can't go on the ground with that, like."'

With so much close air support the Paras soon regained control of the landing zone and moved forward to their objectives. It was astonishing that none of them was killed, even more so that none of the Chinooks was destroyed. 'How they missed us,' said Jones. 'I just can't see how they missed us, you know? I'm surprised – absolutely amazed – that we didn't lose an aircraft. All of us are.'

The Task Force, it turned out, had taken a huge risk for a very small return. The resistance at the landing site melted away, leaving ten dead bodies behind them. In one of the compounds further on, the Paras found a vehicle loaded with two 107mm rockets; in another, half a dozen RPGs were uncovered. There were also a lot of recently slept-in beds squeezed into small rooms, but whoever their occupants had been there was no sign of them now, nor of the

Taliban commander whom the Paras had hoped to capture. The near-misses against the Chinooks were noted by the chiefs of staff. So was the fact that one of the assault force had been shot even before he could get off his helicopter. Operation Augustus was an experiment that was never repeated.

Britain possesses a grand total of forty Chinooks, almost all of them based at RAF Odiham in Hampshire. They have long been a familiar sight to motorists on the nearby M3, scudding along the horizon in pairs, the ominous thump of their enormous rotors audible even above the noise of a speeding car with its windows shut. When I visited the base, thirty-four Chinooks were in service – the other six were 'in storage' – with thirteen of them operating overseas. The fleet is distributed between three RAF squadrons, two of which, 18 and 27, flew in Herrick 4. They were a close-knit community. The total aircrew of 18 Squadron, which was much the largest of the three, numbered fewer than a hundred people. In fact, there were no more than about 40,000 people in the entire air force – 'fewer than a Saturday crowd at Old Trafford', as one of them put it.

They were a different breed from the Army personnel I had met. There was none of the regimented, head-up-shoulders-back posture that is recognizable in some soldiers, even when they are out of uniform. The all-in-one green flying suits they wore, baggy patchworks of transparent map-pockets, useful pouches and loops to clip things through, were designed with comfort and efficiency in mind, not smartness. They even had their nicknames stitched on patches on their chests, suggesting that the informal style was formally sanctioned. Good flying, I understood, required an element of creativity, an autonomy of thought that is drilled out of

Army recruits and discouraged in all but the most senior ranks. A culture of self-reliance extended even to the so-called 'grease-monkeys' of the engineer ground crew. Some of them had worked alongside the Army Air Corps mechanics at Kandahar, and been amazed at how differently they operated.

'I haven't got the time to go out and check every piece of work an engineer has done, so you have to have a level of trust,' said Flight Sergeant Phil Westwood. 'In some cases that erodes the rank structure. We find the more relaxed approach works better, but the Army can't seem to take that on board.' 'It's a very open system that encourages people to speak up if something's wrong,' added his colleague Adrian Bolton. 'A mechanic is more likely to say, "Excuse me, sir, I've made a bit of a whoopsy here," rather than covering the problem up or just passing it up the chain.'

The Chinook pilots were also physically different from their Army peers, for there was no premium on muscles at Odiham. One or two of them had the delicate hands of pianists. Operating a helicopter is an art that requires quick reactions, mental stamina and exceptional hand-to-eye co-ordination. According to Flight Sergeant Angus Highet, the latter quality is innate and cannot be taught. Highet was forty, and had been crewing Chinooks since the First Gulf War in 1991, but although he knew how to fly one 'in an emergency', he had always known and accepted that he did not have the natural skill necessary to qualify as a pilot. 'I can take off, climb to height, fly straight from A to B, but the difference between flying and operating is huge,' he said. 'As soon as you're hooking on loads, with a crosswind, within a foot of something puncturing the aircraft, at night, on goggles, flying by your ears . . . then it gets very complicated. The minute details and distances these guys work within? Nah. I couldn't do that.'

Highet and one of the pilots showed me around a Chinook parked out on the tarmac. Like many of his colleagues, the pilot asked not to be identified by name. The possibility of publishing his photograph was emphatically ruled out as well. He said this was to protect family and friends from finding out precisely what he had faced in Helmand. Unlike most soldiers, the helicopter crews knew for certain that they would soon be going back to Afghanistan – and not just soon, but repeatedly. In June 2007, 18 Squadron was preparing for its third tour of Helmand in a year. Highet, too, was wary of sharing the gorier details of his experiences with me. 'I have an agreement with my wife that I don't talk about it,' he said. 'And she doesn't ask. Otherwise, how's she going to cope when I go away again? Breaking it down into the nuts and bolts of what I do when they know I'm going back out there again ... that's very difficult for us.'

This is the debit side of the shortness of the RAF's operational tours, which at two months are a third of the standard Army one. The infantry consider the RAF a soft option partly for that reason – their common term of abuse for them is 'crabs', because while soldiers go forward, the fly-boys always seem to go sideways – but they couldn't be more wrong. The effects of intensive combat flying, both on machines and crews, mean that longer tours are impractical. Instead, the squadrons complete a greater number of shorter tours, shuttling between home and the war zones with a frequency that is truly bewildering. The pilots commit to a minimum of twelve years when they join a Chinook squadron – double the standard Short Service Commission in the Army Air Corps, and quadruple that in the regular Army. And there are so few Chinooks and crews available that they are all locked into a cycle of deployment that would make any line regiment blench. For the

Chinook pilots that summer of 2007, the war in Helmand was only just beginning.

We entered by the rear loading ramp, stepping over the empty machine-gun mounting in its centre. The cargo bay was lower and narrower than I had expected. Dark and tubular, it felt claustrophobic, even when empty. There were two long benches ranged against the sides where the troops sat. The silver-coloured walls were festooned with buckles and webbing and red nylon straps. It was not hard to imagine what it must be like to head into combat in one of these things. Photographs I had seen – and there were lots of them, because a Chinook ride is always a good opportunity for a snap – showed the men wedged in so tightly with their weapons and Bergen rucksacks at their feet that moving about the craft was impossible. So, because of the engines, is conversation. The troops are routinely offered foam ear-plugs as they come aboard. They sit and sweat in their body armour, with solemn faces and their legs going to sleep, and nothing but their own thoughts to distract them from what is about to come.

We passed along to the hatch to the cockpit where I scrambled down and in. Once again the space was surprisingly tight, although less claustrophobic because it was surrounded top, bottom and to the sides by glass. Only some of it was armoured. The pilots wore special body armour that weighed a massive 70lb ('with the go-kit and everything, it can easily double your body weight', I was told), but it still felt a fearfully vulnerable place to sit. Wasn't it terrifying to be strapped into this goldfish bowl, flaring on to a landing site with balls of tracer streaking towards you? 'You can only see tracer fire from behind,' the pilot replied with a shrug, 'so if you can see it you're OK. It means it's already missed you.' His nonchalance might have seemed affected, but it wasn't. All the pilots were the same. 'You have to worry about incoming fire in a professional sense,' said Flight Lieutenant James 'Birty' Birtwistle (one of the few pilots who didn't mind his name being used). 'There are things you have to do to avoid it. But there isn't any time to concentrate on the psychological side of it. I suppose it's a good defence mechanism.'

It is often impossible to tell from inside if a Chinook is being shot at as incoming fire is seldom audible above the engines. All the pilots hear during a contact is voices on their headphones passing vital information and urgent instructions, which come to them on as many as five different frequencies and radio systems, from other aircraft, from troops on the ground, from headquarters, and from their own crew. Sifting all this information while flying, I was told, is highly 'capacity-sapping' – which is why so much importance is attached to restricting a crew's flying time, and to making sure they receive regulation amounts of rest. 'The aviator's greatest enemy is fatigue' is the pilots' dictum. A lapse of concentration at the controls of any helicopter can be just as dangerous as an enemy bullet, and that leaves little time to feel fear. It helps that they are also physically cut off from the back of their aircraft by a thick Velcro flap that remains in place to protect sensitive avionics from dust. There were times, the pilots said, when they did not even know whom or what they had on board, and so were shielded from the infectious tension in the faces of troops going into combat, and the grisly sight of casualties coming back.

It is different for the crewmen, of course. On Instant Response Team (IRT) missions the Chinooks become flying ambulances, so there were few among the Task Force who had seen as much blood as the loadmasters. 'I had a couple of pilots get out at Bastion and the back was covered in blood,' said Sergeant Graham Jones. 'I'm talking blood trails running down off the ramp and on to the landing site. And they've gone, "Bloody hell! What the hell's gone on in the back of here?" And I went, "Well, you know. The guy lost his leg. You try and stop a femoral bleed." And that's what it is, you know?' The crewmen handled such horrors in different ways. 'How can I describe it?' said Jones. 'It's like an out-of-body experience, it really is. Like, that's happened to a different part of me. Really you've got to be ... I wouldn't say schizophrenic, but ... when you're back here, I think I'm a different person.'

At thirty-three he was older than most in his squadron, and with a background in search and rescue he reckoned he was better able to deal with the proximity of death than some. 'When you pull kiddies out of lakes or the sea ... you just have to, and I've got children myself. I find that more traumatizing, personally. Though some of the young guys have seen some shocking things. A couple of lads have been given help; it's caused them to lose their flying categories.'

What seemed to trouble Jones most about Helmand was the sheer numbers of wounded – together with a suspicion that those numbers were being deliberately suppressed. 'I think they've kept it very well under wraps,' he said. 'Because we're working hard, the IRT in Helmand. The amount we bring out of theatre ... it's never on the news. The only time you see Afghanistan on the news is when there's been a death. But for every death there's a dozen seriously injured, and you just don't see that.'

Like Jones, Flight Sergeant Bob Larcombe, a Londoner, said he had 'lost count' of the times he had collected dead and injured from the front. He was used to it now, but admitted that the first time had bothered him; and although he had no problem with ferrying the plywood coffins the Army had begun to use, he was still oddly haunted by the thought of body-bags. 'I don't know why, but a body in a body-bag just seems slightly more . . . For me, it's worse than seeing someone in bits on a stretcher. You can tell it's a body when you lift it. I think it's that thing about not knowing what's inside – who it is, the state they're in, the colour of their hair and all that sort of stuff. It's . . . a bit weird.' Nevertheless, collecting body-bags became so routine that Larcombe and his crew soon developed the macabre and self-defensive sense of humour of undertakers. 'There was one body we picked up – a soldier from some other ISAF nation. The bag itself was in quite a mess because it had been left outside for a few days. There were some squaddies getting their kit out of the aircraft, and one of them managed to stumble back and plant his boot right in the middle of the guy's chest in the body-bag. It was awful, absolutely awful. And I thought, "I really don't want to know what's inside there."'

At the start of Herrick 4 there were only six Chinooks in Afghanistan, although later there were eight. Two of the six were kept at Camp Bastion while the other four, with which they regularly rotated for repair and maintenance, were kept at the airbase in Kandahar. Flight 1310 was very small, and when the Task Force themselves appeared to complain that they didn't have enough Chinooks, the media once again accused the government of letting the Armed Forces down, in pursuit of the ever-emotive theme that under-resourcing was costing brave British boys their lives. That story was one of the biggest of late 2006, but really the press missed the point. The problem was not so much a shortage of helicopters as the ballistic threat to the ones the Task Force did have. All Brigadier Ed Butler actually said, in response to the Prime Minister's offer to provide whatever extra resources were needed, was that if he had more, he could do more. 'Clearly we could generate a higher tempo, not just on offensive operations but also to crack on with the reconstruction and development.'

It was true, as one pilot acknowledged, that the RAF did sometimes refuse requests for transport, but this was very seldom because a helicopter was unavailable. 'After one casevac mission we were asked to go back on a resupply run the next day, to the same place at the same time,' he said. 'The ambush threat was high. I wasn't very happy, although I was ready to do it. But one of the crewmen said he wasn't sure either. The captain decided to say, "Sorry, boys, can't do it today . . ." It takes a pretty brave person to put the brakes on like that.' Gus Highet added, 'It goes against our ethos. We run a can-do operation. We don't turn things down. If we had fifty helicopters out there, they'd all be flying every day. It's just the way it works.' The US military, he added, sometimes preferred to use British Chinooks rather than their own because the British system was more flexible. 'The Americans have a rigid planning and briefing cycle that starts ninety-six hours before an op. We can get a piece of paper handed through a window and just go and do it.' It was another illustration of the uniqueness of the British Armed Forces – an institution, as the military saying went, that worked like an organism compared to the machine-like ways of the Americans.

The decision to fly was always a complex one. The risks of every sortie were individually and minutely assessed. Were weather conditions suitable for the approach? What was known of the enemy's strength in the drop zone area? How much fuel, how much daylight, how tired was the crew, how many flying hours were left before an essential maintenance check? But all the normal pre-flight considerations were dropped when it came to a casevac. The crews were intensely proud of how far and how often they pushed the envelope in a medical emergency. The suggestion that any soldier died on Herrick 4 because a Chinook would not or could not fly naturally outraged them. Graham Jones described a night-time casevac mission to the Sangin valley that took place twenty-two hours after his crew had first come on duty – long past the time when they should have stopped flying. 'It was a P1 – a Para shot through the chest. We were asked if we'd go and do it, and we volunteered. Initially we landed at the wrong landing site because they were still under contact, and what we thought was a strobe was actually muzzle flash. The medics had already gone off. I had to run out and grab them and get them back on … As we lifted we did see the strobe, so we landed "on". We got the guy on board and he was on a Hercules to Karachi within the hour. It saved his life.'

The press, however, were little interested in these heroics. On one occasion a *Daily Telegraph* reporter was invited on an IRT sortie to rescue five children injured by burning engine oil. Paul Shepherd, the squadron leader, met the loadmaster involved shortly after his return to Bastion. 'I've never seen someone look so grey,' he said. 'Burned kids is not something we train for.' But the published report did not mention this. Instead it spoke about how old some of Flight 1310's Chinooks were. It pointed out that one of them, Bravo November, had first flown in the Falklands twenty-five years earlier. The Joint Helicopter Force HQ in Kandahar reacted with predictable fury, and ordered its crews to refuse all journalists' requests for trips in future.

It was a good story for the *Telegraph*: a machine from the Falklands era still flying in Afghanistan sounded scandalous. But was it? Even the mechanics were divided. 'Put it this way,' said Flight Sergeant Bolton, leaning back in a well-used armchair in the tea-stained sergeants' mess, 'would you drive your 1975 Cortina down the motorway, fully loaded, at eighty miles an hour?' Yet he agreed that the older machines were not dangerous, provided they were regularly maintained and checked – which of course they scrupulously were. They were not even necessarily more prone to untimely failure.

What the *Telegraph* report failed to explain was that the Chinook, designed in the 1950s and still manufactured by Boeing, is a bit like a Lego set on to which new components can be bolted as old ones wear out. So the basic airframe of Bravo November might have seen action in the Falklands but virtually nothing else on board had. The reporter reckoned that the machine's vintage was a good illustration of MoD penny-pinching, and how the RAF was forced to make do and mend. He was right in a way; but it did not follow that the mechanics or anyone else in the RAF were clamouring for newer models. 'We've got some of the new ones too,' said Bolton. 'They're still working as hard as the old ones. It doesn't matter which one the troops get into. Any machine can fail.' More to the point, the newest models were a lot less like Lego sets than they used to be – and on operations, where the workshop priority was to turn around a damaged machine as quickly as possible, this could actually be a disadvantage. 'The new ones have got these single-piece, machined steel frames,' explained Phil Westwood, 'and when they break, we have to start getting specialists in. That's a fact. So sometimes the old ones are easier to keep in the air.' Thrift had its upside. It sounded remarkably like London Transport's dilemma when they decided to get rid of the much-loved Routemaster bus, the simple old design of which made it far easier to repair than its modern replacement. The Paras' jibe that the Chinook pilots were like bus-drivers because they took them to work every day was perhaps more appropriate than they realized.

The engineers took obvious pride in their professionalism and in their squadrons. But there was no hiding a certain discontent at the way the modern RAF was run – and that was worrying, because men like these had always been the Air Force's bedrock, the unsung heroes who kept its machines in the air. As elsewhere in the forces, recent cost-cutting measures meant their jobs were harder and more relentless than they used to be. In the old days, engineering units were attached to individual squadrons and travelled with them on foreign deployments. Now they had been reorganized into a pool, which meant, according to Westwood, that the 'intensity of engineering here is actually almost at the same level as you'd get on an operation. There are always crews generating to go away on ops. So the engineers have become a Monday to Friday operation . . . at the moment we're even working Saturdays and Sundays.'

According to Graham Jones, the fifty-two-strong team that went to Helmand with Flight 1310 were permanently 'maxed out' on the tricky task of maintaining the fleet in the heat and dust of an Afghan summer. Sand built up in the spaces beneath the fuselage floors and had to be cleaned out. Routine maintenance checks had to be carried out every thirty-one hours instead of the usual seventy-five. The rotors had to be reinforced against erosion with special blade tape, and extreme care had to be taken when lubricating the shafts and bearings because excess grease attracted dust and turned into a vicious 'cutting paste'. The engineers split into two shifts of twelve hours each, and had to sustain that for the duration of the eight-week tour. Splitting into three eight-hour shifts might have made for greater efficiency, but the manpower was not available for that. Fifty-two mechanics was all that Odiham had available. It was also the bare minimum they needed to do the job.

Military aircraft engineering, they wanted me to understand, was a much less attractive career prospect than it used to be; and the increasing likelihood of a dangerous deployment abroad was also having an adverse effect on recruitment. Bolton had friends working in recruitment who reported that there were still plenty of people interested in joining up, but that they tended to say that they 'didn't want to go to Iraq or Afghanistan, thank you very much'. Westwood heartily agreed with the Dannatt assessment that the present military tempo was unsustainable. 'My personal opinion is that I don't think we can keep doing what we're doing for the next three or four years without a major impact on people's health, lifestyle and possibly marriages.'

'There is pressure,' Bolton agreed. 'We as a nation don't have the assets to do it. We don't have an awful lot of battlefield helicopters. We are the only Chinook operators in the UK, and everywhere they go they're wanted.'

Westwood was right about the impact on marriages. According to one pilot, the base at Odiham had the highest divorce rate in the RAF: 'What do you expect, when we're always away for eight months of the year?' The can-do spirit of the Chinook wing was magnificent, but as in the Army it sometimes came at a very high price. This pilot was unusually but deeply despondent about his future in the Chinook wing, and the war in Afghanistan in particular. The novelty of Helmand had worn off, and he had only completed two tours there. Dannatt's prediction of a 'generation of conflict' sounded grim indeed to him.

He was not alone when he complained that the public did not understand what the Armed Forces were doing in Afghanistan, let alone appreciate their efforts and sacrifices. 'It's disgraceful that Afghanistan isn't properly publicized,' said Graham Jones. 'Obviously we've got our hands full with Iraq, and it's better all round if they can keep as much of Afghanistan under the hat as possible. Because in reality we have got two Iraqs now. But I don't think people realize that. My friends go, "How's Iraq going?" I tell them, "I'm not in Iraq." And they say, "Oh, I didn't realize we had Chinooks in Afghanistan, I thought we only had peace-keepers and that out there."' Flight Sergeant Bob Larcombe recalled an email from a civilian friend who moaned that he had been ordered to park at the back of his workplace instead of the front, following a policy decision to let female office-workers park there for personal security reasons. 'I thought, "Is that the most important thing you're worried about? Is that really it?" The week before I was at Sangin. There were 105s [artillery shells] landing two hundred metres from the landing site and the airframe was shaking. It's surreal.'

Flight Lieutenant Adam Thompson worried that the precious mystique of the Armed Forces, the RAF included, had somehow been allowed to drain away. Piloting a Services helicopter used to be seen as a glamorous role by the public, he said, but the old respect for it had gone. 'It's just another job to people these days. They don't wave at you when you fly over them like they used to.' He had noticed this change even before joining the Chinook wing, when he was still in grey-painted Sea Kings. On search and rescue missions, he'd found, people were just as likely to flick a V-sign at him as wave. This, perhaps, was the sorry downside of what Paul Shepherd called the 'civilianization' of the Air Force. There had been a concerted effort in recent years to integrate the Chinook wing into peacetime civilian activity, in a bid to maximize an expensive government asset. Chinooks cost about £15 million each, fully fitted. Allowing any of them to sit around on the tarmac unused didn't represent good value for money. And so it was that, in June 2007, the veterans of Helmand found themselves ferrying aggregate to stem the floods along the River Humber near Hull.

Did the RAF deserve better? There were plenty who thought so, and many of them blamed the government, which seemed no longer to regard the Armed Forces as a treasured national institution and the noble defender of society, but as an 'asset' like any other. The pride of servicemen such as Adam Thompson was hurt. Their dignity was damaged, too, by the adoption of New Labour-style management techniques within the Forces. The Blairite obsession with presentation and publicity clashed particularly badly with the traditional values of the past. One egregious example concerned the RAF roundel, the famous tri-coloured insignia that first adorned the wings of Sopwith Camels above the trenches of Flanders. Some insensitive modernizer in the Air Force saw fit to allow the roundel to be remarketed on a line of casual clothing that included bikinis. 'Jesus H Christ,' wrote one contributor to Pprune.org, an online forum for the RAF, 'I've seen the bloody trainers before, but this is even worse. Trenchard, Bader, Harris, Dowding, Gibson and practically everyone who has ever earned the right to wear the uniform with pride would weep to see this. The RAF has been reduced to a f----g catalogue store.' Another commented, 'Has there ever, ever, ever been anything quite so tacky in the history of the Royal Air Farce [sic]? How utterly ashamed I am that this once proud service has allowed itself to stoop to such levels. Can you imagine what our fellow aviators around the world must think?'

In the end, they reckoned at Odiham, it all came down to money. The media cry of 'not enough helicopters' was a simplification of a widespread and debilitating malaise that was affecting all of the Armed Forces, not just the RAF, and under-funding was one of its root causes. 'It's all money-driven now,' said Adam Thompson sadly.

6

Apache: A Weapon for 'War Amongst the People'

The Chinook wing certainly looked old and under-funded compared to the Apaches. At £38 million each, an Apache cost more than twice as much as a Chinook – and Britain owned sixty-seven of them. There were no complaints from the crews, either, about under-funding. It took a year to train a Lynx or a Gazelle pilot to fly one, and the conversion course alone cost £3 million per head. This made them very highly valued indeed by the MoD, and the men of 656 Squadron knew it. After all, they were the first in the country to be equipped with these world-beating American machines.

At their new headquarters at Wattisham, in Suffolk, I was struck at once by the glamour and confidence of the crews. The squadron leader, a thirty-four-year-old major, once won a flying competition in the US and was actually awarded 'Top Gun' status – the title of the famous Tom Cruise movie, which I had previously assumed to be the invention of a Hollywood scriptwriter. His squadron was the apogee of many decades of close Anglo-American cooperation. Wattisham itself, appropriately, had once been an important US airbase, from where USAF Mustangs and Lightnings flew out to patrol the beachheads during the Normandy invasion. The hangars retained a mournful period atmosphere, as did the cracked concrete aprons across which young Americans in Mae Wests and bomber jackets once scrambled.

The final cost of Britain's Apache programme, which began in 1993, is expected to be more than £4 billion. In the wake of such investment it was politically imperative that the Apache's first deployment in combat was seen as a success – and so it was. Everyone was pleased with the machine's performance in Helmand. Its state-of-the-art targeting and weapons systems, particularly the 30mm chain gun, worked just as they should have. So, rather to the chagrin of the Americans, did the new Rolls-Royce engines, which could deliver 25 per cent more power than the General Electric originals, and proved very useful when taking off in the hot, thin air of Afghanistan. The squadron's human element performed superbly too. The crews won widespread respect from the hard-pressed ground troops for the promptness and willingness with which they supported them.

When the Apache procurement programme was first announced there was fierce competition between the Army and the RAF over who was going to operate it. The Army won, arguing that in the ground-oriented, interventionist missions of the future, the closer cooperation that would result from bringing the Apaches under their command would be essential. Now their argument seemed justified. 'Flown by soldiers for soldiers' was the Army Air Corps' proudest boast. On one extraordinary occasion, following an operation near Garmsir in southern Helmand in January 2007, a wounded Marine who had accidentally been left behind was retrieved by four of his colleagues who strapped themselves to the sides of two Apaches which flew in low and slow with their cannons blazing to cover the rescue mission. It was a brilliant and daring piece of improvisation, as good as any James Bond stunt. The ministry fell over itself to publicize it, and the public were duly thrilled by the story – which of course also served as a potent advertisement of the versatility of the Army's expensive new toy. It was in fact quite a coup for the MoD press office. In all the excitement the media somehow forgot to mention that the wider Garmsir operation, a frontal assault on a heavily defended fort involving up to 300 British troops, was a failure. So, in fact, was the attempt to rescue the wounded Marine, who was already dead by the time his would-be rescuers reached him. (The rescuers didn't know he was dead at the time, however; and it was psychologically important, both for the troops and for the Marine's next of kin, that his body was brought back.)

Like the Chinook wing, the eight-strong Apache flight of 656 Squadron was committed to combat tours in Afghanistan for the foreseeable future. The only differences were that their commissions were shorter – four and a half years, after preliminary training, rather than twelve in the RAF – and that their tours lasted for three months rather than two. The pilots were even more insistent on anonymity than their counterparts at Odiham, and asked to be referred to only by an initial. They, too, were anxious to spare their families the gory details of combat, although they had another reason: as pilots of helicopters, which were the visible linchpins of the British operation in Helmand, they were obvious high-value targets for the enemy. Both on and off the battlefield, therefore, they considered themselves prone to kidnap – or worse.

None of them was allowed to forget John Nichol, the Tornado navigator who was tortured and paraded on Iraqi television in 1991. The American Black Hawk pilot who was shot down and captured by an angry mob in Mogadishu in 1993 (an event later turned into a best-selling book and film, *Black Hawk Down*) provided another cautionary tale. Early on in Herrick 4, furthermore, the members of a French Special Forces patrol had been captured, tied up and gutted alive. This was one reason why the British went to such extraordinary lengths to rescue any of their own. It was also why the distinctive pink-hued flying suits the Army Air Corps usually wore were rapidly abandoned at Bastion in favour of drab fire-retardant overalls that made them look like everybody else.

The threat to aircrew, furthermore, was no longer confined to the war zones. At the time of the Garmsir rescue operation, the West Midlands Police uncovered a plot to kidnap a British Muslim soldier who had recently returned from deployment, and behead him live on the internet. The plotters, from Birmingham, had obtained a list of the names and addresses of twenty-five British Muslim servicemen around the country. According to some press reports, their source was thought to be a mole working at the MoD. The Apache was originally designed as an anti-tank helicopter during the Cold War, when the West's greatest fear was a massed mechanized invasion of Europe by the Soviet Union. That its pilots now had to worry about betrayal from within its own defence ministry illustrated how dramatically the role first envisaged for it had changed.

Despite all the precautions, flying an Apache in Helmand was not nearly as dangerous as crewing a Chinook. None of the squadron received a DFC, and there were only two Mentions in Dispatches for them at the end of their tour. Apaches were small, fast and heavily armed, and therefore far better able to defend themselves than the support helicopters. More to the point, although Apaches were occasionally hit by small-arms fire from the ground – and although they faced the same threat from surface-to-air missiles – they seldom had any reason to put down in enemy territory as the RAF so constantly did. The Garmsir rescue mission was a one-off. The majority of the Apaches' time was spent escorting the vulnerable Chinooks, flying high above them in pairs. Even in direct attack mode, the Apaches typically operated 2,000 to 3,000 feet above the ground.

This was noticed by the ground troops, a few of whom complained that their close air support did not always feel very close. US Apache pilots, it was observed, tended to be far readier to attack at low level, which led some to assert that the Americans were the better and braver allies in a fire-fight – a judgement with which the Americans naturally agreed. 'The Brits are good but they don't have the extreme aggression that we do,' said one pilot, Captain Larry Staley. 'When you are on top of the enemy you look, shoot, and it's, "You die, you die, you die",' said his wing-man, Lieutenant Jack Denton. The pilots at Wattisham were predictably dismissive of this. 'I can see what's happening on the ground far better from higher up,' said Major A, the Top Gun squadron leader, 'and I can be far more useful to the boys on the ground from there.' Flying at low level had its place. It could be helpful if a 'show of force' was required, to intimidate the enemy or even to boost the morale of friendly forces, but it also carried risks that the Army Air Corps thought unacceptable. American Apaches sometimes flew low to evade missile fire, but the British defensive aid suite was better than theirs and made such tactics unnecessary. 'You've only got to look at US helicopter losses compared to ours in Iraq and Afghanistan,' observed Major A. Although the Americans had many more Apaches in service than the British – 800 of them – it was nevertheless true that they had lost more of them than any other type of aircraft. Twelve of them had been shot down since 2003, with another dozen lost to low-level collisions and crashes. The British over the same period lost only one helicopter to hostile fire, a Navy Lynx over Basra in May 2006.

Besides, British Apaches did drop into a low-level attack when necessary. Captain D recalled a mission to rescue a casualty just south of Musa Qala in July 2006. A large American convoy had been attacked with the loss of three vehicles, and had gone into a defensive wagon circle in a dangerously exposed wadi. Captain D agreed to 'ride shotgun' for the IRT Chinook, following it all the way down to the landing zone. 'It wasn't a standard operating procedure or even a tactic we'd practised before, but that was what I agreed to do,' he said.

They dropped quickly to about 300 feet when they were ambushed from a dozen firing points on two sides. 'It was dusk, the light was fading. Suddenly the whole sky was lit up with tracer going in every direction ... I replied with my 30 mil into the nearest wood line.' The greatest danger, perversely, came not from the gunmen hidden in the trees but from the Americans. There were more than a dozen Humvees laagered up in the wadi, and all of them responded with their turret-mounted .50 cals, blazing away not just at the enemy firing points but randomly, to every point of the compass. 'At least half the tracers were ricochets off the ground from the .50 cals. There were these red flashes all over the place, and the bullets were going straight up. They were far more dangerous than 7.62s.'

At 200 feet, the Chinook pilot, Navy Lieutenant Nichol Benzie, realized he had overshot the landing site. He explained afterwards that the tracer fire was so bright that he had lost all his outside visual references. There was too little fuel for a second attempt and the mission was aborted. (The casualty was rescued later that night by a Black Hawk helicopter equipped with specialist infrared night vision.) 'Honestly, it was like the last scene in *Star Wars* when Luke Skywalker flies down that gulley on the Death Star and you think there's no way he isn't going to get hit,' said Captain D. Astonishingly, just like Luke Skywalker, neither the Chinook nor the Apache was touched by a single bullet.

As the Gurkhas at Now Zad could confirm, the close air support a pair of Apaches provided on the day of their famous hand-grenade exchange could hardly have been any closer. 'I was firing 30 mil within ten metres of them,' said Captain J, the lead pilot. 'That's the closest any Apache has fired to friendly forces. It was an extreme measure.' It worked, though. The Gurkhas later retrieved and engraved one of his empty shell casings and presented it to the squadron as a thank-you present.

From the air at dawn on 16 July, it was apparent that the Gurkhas were in serious danger of being overrun. Captain J, an Anglo-Dutchman who was brought up in Antigua – he called himself a 'Biwi', short for British West Indian – was one of the most experienced pilots in his squadron. The clinic, the building across the road from the compound which the Taliban had occupied, at first appeared to be on fire, but then he realized that he was observing the detonations of grenades. He could see muzzle flashes, and then enemy grenades exploding within the compound walls. He and his wing-man, Captain M, had been scrambled from Bastion less than an hour before. A pair of RAF Harriers had also responded to the Gurkhas' call for help, but the Apaches had arrived first in spite of the jets' faster response times. The Harriers were powerless in this situation anyway: they could not risk dropping a bomb so close to friendly forces. Ten metres was theoretically too close to deploy any airborne weapon system, let alone a 500-pounder. Even Captain J had his doubts, but he could hear the urgency in the voice of the resident joint tactical air controller, Sergeant Charlie Aggrey from 7 Para RHA. 'We were never trained to fire that close,' Captain J explained. 'You can't be. But you're not going to go, "Sorry, I'm just going to stand back and watch because they're too close for me to fire."' Even so, he insisted on 'swapping initials' with Aggrey before attacking. He wanted him formally to acknowledge that the target's proximity was unprecedented. If things went wrong, responsibility would at least be shared.

The Apache's arsenal included rockets and missiles, but in this situation the 30mm cannon, although classified as an 'area weapon', was the most accurate and appropriate option. The Apache carried 1,200 rounds of 30mm shells which it fired at a rate of 625 a minute. Like the helicopter itself, these rounds were intended for Cold War combat – its high-explosive tip was designed to penetrate the skin of a Soviet armoured personnel carrier before fragmenting and killing everyone inside – but it was effective in urban fighting too, since the tip generally had no problem breaching bricks or the thick mud-wall architecture of Afghanistan.

The Apaches set themselves up in an 'opposing race-track pattern' above the compound. The plan was to attack the clinic from its east and west sides in rapid alternation. Captain J went first, approaching from the west and keeping the aircraft as steady as he could. He dialled up a twenty-round burst – the standard combat amount, at least in training – aligned the cross-hairs of his gun sight on the roof, and squeezed the trigger.

There was an immediate yell of 'Stop! Stop!' from Aggrey. Some of the rounds had detonated in the Gurkha compound. 'I suddenly thought, "Oh my God, have I hit one of my friendlies?"' said Captain J. He hadn't, thankfully. 'Roger that, breaking off,' he replied – even though he knew he was powerless to shorten a burst once his trigger was pulled. His semi-automated cannon was slow compared to the Gatling on an American A10 (which, remarkably, fires 3,900 rounds a minute) but it still took less than two seconds to fire twenty shells. The Gurkhas worried that the Apache's targeting was slightly off, although Captain J reckoned the likelier reason was ricochet caused by the near-simultaneous fragment-ation of so many shells. His backseat co-pilot, Staff Sergeant L, thought the roof of the building was probably concrete, which the 30mm cannon shells wouldn't necessarily penetrate. 'I thought, "Fuck this," if you'll excuse my language . . . I said to [Captain J], "Look, mate, you want to be putting them through the windows." There were a number of windows on the western side . . . I can still visualize how many there were. So that's what we did.'

Captain J and his wing-man switched to ten-round bursts to reduce the risk of spreading, warned the Gurkhas to keep well down, and carried on with the attack. The clinic's occupiers some-how survived several passes by the Apaches, and even shot at their tormentors as they swept overhead. ('That was a bit cheeky,' Captain J remarked.) Between them the Apaches fired some 500 shells at the building, working methodically along it, window by window. They only broke off the attack when Aggrey reported that the shooting had been replaced by the sound of screaming. That detail caused Captain J some unease. 'It was my first definitive kill without a doubt,' he said. 'It was a little bit chilling. I started to think, "Were they all Taliban in there, or were there civvies as well?" It didn't stop me from doing what I was doing, by any means. But it did send a bit of a question.'

The fact that the building was one of Now Zad's few formally designated medical establishments had not passed the Taliban by, and their propaganda machine reacted with great speed. By the time Captain J and the others were back at Bastion – a mere twenty-five-minute flight away – the news that they had attacked a 'medical clinic' was already on Sky News, which was always playing somewhere in the background at headquarters. 'Everyone was giving me banter, like, "Oh, right, so you shot up a hospital." And I went, "No, the Gurkhas were being engaged from there..." Obviously you do a full debrief afterwards, and show the video, so there was no doubt that it was justified.'

The Taliban had deliberately exploited the ambiguity of the term 'clinic'. The building was not a hospital so much as a cross between a small doctor's surgery and a pharmacist's dispensary. No one could be certain that it didn't contain civilian patients at the time of the attack, but given its extreme proximity to the compound it seemed very unlikely. Major Dan Rex's men never heard anything to suggest that innocents had been hit, and no civilian bodies were ever found in the wreckage – although that of course proved little, because the Taliban always made a point of extracting their dead and wounded.

It was a long day for Captain J's Apaches. That night they were called to Now Zad once again, this time to shepherd a Chinook bringing in much-needed reinforcements. While Captain J was in overwatch, Captain M was fired on by an anti-aircraft gun set up on a rooftop near the town bakery, a scant 100 metres north-east of the compound. The gun type was never identified; the Gurkhas said only that it spewed slow green tracer shells like an erupting volcano, and was strangely silent as it fired. 'The fire was sustained and very accurate,' Captain J said. 'We were a hard target to see because we always flew without lights. This was the first time that we knew for sure that the Taliban had night vision capability.' It was only Captain M's flying skills that saved him. 'He's a very good aviator. You could see these tracer rounds following him around the sky trying to shoot him ... he was jinking and diving around the bullets, accelerating, changing altitude, slowing down again.'

Captain M responded with his 30mm cannon and then proposed a Hellfire missile – the first ever to be fired in anger by a British Apache. This, too, was a weapon originally designed for the Cold War. It followed a laser beam down to its target, generating a million pounds of pressure per square inch as it blew – enough to penetrate the armour of any tank. The strike had to be cleared through the JTAC, Charlie Aggrey, who was so worried about the proximity of the target that he aborted the Apache's first approach while he checked that everyone in the compound was under cover. By the time the Hellfire was released, the enemy machine-gunners had collapsed their weapon and escaped to safety. Still, the top floor of their building was turned to rubble, making that rooftop unusable as a firing point in future, and the gun was probably also destroyed, for it was never heard from again. At £60,000 each, the Hellfire was an expensive way of dealing with such threats, but it was to be used more and more in the months that followed. The squadron fired eleven of them during their first three-month tour, but ninety-eight in their second, at a cost of nearly £6 million. However, the accuracy of the missile meant that it was a sought-after capability.

*

The Apache is probably the most sophisticated cog in the Coalition's high-tech war machine. To fly one demands much expertise. Like the Chinook pilots, Captain J and the others spoke of operating in a curious bubble of concentration that left little time to feel fear; and because they normally flew hundreds of feet from the ground, they were even more detached from the action below. In Chinooks, pilots are subjected to instructions from five different radio channels; in Apaches, there are as many as seven.

In some ways they are more like computer operators than pilots. Their job is as much about the rapid interpretation of complex information as controlling the movement of the aircraft which, under the right conditions, could virtually fly itself anyway. The avionics, connected by thirteen kilometres of wiring, contain so many processors that even the specialists are unsure quite how many there are. Each one is duplicated and cleverly hidden away in some asymmetric corner of the airframe, as a back-up in the event of a successful strike from a bullet or missile. One electronic warfare officer told me that he had found sixteen of them, 'although there could be more'. All the computers are talking to one another all the time, and a glitch in any of them can necessitate the rebooting of the entire helicopter.

Sensors automatically detect a thousand potential targets, of which 256 are classified before the top sixteen are prioritized. A monocle attachment to the pilot's right eye relays footage from a telephoto lens in the aircraft's nose. At the touch of a switch it is possible to 'slave the head', causing the underslung cannon to swivel wherever the pilot is looking, and to fire where he focuses his eye. As the former squadron leader of 656, the newly promoted Lieutenant Colonel Andy Cash, remarked, there were times when

229

flying an Apache was disturbingly like some futuristic shoot-'em-up video game – a video, moreover, that can be replayed, since every move a pilot makes is captured on a gun tape for later analysis.

Yet however advanced the technology, there is always room for human error. Night vision goggles and powerful telephoto lenses can help, but it is ultimately the pilots who have to decide what constitutes a target and what does not. That is the heaviest responsibility of being in charge of a machine of such awesome destructive power. In a campaign for hearts and minds, proportionality of response is politically vital.

It didn't help that some of the armaments at the pilots' disposal were quite inappropriate for the task, particularly in the early stages of Herrick 4. The rockets attached to Captain J's Apache on the day of the clinic attack, for instance, carried armour-piercing incendiary warheads designed to disable ships. The clinic was an important part of the town's civilian infrastructure; Captain J needed to kill the gunmen occupying it, not incinerate it. The anti-tank Hellfire was also wrong for this kind of warfare, since the Taliban possessed no armour of any kind. 'We're getting a different kind of Hellfire now, with more fragmentation, because we're firing at buildings and people rather than tanks,' Captain J said.

Meanwhile, it was decided that a potentially more useful weapon, the medieval-sounding 'flechette' rocket, should not initially be used during Herrick 4. Fired in pairs, each of these terrifying weapons is packed with eighty five-inch-long tungsten steel darts. Travelling at supersonic speed, the projectiles spread out into a flying metal wall that can pass through brickwork and thick trees and still kill any living thing in their path. Careful forethought was always needed when firing a flechette because the risk of collateral damage was high.

It is perhaps just as well that the crews were trained to err on the side of caution. Of course there were times when they got it wrong – as they did, for example, at Now Zad, when a pilot declined to fire on an enemy mortar team and ended up having to apologize to the Fusiliers. But just as often they got it right. In one incident, Major A was urged to attack a building the local JTAC insisted was being used as a fire point. 'But I couldn't see any evidence of that at all,' he recalled. 'The JTAC was screaming at me, but I wasn't going to pull any trigger without being sure of the target. In the end I aimed off and fired a burst at some nearby empty ground. Then the JTAC reported that the shooting had stopped. He even thanked me for it. I never owned up to what I'd done. Sometimes, with Apaches, less is more.'

Like the Chinook crews, Major A and his pilots were intensely and justifiably proud of their achievements in Helmand. Their confidence in the capability of their machines was supreme. As Andy Cash said, the Apache was the 'perfect weapon for "war amongst the people"' and its performance would only improve as the weapons systems it carried were upgraded and refined. Brigadier Ed Butler described the Apache as 'the real battle-winner . . . Without dedicated AH support, especially the surgical ability to put 30mm cannon fire down within twenty-five metres of our troops, the Task Force could not have achieved what it did in 2006.' The extreme environment of southern Afghanistan had proved the Apache's versatility, and a role in all military deployments of the future looked assured.

So morale at Wattisham should have been soaring, yet it was not. Instead, the Squadron Leader had a serious crew retention problem. Despite the honour and prestige of being the first to fly Apaches in combat, all bar one of 656 Squadron were getting out as soon as they could. On his next tour, Major A was likely to be leading a group of pilots who had never flown in Helmand before. The hard lessons of Herrick 4 would have to be learned almost from scratch.

The glamour of flying Apaches, it seemed, was a veneer; the reality was that many of the pilots felt trapped and exhausted by their jobs. The Apache's great strength, its technical sophistication, was also partly to blame. It takes six months to learn to fly one, even for previously qualified pilots, and then another six months of CTR, the conversion-to-role course that teaches them how to operate its futuristic weapons systems. Both courses are intensive, and the Herrick 4 crews had hardly completed them when they were deployed to Helmand, with the promise of many more such tours in the future. They were, as Warrant Officer G explained, 'away all the time'. No doubt this lifestyle suited young men without families to worry about, but the Air Corps had made a point of hand-picking older and more experienced men for the first training intake – 'the old and the bold', as Warrant Officer G put it – and now many of them had had enough. 'My boss has lived in thirteen houses in the last fourteen years,' said Captain D, who was thirty-one. 'That's not good at all. And I got married last Christmas. It's time for me to settle down.'

Warrant Officer G's nickname was 'Fog'. 'It stands for Food or Google,' he explained, 'because I'm usually doing one or the other. Although some people have suggested it stands for Fucking Old Git.' He was forty-four, and about to leave the Army after twenty-eight years of service. 'This aircraft burns people out,' he said. 'The hours you've got to put in are unbelievable.'

Fog was the squadron's acknowledged expert on the Apache's electronic defence systems. He spent two years studying them during the machine's critical development phase, but despite that, and despite the £3 million it had cost to teach him to fly the Apache, there was no real retention package, no financial incentive to persuade him to stay on. Being away for seven months of the year, he said, had cost him his marriage. His accommodation at Wattisham was a soulless 'box'. He was desperate for a different kind of life, but the war in Afghanistan had ensured that there was no prospect of that. 'The way things are going, we're going to be in and out of Afghanistan every eighteen months, at best. And that's if we're fully manned. But we're nowhere near fully manned right now.' An inability to retain its crews was a serious problem for the Army Air Corps, though not nearly as serious as its failure to attract replacements. 'There's no one coming through the sausage machine. We were a bad advert, chatting in the bar with blokes thinking of doing it. They've seen us with black eyes, the sixteen-hour days on CTR; they've seen us going out to Afghan. And certainly after the first tour we came back absolutely knackered. You don't get a day off.'

Man and machine were not in harmony at Wattisham. Fog's disenchantment encapsulated a wider problem in the Armed Forces identified in a report published in November 2007 by Demos, the left-wing think tank. 'Stretched budgets remain tied up in big-ticket, high-profile hardware,' the report stated, 'while the "software" – the men and women who make up the armed forces – are overlooked.'

Unlike in the RAF, Army Air Corps pilots are drawn from non-commissioned ranks as well as officers, an egalitarian arrangement that represents an unusual opportunity for NCOs. For ambitious officers, however, the conversion to Apaches is not necessarily attractive. 'An officer has a career path to follow,' said Fog. 'He's got to jump through the hoops if he wants promotion. But if he goes Apache, he's already lost a year on basic helicopter training, then another year converting to type and role. And if he misses the chance he'll be left behind.'

Fog might not have liked the Apache pilot's lifestyle, but the clincher, for him, was his disillusionment with the conduct of Britain's Afghan campaign. Like the rest of the squadron, he had spent a lot of time hovering in 'overwatch' above the district centres. The Apache crews' perspective on all the destruction was unique, and none of it, in Fog's opinion, should ever have happened. 'The platoon-houses only had to be occupied because the Afghans legged it,' he said, 'and that left no one to secure the golden triangle. It was never planned for, and it put all the reconstruction work on a backburner. We certainly should have found a way of sticking with the original plan.'

He had flown many missions during Herrick 4, including Operation Augustus, but the one that summed up his tour came earlier, on 24 May, when he was tasked to escort two Chinooks full of Paras to Baghran in the far north of the province. Their orders were to rescue the local police chief, Hajji Zainokhan, whose town had supposedly been overrun by the Taliban. Zainokhan was yet another 'key ally' of Governor Daoud, who had effectively ordered the mission through Charlie Knaggs, the designated British Task Force commander in Helmand. Although simple in theory, the mission nearly went badly wrong. Baghran was at the helicopters' maximum range from Bastion, and required a quick turnaround if everyone was to get back without running out of fuel. The police chief had been instructed to light a smoky fire as a landing beacon as soon as he heard the British coming. Yet there was no sign of any fire when the helicopters arrived over Baghran. 'We circled for what seemed like ages, biting our fingernails and wondering whether to abort,' said Fog. 'They lit a fire eventually, but only just in time.'

Hajji Zainokhan's lack of urgency was typically Afghan. Did he need rescuing, or not? The Paras and pilots had put their lives on the line for him! There was a sorry symbolism to the story, and Fog's frustration was clear. 'In my opinion it was incidents like that that caused the Task Force to become so spread out. What I'm saying is, we bent over backwards to keep the Afghans satisfied, and I'm not sure that we should have.'

His squadron, he feared, would suffer in the end. The eventual price would be Apaches flown into combat by crews without the necessary experience – or even, God forbid, £38 million war machines grounded in Suffolk for want of anyone qualified to fly them.

7

Tom's War

In mid-October 2006 the BBC correspondent David Loyn set out for Helmand to meet the Taliban. Herrick 4 was drawing to a close by then, and the fighting was beginning to subside, although the platoon-houses at Now Zad and Sangin were still under sporadic attack. Only Musa Qala was quiet, thanks to an experimental ceasefire that had held for almost a month. Loyn joined a band of fighters who took him on a tour of northern Helmand in a convoy of speeding trucks, apparently with complete impunity. At one of their bases the Taliban were seen showing off some captured Coalition equipment: a machine-gun in a wheelbarrow, an American helmet which they had fired at in order to test it, and, most memorably, a pair of night vision goggles that one fighter struggled to put on over his enormous black turban.

The report, broadcast on *Newsnight*, generated much controversy. Some accused Loyn of giving succour to the enemy. The Conservative defence spokesman Liam Fox called the piece 'obscene'. On the other hand, soldiers quite liked it. In a poll on the

Army Rumour Service website, 62 per cent of respondents agreed unconditionally with the question 'Is it right for the BBC to interview members of the Taliban?' A former intelligence analyst for the Allied Rapid Reaction Corps in Bosnia, an ex-Fusilier officer who called himself 'Stonker', wrote, 'I was always happy to read-hear-watch interviews with tw-ts [*sic*] like Arkan;* because (taken with a pinch of salt, and in conjunction with material from other sources) it was a "way in" to their world view, which was advantageous.'

Perhaps the most troubling shot was of a military vehicle lying mangled at the side of a road just outside Musa Qala, the white-on-black British number plate 04 FF 31 plainly visible – 'a Spartan', Loyn commented, 'destroyed with the loss of three lives'. During the trip, Loyn was offered some grainy video footage of what his hosts said were members of the vehicle's unfortunate crew: a pair of corpses, badly burned, swinging by the neck from a Musa Qala lamp-post. The claim seemed plausible. The Taliban had a tradition of hanging their trophy victims in public – President Najibullah in Kabul, for instance, when they deposed him in 1996. But the pictures were too gory to use in the package that Loyn was preparing for *Newsnight*, even if he had been able to verify the identities of the victims.

This was just as well, because whoever the unfortunate people were they were certainly not British. Loyn had almost fallen foul of a crude propaganda trick. Three people – 2nd Lieutenant Ralph Johnson, Lance Corporal Ross Nicholls and Captain Alex Eida of 7 Para RHA – had indeed died in the Spartan, a vehicle operated

---

* the *nom de guerre* of the notorious Serb paramilitary leader Željko Ražnatović, who was assassinated in 2000.

by the Household Cavalry (HCR), which had been ambushed ten weeks earlier. But immediately after the strike, and as a matter of policy, the Paras led a counter-attack to recover their remains. Some of the body parts were pulled from the wreckage by Lieutenant Colonel Stuart Tootal himself. The sole survivor of the blast, the driver, Trooper Martyn Compton, had already been rescued by fellow patrol members.

I heard the details of the ambush from my wife's cousin, Tom Burne, who was there when it happened. His squadron was taking part in Operation Nakhod, which was intended to relieve a platoon of Pathfinders holed up in the Musa Qala platoon-house. Some of his unit reckoned the Taliban had simply been lucky, although the attack looked to him like the work of experts. The bombers had anticipated the lead troop's route and sited an IED (improvised explosive device) to perfection, well buried in a choke point between a high wall and an orchard in the southern outskirts of the town. They allowed the first vehicle in the troop, Call Sign 31, to pass over the spot before halting it with a pair of well-aimed RPGs. The second vehicle, the Spartan, Call Sign 40, stopped and began to reverse – as the ambushers apparently guessed it would. They undoubtedly knew what they were doing. The Spartan, a command and control version of the Scimitar, was the only one in the four-strong troop and easily distinguishable because it carries no 30mm cannon. The IED, probably comprising two or even three Soviet-era anti-tank mines stacked one on top of the other, was powerful enough to blow the back off the eight-ton vehicle.

Tom was commanding another Spartan, Major Alex Dick's Squadron HQ vehicle, about half a mile to the rear when he heard the tremendous bang. The initial contact at the head of the formation had been reported by Corporal of Horse Mick Flynn, who was in command of the lead Scimitar. Unfortunately the pressel on his hand-held radio unit had become stuck on permanent send (the pressels were badly designed, and prone to this). For what felt like minutes, therefore, all Dick could hear was Flynn's instructions to his crew, so he could only guess what was going on at the front of his column.

'You train for this situation but there's no preparation for what it's really like,' said Tom. 'The waiting is the worst. You have to sit and wait and let whoever's been contacted get on with the situation in hand.'

But then they heard from Lieutenant Tom Long, who had taken command at the ambush site and was looking on from one vehicle back. His words sent an awful frisson through everyone who heard them. 'Call Sign Four Zero does not exist,' he said.

The men in Dick's Spartan looked at one another. And then they all looked at Bombardier 'Fitz' Fitzgerald, who had been riding in the back. Fitz was Alex Eida's 'ack' – his number two. Eida himself was a forward observation officer (FOO) responsible for coordinating the fire from six 105mm guns which had been brought up to provide supporting fire for the operation. FOOs and their acks, whose battlefield role is dependent on excellent communication, tended to be close, and the pair had already been through a lot on this operation. Twelve hours earlier they had been riding in a third Spartan when it was struck by an old Russian mine on a ridge just west of the town. There wasn't much the squadron could do about these so-called 'legacy' mines, of which there were an estimated four million scattered about the country, the majority of them unmarked. 'Everywhere we went,' said Tom, 'whenever we recce'd a position we thought was good, the Russians had had the same idea and mined everything around it to protect themselves.' The blast obliterated the engine decks and threw the vehicle into the air, turning it 180 degrees. Miraculously, nobody was hurt. The Spartan's driver, Trooper Jason Glasgow, simply stood up in the driver's cab, touched his body up and down to check everything was in place, did up his body armour and popped a couple of pain-killers. The vehicle's commander, Corporal of Horse 'JC' Moses, was so relieved that he stood up in his turret and went into a war dance.

Now, Eida's luck had run out. The crew and passengers from the disabled Spartan had been redistributed around the squadron – which was why Fitzgerald had been separated from his boss, who was now almost certainly dead. 'It was awful,' said Tom. 'You could see it in Fitz's eyes. But he was focused on his job. We were debussed and he was on the net to the guns in the rear, calling in target grid references. He was incredibly professional; but once he had done all he could, after five or six minutes, he started crying. He just cracked.'

It was a grim moment for all of them. This was the first large armoured vehicle the British had lost in Afghanistan. Until now the eighty-nine men of D Squadron, a forward reconnaissance formation of about twenty-five vehicles, had felt almost invincible behind their armour, secure in the knowledge that they were the biggest thing out there. The vehicles even seemed to offer good protection from mine strike. Musa Qala had just stripped this happy illusion away.

Ralph Johnson's death was particularly shocking for Tom and the other young lieutenants. 'He was in the intake below me,' Tom said. 'He was still a second lieutenant, he'd come straight from training, but he was a key part of the young officer gang as there were only ten or twelve of us. He was a very unassuming guy, very chilled out, a good lad. His dad had been in the South African Army. He was a top-quality soldier. His boys thought the world of him because he was doing everything right, and highly professional. They were absolutely gutted. They were getting close to him because of his competence. He was one of the boys, loving it.'

For Tom there was the added realization that he was the first in line to replace him. Although a qualified troop leader, he had originally been deployed to Helmand in a liaison officer role, which was why he had spent the first three weeks of his tour in the relative safety of Bastion. Now that there were only four troop leaders left in theatre, it was just a question of time before he stepped into the front line.

The death toll of three could easily have been worse. The ambush had blocked the narrow road with burning wreckage, cutting off the lead Scimitar from the rest of the squadron. The commander, Corporal of Horse 'Mad Mick' Flynn, forty-six, from Cardiff, was a regimental legend. He had fought in the Falklands and won a Conspicuous Gallantry Cross (CGC) before quitting the Army, but had found civilian life so dull that he joined up again after an eight-year gap. Now, he decided to try to force his way back through the ambush. The site was swarming with gunmen, with a main killing group of twenty or thirty who were no more than ten metres away. Flynn fired phosphorus grenades at them, taking out the machine-gun posts to the front and killing three others as they assaulted up the lane. But the wreckage on the road had forced Flynn's Scimitar into a ditch, and when a third RPG struck, setting the machine alight and mangling its outer bar armour, it was clear it could go no further. Flynn and his crew dismounted and fought their way along the ditch to the relative safety of the nearest Scimitar, Call Sign 30 under Tom Long, passing the wreckage of the bombed Spartan as they went. 'Inside I could see one body,' said Flynn. 'The one outside was blown up and was just a mass of meat. It was just another dead body. Without trying to sound callous, I don't have any feelings. I think I have become immune to it. You can't – they are finished, that's it. I just accept that they are dead ... My driver was having problems and I said, "We have to move, otherwise they are going to kill us."'

While this was going on, Long saw something out of the corner of his eye: a pair of legs poking out from behind a low wall. 'At first I thought he must be Taliban. But then I saw the trousers were desert DPM [disruptive pattern material]. He was one of ours.' It was the driver, Trooper Compton, who had somehow escaped the carnage of Call Sign 40. Horrifically burned, he had scrambled from the wreck and run into cover about twenty-five metres away, where he had then been shot. The fire-fight was still intense but Long's driver, Lance Corporal Andrew Radford, didn't hesitate. He scrambled out and sprinted through the ambush site towards Compton, where he was joined by Flynn. 'I could see it was one of the lads,' said Flynn. 'When I first looked at him he had fish eyes and I thought he was dead, but as I moved his leg, which was jutting out at an angle, he screamed.' Flynn heaved Compton on to Radford's back and they staggered back, shooting as they went. Compton, unconscious now, was dumped on to the front decks of Call Sign 30, which then reversed out of the fire-fight as quickly as Radford could manage. Compton's life was saved. Radford was later awarded the CGC. Flynn already had one of those, so he was awarded a Military Cross – which, as his squadron leader proudly pointed out, made him the most decorated serving soldier in the entire British Army.

While passing the destroyed Spartan, Flynn had spotted only two dead bodies, which left one unaccounted for. Further back, Dick had already requested help from Bastion, which arrived about an hour later: two Chinooks full of Paras who, guided by the redoubtable Flynn, assaulted through the town until the ambush site was secured and all three bodies could be extracted. In the meantime, the Spartan and the ditched Scimitar were guarded by an Apache. 'We were in overwatch for forty-five minutes,' recalled the pilot, Captain D. 'We saw a couple of cars approaching from the west out in the desert and went to have a look. When we came back we saw two Taliban guys jumping off the disabled Scimitar. They'd picked up a bag, somebody's rucksack. They'd been hiding in the orchard, waiting ever since the attack to see what they could loot. On the gun tape later on I could see them peeking out. I chased them down with the 30 mil and certainly killed one. The other wasn't in a particularly good way; he hobbled off into the orchard.' The would-be looter was Captain D's only confirmed kill of the tour.

His day would have been memorable anyway, for he was very nearly the victim of a freak accident. Before flying into his over-watch position he had spoken to the JTAC accompanying the Paras to check that their supporting artillery barrage had stopped. In all the confusion the JTAC told him, wrongly, that it had. 'We came back into the overhead. I still don't know if it was my imagination or if I genuinely heard it, but I thought I heard a kind of whiz past the aircraft. Now, I don't know what an artillery shell going past at thirty feet sounds like, but if I had to guess, it would be a zip, a whizzy sound . . . which was followed very briefly afterwards by an incredibly big explosion right underneath the aircraft. I radioed the JTAC again. "Can you just confirm that the guns are cold?" "Er, no," he says! But I wouldn't hold it against him. I badgered him about it in the bar afterwards, you know . . . It would have been very unlucky. It's a big old sky.'

Shocked and battered, the rest of D Squadron retreated to Bastion. 'The miracle of the whole thing was that Compo got out,' said Long. 'Everything was blown to pieces. It was his strength of character that saved him. He had seventy per cent burns . . . no one thought he would survive, from the moment the medics first saw him until today.'

On the evening of 4 August a memorial service for the dead men was held in the cookhouse. The venue wasn't nearly big enough. Half the battle group seemed to be there, not just the Household Cavalry. The loss of the three men was felt by everybody, especially in such vicious circumstances. It was the first major IED strike of the campaign, an escalation of the insurgency bitterly familiar to those who had served in Iraq. Neither Flynn's nor Moses' vehicles could be recovered and had to be destroyed, the former by high-explosive barmines, the latter by a couple of Hellfire missiles. By the end of 1 August, therefore, two Spartans and a Scimitar had been reduced to smoking piles of metal. Operation Nakhod had failed, handing the Taliban a valuable propaganda victory, and prompting a serious rethink of the way the squadron should be used in future. 'That was the first and last time we went into a built-up area without infantry,' said Long.

The weakness of the chain of command had been shown up too. The squadron had deployed to Helmand as a Brigade asset, which meant taking orders not from the battle group HQ at Bastion but from Brigade HQ in far-away Kandahar. The staff there had no 'situational awareness'; they were instead concerned with 'big picture' tactics which, in this sort of close country fighting, did the

Household Cavalry no favours at all. 'They were just coming up with orders like, "Go and have an effect in Musa Qala,"' said one officer. 'I mean, what sort of a mission statement is that?'

The arrangement was another hangover from the Cold War. The squadron was structured and trained to operate as a fast-moving reconnaissance unit. Its main intended role was to range eighty to a hundred kilometres beyond the front line looking for concentrations of Soviet armour, allowing the generals in the rear to manoeuvre their tank divisions accordingly. But the Task Force, as the squadron had been pointing out for weeks, was fighting a very different sort of war in Afghanistan. The Scimitars were not being used for reconnaissance but as close fire support for ground troops – yet another example of the Army adapting old ways of thinking to a new kind of enemy. Operation Nakhod was salutary: from 1 August, D Squadron was at last switched to battle group command.

The Scimitars were equipped with excellent night vision optics and a fast and accurate 30mm cannon. They looked like small tanks; and that, in a country with a long memory of the scorched-earth policy executed by Soviet armour in the 1980s, was perhaps the most useful weapon of all. On 23 July, when Major Dick was ordered to resupply the Gurkhas at Now Zad, he made a point of manoeuvring his vehicles noisily and as often as possible around ANP Hill. 'We only had about eight Scimitars up there, and the Taliban panicked. We heard later that they had said they were surrounded, that we had eighty to a hundred tanks on station. They definitely don't like tanks.'

Whatever the locals may have thought, Scimitars are not tanks. They, along with Spartans, are actually classed as CVR(T)s – combat vehicles reconnaissance (tracked) – and at eight tons apiece are the lightest mobile armour the Army possesses. In Iraq the troops could rely for support on twenty-five-ton Warrior fighting vehicles, and even fifty-five-ton Challenger II battle tanks. These, however, had been deliberately excluded from the Helmand mission. This was mainly because of the difficulty of keeping them fuelled and supplied by air, but also because some in Whitehall thought the bigger vehicles would be too intimidating. The deployment of Scimitars was in keeping with the 'soft' intentions of Herrick 4, in other words; but the IED strike at Musa Qala suggested that something heavier might have been a good idea after all.

Even as CVR(T)s, the vehicles were far from the best available. Musa Qala, according to Major Will Bartle-Jones, who took over D Squadron halfway through the tour, demonstrated that the cannonless Spartan was 'not really a fightable vehicle'. Its only weapon system, a turret-mounted 7.62mm machine-gun, was squeezed into a tight circle of other equipment that severely restricted its arc of fire. 'You almost need hands like a Tyrannosaurus rex to operate it – a cocking lever here, the firing system here.' Reloading it or clearing a stoppage required the gunner to climb halfway out of the narrow turret, which was never designed for a man wearing body armour. 'You can fire it, but one stoppage and you're in deep trouble. At Musa Qala the Spartan was constantly having to fire one round and re-cock each time.' The problem was being addressed with the addition of a second gun system on a separate pintle. 'That'll be easier, but the gunner will still have to climb out of the turret to operate it. It's just another quick fix from the Army.' The British vehicles certainly compared badly with the Canadian light armoured vehicles alongside which they sometimes fought. The Canadians didn't even have to open their hatches, because their guns could be controlled from the interior with a joystick and CCTV. 'We could buy LAVs off the shelf tomorrow. Why don't we?' Bartle-Jones shrugged. 'In the end, everything comes down to money.'

The squadron's communications equipment was badly out of date. The most important piece of it was the TACSAT, the tactical satellite radio that linked a vehicle to HQ. There should have been a set for each of the four troops, deployed as they were at different locations across the province. Instead there was one TACSAT for the entire squadron, and it could not be used on the move without a special antenna – which they did not have, although the Canadians did.

It was a similar story with the air-conditioning. The need for it had been identified years before in Iraq, but although the necessary extra equipment had been ordered, it still hadn't been fitted. Temperatures in the high fifties (130 to 140°F) were therefore the norm inside the vehicles. The metal became so hot that the crews had to keep their sleeves rolled down and wore gloves to prevent burning. 'The environmental health guys went down into a vehicle to see what we were complaining about,' said Bartle-Jones. 'But they went first thing in the morning, when it was at its coolest. They only ran the engine up for two minutes. Even so, they came back with a temperature reading of 53°C.' It did not help that the crews could not turn off their engines while on operations. Thanks to a built-in thermal cut-out switch, they were often unable to start up again if they did so. By far the hottest position inside was the driver's cab, particularly in the Spartans, whose operators are obliged to sit by a hot air vent from the engine. The crews reckoned the temperature there could touch 70°C.

'Heat stroke was a problem almost immediately,' said Major Dick. 'On our very first op we had a guy, Ramon Rayner, whose core temperature got up to 41.7°C. That's 0.3°C from the temperature that an egg starts to turn white in a frying pan.' Trooper Rayner was semi-conscious and babbling. His crewmates tried to rehydrate him with a drip from their standard-issue medical pack, but could not insert the needle because the rubber cannula had softened in the heat. He was saved by the brigade's token attachment of Estonians, one of whose six-wheeled 'Sisu' vehicles happened to be nearby. Their machines were twenty years old and had been bought second-hand from Finland, but they had air-conditioning. Rayner was transferred aboard and his life very probably saved.

The root problem with the CVR(T) fleet was its age. Some of the Scimitars had been in service since 1969. However tough their exteriors, they required surprising amounts of maintenance to keep them operational in the harsh environment of Helmand. They were designed to go out on long-distance patrols and return to base, where mechanics from REME, the Royal Electrical and Mechanical Engineers, could rectify any fault. Instead, individual troops were increasingly fixed in place in the outstations, where there were no proper maintenance facilities and all spare parts had to be flown up by Chinook. Securing spares was difficult even at Bastion, for the supply chain from Britain was already creaking under the strain.

It was no surprise to the Household Cavalry when, six weeks into the tour, the vehicles began to break down. With the engines running for so much of the time, moving parts were bound to wear out. The heat burned out laser sights. Track links and bar armour got bashed and bent. Gearboxes seized, fuel bags split, and the torsion bar suspension systems started to collapse. Back at Bastion after the disaster of Operation Nakhod, Dick warned battle group HQ that he needed at least five days to overhaul his vehicles. Forty-eight hours later, however, he was ordered northwards for a second try at relieving the platoon-house at Musa Qala. His formation had barely covered a kilometre when three of his four Scimitars broke down and had to limp back into camp. Even then the lesson was not learned. The following day he was told that the squadron would be needed at Garmsir, a hundred miles to the south, in three days' time. This time, Dick flatly refused. Had his vehicles even been capable of travelling that far, which was doubtful, they would be horrendously vulnerable in the event of a mine strike or any kind of breakdown.

The crews battling to keep their vehicles in working order were taking enough risks as it was. On 12 August, at Sangin, Lance Corporal Sean Tansey, twenty-six, of Number 2 Troop, was crushed to death when a jacking strut collapsed as he tried to replace a snapped torsion bar on a Spartan. It was a major job that would ordinarily have been carried out on a hard standing at Bastion or Kandahar, but through necessity had been attempted in situ in the soft and dusty earth of the compound. Number 2 Troop, commanded by Lieutenant Toby Glover, had been sent to Sangin on an operation that was supposed to last seven hours; when Tansey died they had been there for thirty consecutive days. It was eighty-two days before their four vehicles were withdrawn for a proper mechanical overhaul. 'The boys were just about coming back online [after the deaths of HCR colleagues Johnson and Nicholls] when the news came through,' recalled Major Bartle-Jones. 'It was difficult for them to take, especially because Sean wasn't killed by enemy fire. It was just a sad accident. But they got on with it superbly. They were magnificent.'

This was cousin Tom's moment. Glover's troop was due for relief in four days' time, but with Tansey's death the changeover was brought forward. At first light on 13 August, Tom flew up in a Chinook at the head of a dozen men, the new and untried commander of the late Ralph Johnson's Number 4 Troop. Glover met him on the drop zone with a cheery high five and a handover letter, before piling aboard and disappearing back over the horizon in the Chinook Tom had come in on.

The four vehicles he had inherited were in a bad way. Only one Scimitar was in full working order; the other had been cannibalized to keep the first one going, and had no clutch and had lost much of its bar armour. The Spartan still had no suspension and was 'completely bust'. Even the Samson recovery vehicle, though just about roadworthy, needed a complete new set of track. It was to be a fortnight before they were all working again. Much of Number 4 Troop's first week was spent guarding a small company of engineers who left the camp each night to collect spoil to pack out HESCOs, a wall of which they were building as fast as they could around the desperately exposed compound. The garrison, led by Major Jamie Loden of 3 Para's 'A' Company, were well and truly besieged by now. Mortar and rocket teams in the surrounding tree lines, particularly in an area to the north-east known as Wombat Wood, had had weeks to gauge the range to the compound and were unnervingly accurate with their shells.

The Paras felt trapped and frustrated. This was not what they were supposed to be doing. They were a manoeuvrist group who had been trained to take the fight to the enemy, not sit in a compound being bombarded. The Fusiliers at Now Zad had been specifically banned from conducting foot patrols or any other sort of deliberate operation in the town, but the same stricture did not apply to Loden's Paras. Sangin was a part of the battle group's 'main effort' now, a key Helmand valley town in their over-extended battle ground. Loden felt certain that they would never dominate the district if they stayed in the compound, so he determined to mount a series of aggressive patrols to deliver what HQ had begun to call 'the Sangin effect'. His men were more than ready for it. As a poem scrawled on a compound wall illustrated, aggression was what the Paras did best:

Message for Terry Taliban

Watch out Terry, we're hunting you down.
There's nowhere to hide in Sangin town.
You shit yourself when .50s are fired.
No point in running you'll only die tired.
Got A10s on call for brassing you up.
No food or water we don't give a fuck.
So do one, Terry. You've plenty to fear.
We run this town now. The Paras are here . . . Airborne for ever.

A patrol left the gates on Tom's second day. With flanking support from the Scimitar and the Samson, the Paras fanned east-wards through the town. Then they were attacked and came back again under more or less constant fire. That afternoon, Terry Taliban retaliated with a sustained mortar attack from Wombat Wood, as well as small-arms fire and RPG attacks from multiple firing points in the town.

Two days later Loden tried again, this time pushing a patrol out to the south-west. Tom hadn't taken part in the first patrol because his troop didn't have enough working vehicles. This time, however, he was determined to accompany them – 'I wanted to get out on the ground,' he said – and commandeered a WMIK* in order to do so. Together with the Scimitar and Samson, he set up a position on the Helmand river's flood plain that would give covering fire to the patrol.

In a lane between fields of tall wheat and maize the Paras came across two young 'dickers' on motorbikes, and arrested them. Soon afterwards they bumped into a Taliban patrol coming the other way. A twenty-minute fire-fight ensued during which the captives, handcuffed and blinded by black-out goggles, were killed by fire from their own side. The patrol began to pull out towards base, hotly pursued through the crops by gunmen who seemed unaware that the dickers were dead, and were intent on getting them back. The Paras turned and mounted one and then another snap ambush.

Then, as they fell back on the three Household Cavalry vehicles which were pounding the fields beyond with machine-gun and cannon fire, the small-arms fire was switched to Tom and his men. There was little threat to the Scimitar and Samson, but Tom was now in a lightly armoured WMIK. 'It basically had some bits of body armour bolted to its sides,' said Tom. 'It's a typical British Army piece of kit.' He manoeuvred the WMIK behind cover and hoped for the best. Meanwhile the Samson, commanded by Lance Corporal of Horse Leigh Preston, became stuck in a bog as it tried

* A WMIK (weapons-mounted installation kit) is a combat patrol variant of the Land Rover.

252

to jockey into a better firing position. The crew, still under attack, were forced to abandon their vehicle and run for it under covering fire from the Scimitar and the WMIK.

Miraculously, the entire patrol made it back to base without anyone being killed or injured. It was Tom's first time in a contact – the first time he had been shot at, or indeed shot at anything other than a target on a range – and it had been a very close-run thing. The abandoned Samson, close enough to the district centre for the garrison to be able to watch over it through the night, was recovered with great difficulty the following day with the help of the engineers.

The pattern of Tom's war was set. Months later he showed me a DVD compiled from footage taken by the garrison. ('The amount of video footage that has gone around,' he remarked. 'Everyone was filming themselves at Sangin.') It was of a higher quality than other tour compilations I had seen. Indeed, there was a terrible, spell-binding beauty to parts of it. Tree lines erupted into flames as though choreographed. Mortars popped, machine-guns hammered and helicopters clattered in satisfying counterpoint to the compiler's soundtrack, 'Zombie' by the Irish band The Cranberries – a lament on the futility of violence, inspired by an IRA bombing atrocity in Warrington in 1993. 'When we arrived at Bastion there were big calls for us to come on,' said Tom. 'It was "Bring on the Cavalry". It was another Charge of the Light Brigade.' But three Household Cavalrymen were dead now, and there was no charging, no manoeuvring for the men at Sangin. Tom's troop hit their mechanical low point on 18 August, one week into his time there, when they had just one working Scimitar and a commandeered WMIK between them. Two days later, a fresh crisis overtook the garrison when another patrol, this time to the north of the base, got into a heavy fire-fight in a field of maize. This was the celebrated engagement that won Corporal Bryan Budd, twenty-nine, a posthumous VC. Two of his eight-man section had been badly and simultaneously wounded in an attack on a group of gunmen, and two others were hit in the plates of their body armour. This in itself was a kind of record. The press later reported that every man in Budd's section had now been hit in some way during their tour. This time, the enemy were no more than eighteen metres away. To give his men time to get clear, Budd charged forward, firing as he ran – and was never seen alive again.

The Paras were in deep trouble. Back at the compound, Loden had already sent forward the rest of his company to secure the casualty collection area when he learned that Budd was still missing. He needed to push his troops further forward again to rescue him, but now he had run out of manpower. The folly of the platoon-house policy was once again laid bare. The Soviets had struggled to secure Afghanistan with an army of 104,000. In a region as volatile as this one, a town like Sangin would have been garrisoned by a battalion at least – as many as 400 men. Yet the British had gone to Helmand with only 650 combat troops, and could barely field a single company for an outstation the battle group's own commanders now considered a cornerstone of their mission.

Loden's solution was to scratch up a platoon from anyone who was left in the base. The sentries on the perimeter formed one section, leaving each sangar manned by a single man. A second section comprised four engineers, two snipers, and the two military policemen who were at Sangin to investigate the accident that had killed Sean Tansey. And the third section, made up of two REME mechanics and the crews of the disabled HCR vehicles, was commanded by Tom.

The beauty of being in a fast-moving reconnaissance unit like the Household Cavalry, Tom always said, was that it offered a unique perspective of any battlefield. One of the reasons he had chosen the regiment when he passed out of Sandhurst was that being in armoured vehicles promised to be so much more interesting than infanteering. The dummy 'section attacks' he had practised in training had never much appealed to him. Now, however, he found himself rushing out of the compound gates on foot, with orders to picket the route up to the contact point to prevent the Paras from being attacked from behind.

No sooner were his men in position than they were shot at from across the river. 'It was awesome,' he said. 'I was pretty sure where their firing point was, so I shouted at the others to follow my mark and fired back with tracer rounds . . . I don't know if we got them, but the shooting certainly stopped.'

They weren't out there for long. The Paras had pushed forward and found Budd's body, surrounded by three enemy dead lying where he'd killed them at the edge of the maize field. Budd was put on a quad bike and then the entire patrol doubled back into the compound, harassed by mortar and small-arms fire all the way.

It was fifty-two days before Tom left Sangin again – fifty-two days of terrifying attack and counter-attack, interspersed by desperately dangerous patrols. On one occasion a carload of fighters tried to ram one of these, but was diverted from its course by sheer weight of fire. Automotive problems permitting, the HCR always went along to provide fire support. And if they were not out on patrol, they were detailed to go out and protect the detachment of engineers who, as well as endlessly collecting more spoil, had begun to construct a motorized ferry across the river to the north to improve the garrison's 'manoeuvre capability'.

There was little sleep for any of the defenders. The incoming fire seldom ceased. Nevertheless, Tom soon became used to life in the compound. It is obvious from his private diary that the extraordinary quickly became routine, until only the most unusual incidents were worth recording. On one occasion, a Scimitar went into the town to suppress a firing point that had already been hit so many times from the air that it was known as the 'JDAM building' (a JDAM is a joint direct attack munition – a satellite-guided bomb). The Scimitar was firing at a range of only thirty-five metres when a 500lb bomb was dropped on the same target – a redefinition of the phrase 'danger close'. On another occasion, an RPG man tried to shoot a Scimitar at close range but was hit by one of his target's high-explosive shells first, obliterating the fighter and causing the grenade to streak straight up into the air.

The diary entry for the evening of 21 August, written up only eight days after his arrival, was so typical that I almost skipped over it. Two 107mm rockets were fired from Wombat Wood, followed by a five-minute barrage of RPG and machine-gun fire that turned the metal 'tank sheet' under which he had just been sheltering into a sieve. A Scimitar manoeuvred up a newly built earth ramp and suppressed the wood line with twenty-one rounds of high explosive. An air strike was called on a rooftop firing point on the JDAM building once again. On this occasion three bombs were dropped, along with mortars and artillery fire. 'Establishing that we could have no more effect on the ground,' Tom wrote, 'Corporal of Horse [David] Simpson and myself sat next to the

ISO container* by the tank park with a cup of tea and enjoyed the fireworks.'

The occasional quiet day, when intelligence suggested the Taliban were regrouping or waiting for reinforcements, was almost more noteworthy than the periods of violence. At such times the soldiers took turns to bathe in the stream that conveniently ran through the compound – a welcome respite from the remorseless heat.

'That night in the accommodation,' runs the diary, 'Tpr [Rich] Hannaford found a Black Widow spider under his bed. Tpr [Jason] Glasgow having played with it for a while in a shoebox destroyed it under the sole of his shoe.'

At the end of August, the Paras' 'A' Company was relieved by 'C', together with a platoon from the Royal Irish Regiment. There was no relief for Tom's troop, however. An attack a week later, on 6 September, brought renewed tragedy when a group of Royal Irish was caught by a mortar shell as they gathered for a briefing in the compound's orchard. Four were injured, two of them seriously. Tom's Spartan, back on the road, was used to casevac them to the helicopter landing site – a terrible task that had become all too familiar to the crew. One of the injured, Corporal Luke McCulloch, twenty-one, died of a shrapnel wound to his head long before he reached Bastion. He was a popular soldier who had completed two tours of Iraq and another in Northern Ireland. His mates, who nicknamed him 'Skywalker', nailed a clover-embossed memorial to a tree where he had fallen. The orchard was known from then on

---

* sometimes known as 'Isotainers'. International Standards Organization containers are a very common sight in Afghanistan, where many market streets are made up of little else.

257

as 'McCulloch Lines' – an old Royal Irish term for a defensive rear position. The following month, McCulloch's devastated father posted a memorial poem on the Army Rumour Service website, which had filled with messages of condolence. 'My son, L/Cpl Luke McCulloch of 1 Royal Irish' it was headed. 'Killed in Sangin in the compound while eating lunch'.

> No farewells were spoken
> we did not say goodbye
> you were gone before we knew it
> and only God knows why.
>
> We seldom ask for miracles
> but today just one would do
> is to leave the front door open
> and see you walk right through.
>
> We would put our arms around you
> and kiss your smiling face
> because you were one in a million
> and no one can take your place.

Not long before the fatal attack, Tom had requested an armourer to come up from Bastion to clear a stoppage on a Scimitar cannon; he had also asked that the armourer pack a new pair of boots for Corporal of Horse Simpson, whose originals had completely worn out. Earlier in the siege a column of Canadian LAVs had made its way to Sangin to deliver emergency supplies. Even then, the Canadians were astounded by the conditions the British were living in. 'They were running out of food and were down to boiling river water,' one officer wrote in an email home, which was passed to the press at his request. 'They had tried to air-drop supplies but they had ended up landing in a Taliban stronghold (thank you, air force) ... We headed off to what can only be described as the Wild West. When we arrived the locals began throwing rocks and anything they could at us. This was not a friendly place.' The Canadians were supposed to drop their supplies and leave again, but a mortar attack came as darkness fell and they were forced to stay. 'We were attacked with small arms, RPGs and mortars three times that night. I still can't believe that the Brits have spent over a month living there under those conditions. They are a proud unit and they were grateful but embarrassed that we had come to save the day. And as good Canadians we didn't let them hear the end of being rescued by a bunch of colonials!!'

It was through such fragments of news that the world woke up to what was happening at Sangin. The first journalists to reach the town, ITN's Bill Neely and his cameraman Eugene Campbell, did not arrive until 20 September, fully four months after British troops had first arrived there. It was this ITN report that stunned Tom's family, watching at home as Neely's Chinook was ambushed and three RPGs whistled at head height between two HCR vehicles, one of which was commanded by Tom. In his family's words it 'looked like hell on earth', although to Tom it was just another day at Sangin. Neely stayed for forty-eight hours, during which time he was also able to film two small-arms attacks on the compound, and the Paras retaliating with Javelin missiles – a source of some satisfaction to the garrison, who for some reason had worried that there might not be anything very spectacular for ITN to film.

Tom's time at Sangin had undoubtedly been the most exciting

time of his life. He was understandably proud of how the garrison had pulled together, and still on a high when I saw him at the end of 2006, a few weeks after he had returned to Britain. 'It was all hands to the pumps,' he said. 'It was a great team effort and a huge bonding experience. Getting the job done – that's the British Army's forte.' His Officer Commanding, Will Bartle-Jones, observed that he could hardly stop talking about it.

When I saw Tom again at his barracks at Windsor in mid-2007, however, a stunning change had come over him. He was clearly a good and popular officer who had won the respect of his men in Helmand. A promising future with the Household Cavalry beckoned. Yet, eight months after Herrick 4, he had begun to talk about swapping his Army career for a new life in the City.

The catalyst for his apparent change of heart was his girlfriend, Katie. There were only so many times, he said, that he wanted to put her through an operational tour. General Dannatt's warning of 'a generation of conflict' had clearly resonated with him, too. I sensed that he also felt he had to a large extent 'proved himself' in combat now. In this he was like the young men described by the Fusilier doctor, David Baxter. The questions that lurk in every untried soldier's mind – How will I perform under fire? Am I brave enough to fight? – had been satisfactorily answered. It was natural if the lust for this kind of adventure was not as strong in him as it had been.

Small as it was, the part he had played in the celebrated operation to recover Bryan Budd's body had given him pause for thought. That mission had been an emergency; he readily accepted that Jamie Loden, the Para company commander, had no choice when he ordered a collection of mechanics, military policemen and

Scimitar crews to step into the breach. What was disquieting was how common such desperate extemporizing had become during Herrick 4. Tom had heard countless examples of it, some of them amusing and harmless, such as nurses and chefs having to do sangar duty at Bastion, but others that were rather less so. At Sangin he had made friends with an engineer sergeant called 'Eddie' Edwards who, early on in the tour, had been ordered to guard the entire Kajaki dam area with a group of only a dozen men, who were then obliged to fend off an attack by thirty Taliban. Edwards had also taken part in the engagement near Forward Operating Base Robinson in June when Captain Jim Phillipson was killed.

'The team that Eddie went out with that night was a typical ensemble of anyone and everyone. It was a case of, "Who have we got? Do you want to go out?" "Yeah, OK, I'll do that . . ." Half an hour later Eddie was in a fighting withdrawal, fire-and-manoeuvring with a bloke he'd literally never met before, his life completely dependent on him . . . The next day in the dinner queue, after a night fighting their way back into camp, Eddie didn't even recognize him. This bloke goes, "Um, I think we worked together last night." And Eddie goes, "Oh, right! All right, mate? Do you want to go and have a cup of tea?"'

Tom loved that story. It perfectly illustrated the Army's famed 'can-do' spirit, of which he was proud and had often spoken. But the story was also troubling, because the sortie for which Edwards had volunteered could in no way be classified as an emergency. Its aim had been to recover one of the battle group's Desert Hawk surveillance drones which had crashed – a hand-launched, remote-controlled aircraft that was only three feet long. 'Phillipson died for one of those planes,' Tom said. 'They were always crashing. The battle group had sixty of them when we started but there were only four of them left by the time we finished.'

I had spoken to many soldiers who felt that Phillipson's death, the first of the tour, had been unnecessary. Some could not help but wonder what the point of so much sacrifice had been. For any officer in an armoured reconnaissance squadron, the carcasses of Soviet tanks and troop-carriers that dotted Helmand inspired a dreadful feeling of vulnerability. Parts of the destruction around the northern compounds were reminiscent of World War One photographs of Flanders. At Sangin, Tom's two battered Scimitars had fired over a thousand rounds of high explosive by mid-September alone. And for what?

During a lull in the fighting on 18 September, the Paras, accompanied by some Afghan National Army soldiers, felt confident enough to push a patrol across the Helmand river to the village of Do Ab. The usual promises of future peace and security made no impression on the elders they met there, who replied simply that their way of life was being wrecked. The elders attended a *shura*, a tribal council, at the compound the following day – the only one to be held in all of Tom's time at Sangin – where they begged the British not to return to Do Ab because they had been badly harassed by the Talibs overnight. Despite that, the Paras took encouragement from the meeting: at least the elders had turned up for it. But they were disabused later that day by two suspiciously accurate mortar and RPG attacks on the compound. The Taliban had infiltrated the *shura* in order to reconnoitre their target, just as they had at Now Zad.

Wrecking the lives of villagers was never what the mission to Helmand was supposed to be about. 'It's hard to say for sure, but it looks to me like the war between Islamic fundamentalism and the

West is being fought in Afghanistan now, and it will be the local farmers and villagers who suffer the consequences,' said Tom. Herrick 4, he had found, was no longer spoken of very highly in Army circles, however bravely the Paras had fought. He had met soldiers from other regiments who shook their heads and muttered about the 'mess' left behind in Helmand that would take years to clean up. The fault, these critics said, was the lack of a clear strategy in the northern platoon-houses. Tom had passionately disagreed at first, but now grudgingly conceded the point. 'We were simply reacting to events on the ground,' he said.

His thinking appeared to have been influenced by a military history lesson about the SAS, picked up on a recent training course. Since their inception, and especially during counter-insurgency operations in Oman in the late 1950s and early 1970s, the SAS had developed a behind-the-lines modus operandi that seemed very pertinent now. Travelling in small units, they made a point of dropping in on elders, offering advice and support, making friends and building networks. On their patrols they tended to take along a doctor who would set up a free, snap health clinic for any local who was ill. The effect was dramatic: every parent of every cured child became an ally. The grateful villagers could also provide huge amounts of useful intelligence. A 'light footprint', the SAS had always insisted, was a far better counter-insurgency technique than the blunderbuss approach adopted during Herrick 4. But the clock could not be turned back; the days of light-footprint patrols were decisively over in Helmand. Instead, the British were apparently committed to escalating the war, and begging their unwilling Nato partners for support.

'I was shocked by the British troop number projections for 2008,' said Tom. 'Where are they all going to come from? Iraq, probably

– battle weary, and not having had enough time to relax and get back to their families. Remember that the six months before a tour are just as busy as being out there . . . it can't be much fun banging out two on the trot.'

Like every regiment I had been to see, with the exception of the Gurkhas, the Household Cavalry were struggling to retain their talent. The Royal Armoured Corps was worryingly short of future squadron leaders. In normal times there was fierce competition for the twenty-eight training places available each year; by the end of 2007 only seventeen officers had applied for 2009. The outcome seemed inevitable: officers without the necessary experience or competence would be promoted too soon, and the HCR's usual high standards of leadership would drop. Officers like Tom were desperately torn between their loyalty to the regiment and the lure of a career outside the Army – a safer and less glorious life, perhaps, but one that offered more time for important things like girl-friends, as well as better prospects and pay.

Within weeks of his return from Helmand, Tom was learning to ride a horse. That autumn he found himself dressed as a nine-teenth-century cuirassier for the state visit of Abdullah, the King of Saudi Arabia. The visit was controversial. The acting Liberal Democrat leader Vince Cable boycotted the ceremony on the grounds of Saudi Arabia's 'appalling human rights record'; he also cited the Saudis' multi-billion-pound arms deal with the British firm BAe, and the row over alleged corruption surrounding it. Meanwhile, the King told an interviewer that his country had warned Britain about the '7/7' bombings in London in 2005, but that MI5 had failed to act on the intelligence (an accusation that was naturally denied).

Tom later showed me a photograph of himself peering out at

London SW1 from under his magnificent red-plumed helmet, the sunshine glinting off his breast-plate and drawn sword as he clopped up the Mall, thirty yards ahead of Abdullah's carriage. A year earlier he had been fighting for his life against the co-religionists of the Custodian of the Two Holy Mosques. Britain's money-driven relationship with Saudi Arabia, it seemed to me, was every bit as confused and ambiguous as the international policy in Afghanistan.

8

The Royal Irish and the Musa Qala Deal

By September 2006 it was clear that the battle group was reaching the end of its endurance, and that the platoon-house strategy could not be sustained. The Paras and all their reinforcing units were fixed in position across a large swathe of the province, and there was little sign of any let-up in the violence. The enemy seemed Hydra-headed. The garrisons had killed dozens and dozens of them, but they were always replaced and never seemed to give up. From intelligence gathered at Sangin and elsewhere, it was evident that few of the fighters now ranged against the British were from Helmand. The great majority were incomers from Pakistan. The infidel British were what worried senior officers had begun to describe as 'tethered goats' for any Muslim wishing to have a go at them, and the legions responding to the bait came from across a border where the battle group could not touch them. To many in the garrisons, the platoon-house strategy was now looking like a recipe for a long and perhaps unwinnable war.

In early September General Dannatt paid a visit to Afghanistan where he was warned that the threat to the Chinooks was becoming unacceptable. In Brigadier Butler's view, an 'immeasurable strategic shock to the overall campaign' was now likely every time a man had to be casevac'd. The notoriously exposed drop zones at Musa Qala presented the greatest risk. Chinooks had managed to land there only six times in ten weeks. It was here, on 6 September, that Major Mark 'Sweetcorn' Hammond was forced to abort a landing after his Chinook was narrowly missed by a pair of RPGs, and small-arms fire damaged a wing blade root – just one of the incidents that prompted Butler seriously to consider a unilateral pull-out from Musa Qala.

That option was fiercely resisted by Butler's superior, General David Richards in Kabul. Richards had never approved of the platoon-house policy, which by the time he took over ISAF command at the end of July had already led to what he described as a 'dog's dinner' in Helmand. But neither did he now favour a headlong retreat from it. 'London was worried that we'd lose domestic support if a Chinook went down. But what they didn't see was that if we simply abandoned Musa Qala, they were going to lose the whole bloody war. Because as soon as the Taliban were able to say in Afghan society, "Look what we told you – we just defeated them," the British were going to lose all support in that area and much more widely. We'd have been a laughing stock.'

Something had to give, however – and at Musa Qala on 12 September, the British were fortunate to be offered a way out of the impasse. It came from an unexpected quarter. Musa Qala's tribal elders, led by one Hajji Shah Agha, approached Governor Daoud with a proposal. The elders were dismayed at so much killing and the destruction of their town, and desperate for it to stop. The local

Taliban, they said, were prepared to stop fighting and withdraw if the British would do the same. They themselves would take responsibility for security once the two sides had disengaged; they even promised to put forward sixty of their own sons as the nucleus of a new police force.

Not everyone was in favour of the 'Musa Qala deal', as it came to be known, least of all the Americans, who suspected the Taliban would retake the town the moment the Coalition withdrew. To them the proposal seemed little more than a clever Taliban trick. The Taliban leadership in Quetta, for its part, was equally suspicious. A mutually agreed ceasefire looked to them like a need-less concession to the British. At first, therefore, Quetta ordered its commanders to fight on, arguing that they had the British on the run – an assessment, General Richards observed, that was 'not far from the mark'.

The Musa Qala elders were not the only locals exhausted by the fighting, however. There were intelligence reports that a senior commander's son had been killed by a British mortar, and rumours of a mass grave containing the bodies of 200 dead fighters. With the approach of autumn and the accompanying obligations of harvest time, it was getting harder for the Taliban to find replacements. Morale was low, they were short of ammunition and they were unable to get their casualties to field hospitals. In short, the forces besieging the British had fought themselves almost to a standstill. At the very least they needed a pause in the fighting to reorganize. At Musa Qala it suited them to comply with the elders' initiative; so Quetta, no doubt wary of the dangers of further alienating local opinion, reluctantly gave the go-ahead.

Despite the misgivings of the Americans, the elders' proposal suited British strategy, too. 'I had to create the means by which we could regain the tactical initiative,' said Richards, 'and the only way we could do it, given our level of commitment in Helmand, was to get out of one of the platoon-houses ... Throughout this mid-autumn period, Britain in the eyes of the people of Afghanistan had achieved nothing. We genuinely needed to start reconstructing, let alone constructing, and [the elders' initiative] gave us an opportunity to demonstrate, in an area where we had done nothing but damage, that things could be better with a bit of common sense on both sides.' More to the point, a mutual withdrawal from the town offered Richards a chance to free up badly needed troops without losing face, which in propaganda terms was essential. It was, as everyone involved with the deal said, 'an Afghan solution to an Afghan problem'.

For Brigadier Butler, Hajji Shah Agha's appeal for reconciliation was an eleventh-hour vindication of his strategy. The *'shura* process', as he called it, had in fact begun the previous month with a discreet meeting between Governor Daoud and the tribal elders from Sangin. Daoud had drawn up a fourteen-point plan with them; Butler had commented on the security arrangements. The fourteen-point plan was then picked up by the Musa Qala elders, who were apparently more anxious for reconciliation than their Sangin counterparts. This was the 'tipping point' of popular support for the Coalition that he had hoped to reach: a crucial first chance to drive a wedge between the Taliban and the populace. In his view, the Musa Qala elders were bound to feel let down by the Taliban, who had promised to rid Helmand of the British within six months. Instead, their town had been gravely damaged, many of their menfolk had been killed while fighting for the Taliban as 'hired guns', and the British didn't seem to be going anywhere. Little did the enemy know that Butler was within hours of ordering a withdrawal. 'It was,' said Butler, 'a question of who blinked first.'

For the men in the Musa Qala compound, the ceasefire that took hold at 9.41 p.m. on the evening of 12 September heralded the first night's peace in two months. The garrison, known as Easy Company, had originally been sent there for only ten days. Easy Company was a mixed bag of Paras and Rangers of First Battalion, The Royal Irish Regiment, two platoons of which had been sent to reinforce the battle group in July. In the view of the Household Cavalry squadron commander, Will Bartle-Jones, of all the ground units who fought in support of the Paras – them, the Gurkhas, the Fusiliers – the Royal Irish 'probably had the most horrid time of all'. By the end of the tour three of their number were dead and seventeen were injured, out of a total of about sixty men. Luke McCulloch was killed at Sangin, but it was Musa Qala that they talked about most when I went to visit them.

The fighting there had been as desperate as anywhere, and they were proud of the tenacity of their defence. Towards the end of it they were reduced to a few hundred rounds per GPMG – about ten minutes' worth of firing in a heavy contact. In one month of combat, the garrison fired a quarter of all the 7.62mm rounds used by British troops in the whole of 2006. Meanwhile, the ammunition for the Minimi light machine-guns ran out altogether. It was fortunate that the company of Danes who held the compound before them had left behind several boxes of 5.56mm rifle rounds. Thanks to Nato standardization, these fitted the chambers of the light machine-guns. By pushing the Danish rounds one by one into the expended links, the Minimis were put into action again. Necessity had many children at Musa Qala. When one of the .50 cal machine-guns was destroyed, it was replaced with a dummy; the generators running the water pumps on which the garrison depended were held together with Superglue. The siege of Musa Qala was extraordinary even by Helmand's standards, but what really distinguished the men of Easy Company was that, at the end of it, they were ordered to abandon the compound for which many of them had paid with their limbs and lives.

Even the manner of the garrison's departure on 17 October bordered on ignominy. There were no support helicopters to whisk them back to Bastion: in the delicate atmosphere of the ceasefire, headquarters judged that sending up Chinooks would be too provocative. There was no regular Army road transport for them either. Instead, in an extraordinary departure from usual military practice, the Royal Irish were obliged to leave Musa Qala in a convoy of Jingly trucks provided by the village elders. This was a risky exercise, for although the Rangers were able to line the floors of the trucks with sandbags to give some protection against mine strike, the lumbering Jinglies were otherwise completely exposed to attack. Hundreds of impassive-faced locals turned out to watch their departure, dozens of black-turbaned Taliban clearly visible among them. The British were at least spared the humiliation of leaving behind their weapons. The Jinglies bristled like hedgehogs as they left. 'I wouldn't have been very happy with it,' said Lieutenant Paul Martin, who had prior to this been injured and evacuated. 'There were forty white Toyotas thrashing around the sides and back of the trucks as they left. The boys were waiting for the mother of all ambushes; they said it felt like handing themselves over on a silver platter.' There was no ambush, thankfully; and the Taliban later fulfilled their side of their bargain by withdrawing to at least five kilometres beyond the town.

In Kabul, the Musa Qala deal was hailed as a kind of victory for 'people power'. 'A lot of Afghans including people in the Ministry of the Interior were very much in favour of it,' said General Richards. 'They saw it as the sort of thing one had to do.' On the other hand, the enemy leadership in Quetta successfully portrayed the British pull-out as an important victory of their own. There was no more evocative symbol of the Coalition's discomfort, in Afghan eyes, than British soldiers retreating from battle in a fleet of battered local trucks. Besides, fourteen weeks later the deal collapsed, and the Taliban did indeed reoccupy the town.

The details of how this happened remain sketchy. What is certain is that the Americans, whose tough-talking General Dan McNeill took over ISAF command from Britain's more accommodating General Richards on 4 February 2007, bombed and killed the brother of a local Taliban leader called Mullah Ghafoor. Machiavellians, noting that the Americans had never approved of the Musa Qala deal in the first place, suggested this was done with the intention of precipitating its end. If it was an American ploy, it certainly worked. Mullah Ghafoor accused the Coalition of breaching the ceasefire agreement; the Coalition retorted that the bomb had been dropped outside the town's agreed five-kilometre exclusion zone. Wherever it fell, Ghafoor was incensed, and he stormed into the town to accuse the elders of cooperating with the foreigners. The elders, very bravely, disarmed and ejected Ghafoor and his henchmen. But Ghafoor returned, this time with a larger group, and threw the elders into prison. There were allegations of torture. Hajji Shah Agha was reportedly murdered. The Taliban were indisputably back in charge.

There were plenty of people, some Royal Irish among them, who thought that the Musa Qala deal was not the British Army's finest hour. They had more right than anyone to feel bitter about the platoon-house policy. Not surprisingly, many of them wondered what so much sacrifice had really achieved. 'I think some of the blokes looked upon it in a bad way,' said Martin, one of the platoon commanders. 'They thought, "Why did we do that? How come we lost three men – for what? What exactly did we do if only to hand it back again?"'

I'd asked to meet no more than three or four members of the Musa Qala garrison, but in the event, at the Royal Irish battalion's headquarters at Fort George on the Moray Firth, a sprawling eighteenth-century monument to the Hanoverian suppression of the Jacobites, I met about twenty of them. It was a strange and intense experience. Unable or perhaps unwilling to decide whose story should be told, the officer in charge had invited along anyone who was interested. For eight hours they rotated through my interview room in groups of threes and fours, even queuing in the corridor outside in their anxiety to tell their tale.

Each wore a huge, misshapen beret known as a caubeen ('originally for carrying potatoes', one of them explained); the officers carried a heavy gnarled walking stick fashioned from blackthorn. They came from both sides of the Irish divide, although Ulster was naturally the biggest recruiting ground. They had names like McKeown and McKenna and O'Driscoll, with accents to match. Others were English, and there were also a significant number of Commonwealth soldiers in the regiment, particularly from Fiji. The differences between them didn't seem to count for much; it was clear that their shared experiences had created a powerful bond between them. In fact, Herrick 4 appeared to have brought these men closer together than any unit I had previously seen. They called themselves a 'Band of Brothers' without irony. All of them, unusually, had volunteered to go to Helmand. Most of them were twenty-one years old.

There was a fierce fighting spirit at work at Fort George that felt distinctly Celtic. When I suggested, stupidly, that they had become honorary Paras during the defence of the district centres, one of them replied, with stony seriousness, that it was the Paras who had become honorary Royal Irish. They were certainly well qualified for the type of urban counter-insurgency warfare required in Helmand. Years of practice in Northern Ireland had made them experts in house arrests, cordon-and-search operations, the confiscation of weapons and the setting up of vehicle checkpoints. 'It's exactly what we do,' said Martin. 'We're extremely good at it.'

I was unsurprised to learn that Gerald 'hearts and minds' Templer, the architect of the counter-insurgency in Malaya half a century ago, had been an officer in the Royal Irish Fusiliers, one of this regiment's forebears.

Martin and the others had been back in Scotland for months, yet most were still driven by adrenalin, still chattering about what they had seen and done. One or two of them were still in slings or plaster. Many of them pressed snapshots and email addresses on me, and were understandably keen to know when their names would appear in print.

It was Paul Martin's story that impressed me the most. He had been on holiday in Jamaica when the call for reinforcements came through, and was thrilled when he was selected to command one of the two Royal Irish platoons. 'Anyone who has done the platoon commander's course would be the same,' he said. He was twenty-nine. Like many others in his regiment, there was a long tradition of soldiering in his family. It pleased him very much that his platoon was called 'Barossa' after the 1811 Peninsular War battle in which an earlier generation of Ulstermen had fought. Like other young officers I had met he seemed much older than his years. The softness of his brogue was at complete odds with the brutality of the experiences he described so matter-of-factly. At times I caught a faraway look in his pale blue eyes, and a certain tautness of expression that made me ask if he was suffering from latent exhaustion, or even some kind of delayed battle shock. 'I'm OK,' he replied with a smile. 'The medical officer said to me, "I'm not worried about you now, but I'll be watching you extremely closely the next time you're in a contact. You just don't know how you're going to react."'

Martin was one of what his regiment called 'The Magnificent Seven'. In the early hours of 2 September, during an attack which seemed slightly heavier than usual, a mortar dropped neatly on to the centre of the 'Alamo', as the tallest building in the Musa Qala compound was known. An eight-man section of Royal Irish were manning the roof and seven of them, including Martin, were caught in the spray of shrapnel. 'It was a bit of a blur when the explosion went off,' he said. 'It kicks up an awful lot of sand and dirt and dust and stuff. Everyone is very disorientated. You're deaf, you're bleeding through your ears and your eyes because the explosion has just gone off so close to you . . . everybody's the same.' The only one unscathed was Sergeant Steven Gilchrist. 'I was on the .50 cal one minute, and the next, everyone was lying there screaming – apart from me,' he recalled. Six of the men, who had been crouching behind the low wall that ran around the edge and therefore had their backs to the blast, received 'lower leg injuries, elbow injuries, that sort of thing'. Martin, standing in the middle of the roof because he was commanding the defence, was not so lucky. 'I was hit in the spleen, the lung – that bit just missed my heart – and the top of my left arm,' he said. 'I've still got three pieces left in me. I was extremely lucky. I didn't realize it at the time ... The lung thing was the biggest thing because of the breathing. You think it's just a scratch. The adrenalin's pumping, everything's happening, you're trying to do the best you can, stay in command. But I was starting to choke down on blood so I couldn't command any more and had to drop down off the roof.'

The strike was controversial. Some suspected that it was not a Taliban mortar that had done the damage but a stray shell from a British 105mm battery which had been bombarding the town from out in the desert. Martin was ultimately operated on in Kandahar, where the surgeons presented him with a piece of shrapnel from his body. He had intended to bring it back to Britain for forensic verification – 'just for my own piece of mind, you know' – but lost it in the confusion of repatriation.

Martin actually thought it more likely that the Taliban had been responsible. Over in Sangin, a major relief-in-place operation had 'flushed out an awful lot of people'. Many of the fighters besieging that garrison had simply decamped northwards to Musa Qala until the Paras had finished sweeping the town and they could re-infiltrate down the valley at their leisure. By September, Martin observed, avoiding a confrontation that they could not win in this way had become standard Taliban operating procedure. Among the fighters who had temporarily quit Sangin, unluckily for Martin, was a highly skilled mortar specialist. A night or two before the Alamo was hit, intelligence revealed the details of a conversation between this newcomer and the local Taliban commander. 'They obviously knew each other – it was all very convivial. The commander was asking, "How long are you up here for?" It was almost like it was a holiday break for this guy. And then we heard the commander asking him to stay on for a couple of weeks, to lend them a hand, because we'd given them a thrashing recently . . . The change was dramatic for us. This guy was very accurate, and we started to lose people at that point.'

When Martin was hit, his platoon had been at Musa Qala for a month. As a commander, he explained, one of his greatest challenges was to protect his men from the worst psychological effects of being so close to so much death and serious injury – a job, he made clear, that left little time to think about himself. Every evening at Musa Qala he gathered his platoon together for a briefing session he called 'evening prayers', when the men were encouraged to speak their minds. 'Musa Qala was a close environment. I found myself knowing what questions they were going to ask before they asked them: what's happened, what about the RAF, what about casevac procedure, why, why, why, boss . . . they were quite an interesting bunch.' He acknowledged that it was sometimes difficult to justify the orders from above – about 'why they had to go into the same position [where] someone had just . . . had their head blown off. Or et cetera, et cetera. That's a hard thing to do, being a commander. I spent a lot of time thinking about it. How do I keep the men motivated? How do I do it? How do you push them on?'

His task was relentless. On average, he reckoned, he slept for about four hours in every twenty-four. It was also lonely, for he had no real friends with whom he might share his private thoughts and fears. The only other Royal Irish officer was the second platoon commander, Captain Mark Johnson, to whom he was not especially close. He had never worked with his sergeant, Steven Gilchrist, before. 'You try not to show them how much you're affected by anything, or how much you're tired, because you're the commander. You can't afford to take a wrong decision. I had to get on with it, bottle it up and not let things show. They don't want a friend, they want a leader in that type of situation. Although McKenna, my driver in Iraq – he got to know me very well. He'd make me smile, give me a cigarette. He'd know I hadn't slept in three days.'

Dwelling on the proximity of death did no good to anybody. Martin dealt with morbidity by trying to focus his men's minds on the day to come rather than anything that had just happened. This was the real point of his 'evening prayer' sessions. Too much exposure to what he called 'blood and guts . . . the Vietnam thing' could cause mental devastation. An early illustration of this truth came on 6 August with the death of Andrew Cutts, a private in the Royal Logistics Corps. During a resupply operation in which the Royal Irish were also involved, the nineteen-year-old from Blidworth in Nottinghamshire was providing cover for a WMIK as it crossed a wadi near Musa Qala when he was hit by a bullet that exited through an eye. His vehicle was stuck in a bottleneck, and because of its exposed position two or three minutes went by before anyone could begin to administer first aid. The shock and anguish of watching Cutts at their feet was too much for his crewmates. 'The guys in the back of the WMIK were badly affected. They were screaming; it was slap-in-the-face stuff. The whole team had to be extracted by Chinook.'

Looking at carnage, Martin concluded, was 'not necessary'. But sometimes it was unavoidable – and he was shocked at how he, personally, became hardened to the sight of it at Musa Qala. 'Your heart slowly does become colder – or black,' he said. In the early hours of 27 August a signaller, Lance Corporal Jonathan Hetherington, twenty-two, from Port Talbot in South Wales, was shot dead. Five days later a mortar exploded on the Alamo, this one at head height. Two Royal Irish, twenty-eight-year-old Lance Corporal Paul Muirhead from Bearley in Warwickshire, and Ranger Anare Draiva, twenty-seven, from Suva in Fiji, were hit. Muirhead – 'Moonbeam' to his mates – died of his injuries five days later; Draiva, known as 'D', was killed outright. In the scramble to evacuate the pair from the roof, Martin ordered one of his Rangers to grab the other end of Draiva's stretcher. 'There wasn't much left of him,' said Martin, 'but I didn't think of it. Because it was something I was dealing with all the time, what with us and the civvies and the ANA getting wounded and all the other bits and pieces.'

Not long afterwards, Martin was approached by a corporal.

' "Boss," he said, "I think you need to have a word with -- [the Ranger who had just helped Martin with the stretcher]."

' "Why, what's wrong?" I said.

' "Well," he said, "he's on his hands and knees in his sangar, crying his eyes out."

' "Ah," I said. "Right. I missed that one. Right." '

Martin hadn't appreciated that it was the first time this Ranger had had to deal with somebody 'in bits' and had forgotten the impact this could have. He ordered him out of his sangar and spent three-quarters of an hour trying to soothe him. 'I gave him the choice of staying off the sangar, but I really wanted him to go back on to keep his mind busy.' Martin was nothing if not a conscientious officer, and he still felt guilty about the incident. 'I became a little bit complacent in command. I spoke to him about it. I hope I didn't let him down.'

Following the 2 September attack, from the field hospital at Kandahar Martin was sent first to Selly Oak in Birmingham and then to a specialist unit at the nearby Queen Elizabeth hospital, where doctors could monitor the shard of shrapnel which had lodged so perilously close to his heart. He was glad to be there. 'I didn't have people running up and down the ward having nightmares, screaming themselves to sleep like they do at Selly Oak. Everyone understands the need to have people who shared the same experiences around you . . . you've got a common bond. But for me it was the opposite. I was glad I was on my own, with my family. The last thing I wanted to subject them to was visiting with people with no arms and legs and having dramas – extreme mental dramas – getting up from their bed and running down the street. That's not necessary.'

It was another six weeks before Martin's platoon returned to Scotland, by which time he was well enough to be able to meet them off the plane at RAF Kinross. In the relative tranquillity of Queen Elizabeth's, Martin had begun to think about the formal two-week 'decompression' period that all troops returning from theatre are obliged to undergo, and had worked out what was wrong with it. 'I was lying in hospital, getting myself back on the straight and narrow, and I thought, "Let's look at this." When somebody dies or is severely injured, the last time any of us sees them, or me for that matter, is as we put them on to the back of the Slick [support helicopter] . . . and then they are gone. And the next day brings new things to keep you busy and occupied. There's no closure on it.' At Martin's instigation, therefore, and with the full support of the battalion medical officer, the first three days of the returning platoon's decompression period were spent on a bus. 'We drove down south to England to visit graves. The whole team – two platoons' worth. Fifty or sixty blokes! Paul Muirhead's family were there. It was good. A lot of them laid a bunch of flowers or whatever, and gave the mother a hug. Then we all went to his local pub. A really nice English pub. A couple of drinks with the mum, stepdad, brother and stuff. They didn't want us to leave.'

But leave they did, back up to Morayshire via other graves and the hospital at Selly Oak, where they paid a surprise mass visit to their recuperating injured. Martin's only regret was that they couldn't 'do' Anare Draiva because he was buried in Fiji.

The aftermath of Musa Qala affected the Royal Irish in different ways. Many of the younger men were astonishingly upbeat. Lance Corporal Michael Diamond, twenty-one, who had been heavily involved in the horror of the ambush which killed Andrew Cutts, was typical. As a teenager he had been a promising golfer, and had even been offered a chance to turn pro, but he had joined the Army instead and had no regrets. 'I'd never give up the experiences I've had in the last three years,' he said. Like others in his group, he saw even his platoon's strange retreat from Musa Qala in the best possible light. 'I was happy the ceasefire was called,' said one. 'It was an experiment for Herrick 4. That was our achievement.'

Yet the symptoms of post-traumatic stress disorder often lurked beneath the surface bravado. Even Diamond's group admitted to bad dreams, and that it had taken some time to readjust to normality. 'My first day back I went for a haircut in Inverness,' Diamond said. 'It was fireworks season, and somebody let off a banger a couple of feet away. I took cover under a car.' It was harder for others. 'My wife saw a change in me when I came back home,' said Ranger Craig McLean. 'I was drinking. I was arguing. I went for medical help, I couldn't sleep. I had dreams about [Luke] McCulloch. About six weeks after I got back, it hit me. I just sat in any room thinking about it, 24/7. I couldn't do normal stuff in the house, I was always cracking up. It was that bad – waking up at night at the same times that I did in Afghanistan. There's a psychologist on the base you can go to, but the boys don't go because they don't want people to talk; they think it's gay. The boys here who haven't been to Afghanistan yet are in for a big shock. We tell them what it's like but it makes no difference.'

Among the last Royal Irish I spoke to was Ranger Stuart Devine, from Liverpool. He had served alongside Luke McCulloch in Iraq, and had spent seven weeks at Sangin. He remembered Tom Burne and the other 'Tankies' of the Household Cavalry well. He had also taken part in the operation to relieve the Gurkhas at Now Zad in late July. ('The camp was stinking. It was the most destruction I'd seen in my life. We'd levelled the place, like . . . They were pretty broken, man – they were glad to see us.') He seemed tougher and more cynical than most of his contemporaries. 'Well, it's a chance to save money, so it is, you know?' he replied when I asked him how he would feel about another tour in Helmand.

Devine offered one of the most acerbic analyses of the tour I had heard. His assessment of the strategy that had sent him and his mates to the northern areas was damning. 'We'd have been better not to have bothered,' he said. 'All that happened is the Taliban moved in and the civilians moved out and the towns got destroyed. Every time you kill one he's bound to have a friend, a father, a brother . . . You might have people saying we won, we killed all these people. But you can go out there and kill as many as you want. There are millions of them, and the more you kill, the more they'll fight.'

In his personal message to commanders at the end of Herrick 4, Brigadier Butler judged that the Taliban had been 'tactically defeated for this war-fighting season'. At the same time he acknowledged that the defence of the district centres 'may have appeared meaningless and at too high a cost in blood and treasure', but argued that 'the operational and political imperatives of maintaining these "strategic pegs" was, and remains, essential'. Devine was clearly one of those who thought the cost had indeed been too high. Butler had spoken in person to the Royal Irish at the end of the tour, yet Devine remained profoundly unimpressed by the words offered. 'The way he described it, he said the reason the platoon-houses were set up was to fight the Taliban so that in the south QIPs could go in and fix the place up. But nobody went into Gereshk and did anything. When we came back from Sangin, all they'd done was build a road. And there was never any Taliban there anyway. Gereshk is all about the drugs trade. And it was the same in Lashkar Gah.'

Butler repeated his justification in a foreword to *The Battle for Helmand*, an official account of Herrick 4 produced in glossy soft-back by the Para Regiment's own publishing arm in 2007. 'The Brigade deployed to make a difference to the ordinary Afghan,' he wrote. 'Not only did the brave men and women make a genuine difference, but they also set some really solid foundations for the Other Government Departments, the Royal Marines and sub-sequent follow-on forces to build upon.' But how solid were these foundations, actually? What, specifically, had the Department for International Development and the Foreign Office managed to achieve in Helmand in the year since Herrick 4? Butler argued that Sangin had been transformed into a functional market town, with little overt sign of its recent past as a centre of the narco-trade. However, it was Lashkar Gah, the provincial capital, which really mattered. If reconstruction was failing there, what hope was there for the province as a whole?

I asked Adam Holloway, a Conservative MP, a member of the Commons Defence Select Committee and a former officer in the Grenadier Guards. Deeply suspicious of the MoD's claims of progress, in 2007 he twice visited Lashkar Gah to discover his own 'ground truth', travelling incognito and at his own expense. It was an unprecedented and possibly foolhardy thing for a serving MP to do – 'the ambassador in Kabul went ape-shit when he found out', he told me – but the ammunition he found with which to pepper the Defence Secretary in select committee meetings made it worth it. 'There has been little reconstruction in Lashkar Gah worth speaking of,' he said. 'Des Browne keeps saying that we've spent seventeen million dollars there. But when I looked I discovered the money had mostly been spent on ANP checkpoints, which often aren't even manned at night because the police are too scared . . . All that checkpoints do is to make it easier for the cops to rob road-users.'

It was not entirely the Defence Secretary's fault if his view was rose-tinted. His primary source of information, according to Holloway, was the PRT, the military-run Provincial Reconstruction Team in Lashkar Gah, whose view of the ground from their fortified base was monocular. 'The PRT people hardly ever get out of their base, for security reasons,' Holloway explained. 'When you go there it's like Salisbury Plain with the heating switched up. But the difference of opinion on the other side of the wire is huge.' The PRT reported back to the MoD, who put their own Panglossian spin on events for their own reasons: politics, funding, careers, institutional ethos. Nobody wanted to be the bearer of bad news. Again and again, Holloway found, the authors of upbeat official accounts of progress were deeply pessimistic in private. He called this phenomenon 'groupthink', and the net result was that the minister was being misled. 'The MoD, like the Army, take a "can-do" approach. That's healthy, but I worry that they themselves are allowing their willingness to obscure the scale of the challenge. Even now we've only got about seven thousand people in Helmand. Is that really enough to control it?'

Part of the explanation, he thought, lay in the speed with which British troops were rotated through Helmand, which led to a syndrome he called 'short-tourism'. 'The first two months of each rotation are spent working out what to do, the next two are spent fighting, and the last two on justifying the outcome,' he said. 'You get these strange little spikes of progress in each tour's closing signal report to PJHQ. If you're an MP, and your only source of information is the MoD, you'd think everything was going swimmingly in Helmand. But the military are only deluding themselves.'

Holloway was certain that Afghanistan would be won or lost on 'what the little villager thinks', and equally certain that the high expectations of Western promises were still not being met. 'We're spending money but we're doing it doctrinally, through DfID, and we haven't got time for that. People want their lives changed. And so they have been, but so far only by bombing. Since Herrick 4, all they've had is war-fighting. Britain has spent £1.6 billion so far on the military effect. Just think how much development that kind of money could buy ... We're ignoring the key people in all this, imposing the will of the central government while ignoring the wishes of local *shuras*, and we're at the tipping point, poll-wise.'

General Richards agreed that the development effort was still nowhere near robust enough to counter-balance the destruction and violence the British had meted out. 'In relative and absolute terms we are all putting in far too little money,' he said. 'Only America is putting in the sorts of blood and treasure that can really help Afghanistan. In one case the Americans spent fifty million dollars in just one small valley on roads, job schemes, a new mosque. The British, meanwhile, put ten million pounds into the whole of Helmand province in one year.' He was confident that DfID and the other agencies would deliver eventually; the danger was that they would be too late. Without real and demonstrable developmental progress, there was a real risk that the Afghan people would turn back to the Taliban out of 'tiredness with our failure' – a resigned acceptance that the hardliners, with their promise of stability and security and their perceived lack of corruption, were 'better than our cock-up'.

He thought that the whole structure of the Herrick 4 Task Force, and the battle group within it, was inadequate for the task it had been set. The very term 'battle group' was wrong. 'The Army is structured for short-duration, war-fighting operations. We compensate for the historical shortage of troops with firepower, air power in particular, but you just can't do that in counter-insurgency. You actually want to minimize the use of firepower and maximize the number of boots on the ground, to almost freeze opposition movement. In that state you can do lots of reconstruction. But we couldn't do that during Herrick 4 because we didn't have enough troops.' Britain's Armed Forces, he went on, had failed to adapt fast or far enough to the long-term nature of modern operations. And in trying to perform a job for which they were neither structured, nor trained, equipped or numerous enough to do – first in Iraq and now in Afghanistan – they had become dangerously 'knackered'. What was needed in future was 'many more boots in the Army and a few less fighter jets and aircraft carriers'. The alternative he prescribed was not far from the idea of 'embedded development officials' proposed by Leo Docherty, the disillusioned ex-Scots Guardsman. 'I'd have more mixed groups. Not just engineers but logisticians, contracts officers, people who understand how to create business.' The theory of the comprehensive approach, Richards still believed, was correct. The problem was that the British were simply not putting it into practice. 'I believe Afghanistan can still be won,' he concluded. 'But my goodness, we've got to get on with it.'

Adam Holloway was less certain. 'We may actually be too late now,' he said. 'Winning or losing always depended on the ordinary Afghan, and I am not sure we still have their consent for this project.' He was hard-nosed about the alternative. 'Maybe we should be less ambitious now. Maybe we should accept that we will only ever contain the insurgency, reduce our troop numbers, massively increase support for the Afghan Police and Army, and bring the reconcilable Taliban into the political process. Are we seriously saying that the British public will put up with the deaths, or even the current level of military spending, for year after year after year?'

'In a sense the horse has bolted now, hasn't it?' said one very senior officer gloomily. 'We're now in recovery mode. Helmand is only going to work if the battle space itself switches to the minds of the people. But the Brits came in, they fought the Taliban, they threatened their poppy and all the rest of it . . . It's bloody difficult to come back from that.'

Stuart Devine, the Irish Ranger, also worried that the legacy of Herrick 4 was irreversible. Like Docherty, he believed that an opportunity to avoid confrontation, even in the hostile north, had been squandered early on in the tour. 'I think the Brigadier was looking to win a war. But it wasn't a war then. You're not really winning anything, are you? It's different now, though. It all goes back to the platoon-house thing. It wasn't until the Paras arrived that it really kicked off.' Devine didn't blame the Toms – 'they were as good as us', he said – but he did blame 3 Para's chain of command, some of whom 'didn't seem to like working with other people'. The commander's greatest mistake, he said, was the failure to engage in dialogue with the locals. Even some Paras had muttered about this to Devine. 'There should have been more *shuras* at the start. We should have spoken to the Taliban and told them we meant no harm. We should have had more troops to start with, then talked to them from a position of strength. That would have avoided the fight.'

Devine didn't have the whole picture. In late May 2006 the Pathfinders, the first British soldiers to enter Musa Qala, had in fact held a series of *shuras* with the tribal elders there. The mood then was promising, but the meetings were discontinued with the start of the Taliban-instigated violence. However, I suspected that Devine was right when he said we should have talked to the Taliban directly – something that never happened during Herrick 4, at least at the tactical level. Talking to the Taliban had been advocated many times before, by President Karzai, who pushed for 'reconciliation committees' throughout 2006, and by journalists in London such as Simon Jenkins, who on the very day of the deaths of Rangers McCulloch and Muirhead published a devastating critique of the war prophesying that eventual negotiation was inevitable. Even Brigadier Butler thought that some form of political settlement was likely in the end. 'I think you're absolutely right that the ultimate legacy will be a government in Afghanistan, in x years' time, with Taliban representation,' he said. 'Some people in the UK are starting to think that way, but not publicly declaring it. The Americans, with their emotional ties to the abuse of 9/11, are absolutely, vehemently opposed to that. But then they said the same thing in Iraq.'

If even he thought that was where the violence in Helmand was headed, why had the British fought the Taliban in the first place? Would it not have been better to avoid it by going straight to the negotiating table? Butler, with his 'Hobbesian cycle of violence' theory, believed it had always been necessary to fight the Taliban first. For all its faults, he argued, the Musa Qala deal exemplified a victory for the kind of 'people power' the Coalition ought to be looking for in future. But was he right? Was violence and destruction really a necessary precursor to this or any other deal?

I was sure that the standard Western view of the Taliban as an austere, illiterate band of ideologues bent on jihad and a fight to the death with the hated infidel was wrong. I had met the Taliban and their supporters often over the previous decade and had always been struck by the variety of opinion within their movement. The Islamic utopia they hoped to create was a work in progress, and they often disagreed even among themselves about the direction of their regime. This could hardly be otherwise, given that their doctrine was based on the Koran – a document written in poetic and antiquated Arabic, an elliptical language open to interpretation even in its modern form. 'If you turned all the trees on earth into pens and all the seas into ink, you would still not explain all the meanings of the Koran,' a religious scholar in Kabul once told me.

The Taliban's beliefs are always passionately held, but that does not necessarily mean that they are fixed. With patience and under-standing, even hardliners can be made to see reason. They are as open to persuasion as anyone else, and not always too proud to change their minds. A tradition of slow intellectual deliberation is central to Pashtun culture. Many Westerners find the *shura* system of governance ponderous, with its seemingly endless debates in cushion-filled rooms. Business is always mixed with hospitality at *shuras*, and discussions can certainly meander, but in the end it is not a bad way of reaching a consensus. Even modern Western businessmen recognize the value of 'face time' when trying to strike a deal, and routinely fly across the Atlantic for a meeting when an email or a phone call won't do. Like any revolution, the Taliban's thrives on the exchange of ideas. The main difference is that, while the ideas that drive most revolutions claim to be new, theirs date from the early seventh century. Theology is never far away in an exchange with them, or indeed any pious Pashtuns, who seem genuinely to relish the opportunity for a communal debate with a real-life Christian infidel.

In Jalalabad in 2002, I once argued long into the night with a group of Taliban supporters about Mullah Omar's decision the previous year to destroy the giant sixth-century Buddhas of Bamiyan – an act of vandalism, I thought, comparable to the Egyptians blowing up the Pyramids. As a group, they wouldn't budge: the Buddhas were evidence of idolatry, and their destruction was justified. But later, in private, one or two of them conceded that Omar had been wrong. There was no Buddhism in Afghanistan any more, so no reason to get rid of the statues. The Koran, they admitted, had little to say about the corrupting in-fluence of ancient monuments – and the move spelled obvious disaster for the tourist industry of the future.

For all their undoubted abuses of human rights and crimes against women, the Taliban are not stupid people; they understand how much the West has to offer in terms of economic assistance, investment and technical advice. Nor is their rejection of Western values absolute. Indeed they are theologically inclined to respect all

Christians, if not Jews. Muslims call the Bible 'the Book of the Sky' after all, and Jesus was one of their prophets, too. They may once have hosted al-Qaida, but they have never exported terrorism themselves. Their manifesto has always been inward-looking, and still essentially ends with the local establishment of their version of an Islamic state. For all the sophistication of their propaganda machine, it has never once been used to denigrate the West in any targeted way – as, for example, the Soviet Union did throughout the Cold War, or the Ayatollahs did in Iran in the 1980s. Where, in all this, is the threat to the Western way of life?

However improbable it may seem now, there was a time when even Americans found it acceptable to treat with the Taliban. In December 1997, in the days when Mullah Omar controlled 90 per cent of his country, a black-turbaned delegation travelled to Sugarland, Texas, to discuss the construction of a trans-Afghan gas pipeline with the energy firm Unocal. Their visit enjoyed the formal backing of the US government. In Sugarland, the Talibs dined at the palatial home of a Unocal vice-president, Martin Miller, where they were fascinated by his Christmas tree and, especially, the meaning of the star on top of it. They visited Houston's zoo and the Nasa space centre, and shopped happily at Omaha's Super Target discount store. There was even a rumour that they had played in Miller's garden with a frisbee. Civil war, the emergence of al-Qaida and the hardening of the US's stance towards the regime after the 1998 embassy bombings in Tanzania and Kenya conspired to ensure that the pipeline was never built. But the Sugarland meetings proved that dialogue had at least been possible in the past, and perhaps could be so again.

Finally, the Taliban had a recognizable political agenda – a return to government power – and I felt certain that some of them, at least, understood that violence was rarely the best way to pursue that. I couldn't help wondering what difference a less 'kinetic' approach during Herrick 4 might have made. Even fanatics could agree with Churchill's Cold War dictum that 'to jaw-jaw is better than to war-war'. Might the Taliban not have been prepared – might they not *still* be prepared – to make certain concessions in order to achieve their ambitious political ends? It was time to find out.

9

Amongst the Taliban

Meeting the Taliban was the main purpose of my trip to Afghanistan in February 2007. In London my friend Mir had introduced me to a young Pashtun acquaintance who he swore was competent, trustworthy and in possession of all the necessary contacts. The acquaintance and I met in an Islington café, carefully chosen for its anonymity, where he agreed to help for a large sum of money, and only on condition that I did not reveal his identity. I was not even to use his real name; instead, I would address him as 'Mohammed' – the 'John Smith' of the Muslim world. A down-payment changed hands, discreet phone calls to Taliban High Command in Quetta were made, and within a month I found myself in the Hotel Continental in Kandahar.

Now that Britain was effectively at war with the Taliban, my arrangement with Quetta, 100 miles to the east over the Pakistani border, was necessarily a secret. I had been told to wait for a signal and had no means of contacting the insurgents myself; everything was in the hands of Mohammed. He was supposed to be in Quetta now, arranging my meeting in person. All he had told me was that I would be picked up from the hotel when the time was right, and spirited off to who knows where, probably by a taxi flagged down at random in the street outside. I had been ordered neither to discuss the forthcoming meeting with anyone, nor to call his mobile unless absolutely necessary, because 'spies were everywhere'. I swapped my Western clothes for some local ones, a pale blue *shalwar qamiz* and a dark waistcoat bought from a tailor called Gulab around the corner, and settled down to wait.

After five days in Kandahar there was still no news from Mohammed. James Bays and the al-Jazeera film crew were called back to Kabul, and I was beginning to run out of things to do. On the morning of the sixth day I sent out one of the hotel boys to buy a local, pay-as-you-go *Roshan* SIM card on the black market – a new and unused number, I reasoned, would be impossible for military intelligence to intercept – and dialled the Pakistani mobile number Mohammed had given me. He answered at once, although he was evidently unable to talk.

'Send me some *Roshan* credit,' he murmured. 'I'll call you back on this number.'

I dispatched the hotel boy once again, texted across a string of numbers, and waited. An entire day went by. I sat on my bed in the cold hotel room reading Joseph Heller's *Catch 22* and wondering what was going on across the border.

The muezzins were calling the townspeople to evening prayer when Mohammed finally rang. Our conversation was cryptic. He was even more paranoid than I was about intercepts, and spoke throughout in a dramatic stage whisper. The tension in his voice was so infectious that I found myself speaking in exactly the same way back to him. I learned frustratingly little. The names of the

Taliban we were supposed to meet could not be mentioned, obviously, and nor could the location or time of the meeting. However, I gathered that he was in Chaman (he called it 'the C place') just over the border in Pakistan – the natural entry point into this part of Afghanistan, which was at least promising. On the other hand it was clear that our rendezvous would be delayed, or might not happen at all.

'There's something going on over there,' he whispered. I assumed he meant Helmand. 'It's hard to get good information. I am waiting to find out.'

'How long?'

'Soon, maybe. You must be ready.'

'Like, tomorrow?'

'Just be ready.'

I spent a sleepless night. My bag was already packed. At six o'clock the following morning I repacked it, just for something to do, and then began another day of waiting. I finished *Catch 22* and started a Victorian memoir called *Recollections of Four Years' Service in the East with HM Fortieth Regiment*, by Captain J. Martin Bladen Neill. Finally, at around four in the afternoon, and without warning, Mohammed ambled into view. He was alone and looked very tired. I could tell just from his face that there was a problem with our plan, and that I wouldn't be checking out of the hotel just yet. At length we settled down in a quiet corner with a pot of green tea, and he began to talk.

Chaman, he said, had changed dramatically since his last visit there four months earlier. Along with many Afghan Taliban, the town was filled with Pashtun fighters from Pakistan's tribal areas to the north, spoiling for a fight with the infidel invaders across the border. I said it sounded like the 1980s and the Russians all over again. 'It's *exactly* like that,' Mohammed said. 'It's turning into an old-style jihad. It's a tribal thing: fighting for fighting's sake, or for ancestral honour. I saw a lot of lovely lads with pretty turbans and curly hair. They were Waziris. I asked them, "Why aren't you at home, at work on your farms?" And they said, "No, this is work. It's important to us. These foreigners are in our land, and they don't belong."'

History really was repeating itself. The Waziris fought the British as recently as the 1930s under their elusive leader, the Fakir of Ipi. In Peshawar in late 2002 I had met a Waziri tribesman with an immense peach-coloured turban whose family had fought with the Fakir. 'We killed a lot of your people in the 1930s,' he growled when he discovered that I was British. 'We are waiting for a sign from Allah and then we will launch a war that will *amaze* the Americans.'

It sounded as though the sign had finally arrived.

The atmosphere in Chaman was feverish, paranoid, breathless with the expectation of combat. Mohammed described a street market that was doing a brisk trade in trophies and kit looted from ISAF. Most of it seemed to be American, and included night vision goggles, body armour and ammunition, as well as, more chillingly, personal material, such as letters. Mohammed had bought himself a souvenir: the latest model of Sony PlayStation that its vendor claimed had just been looted from a destroyed American tank. It was certainly American in origin: its previous owner had loaded it with an NBA basketball game. 'It's totally different from the last time I was there,' Mohammed said. 'It's much more dangerous.' He was sure that Chaman was filled with spies – ISI men, CIA men, traitors and turncoats of every stripe – which explained the theatrical whispering on the phone. Even the border had been difficult to cross. 'I had to pay the guards a hundred and fifty dollars. Can you imagine?' Afghan nationals generally expected to be able to enter their country from Pakistan without so much as a passport. A bribe of $150 was a huge amount in this part of the world, and a real indicator of regional political tension.

The trip he had arranged sounded perfect. A senior Taliban field commander in northern Helmand, one Mullah Abdul Manan, had agreed to show us around all the recent battlefields there: the dam at Kajaki and the platoon-houses at Sangin, Musa Qala and Now Zad. I was purposefully being offered the equivalent of what the MoD's press department occasionally granted to British journalists visiting Camp Bastion: a five-day 'embed' with the troops. This was journalistic gold-dust. Mohammed had met Manan before, and trusted him not to kill or kidnap me. Better still, he had extracted a guarantee of safe passage from an even more senior member of the Taliban, Mullah Obaidullah, who was the movement's former Minister of Defence. He had done brilliantly.

Our departure from Kandahar had originally been set for dawn that morning. The obstacle, Mohammed explained, was the new American head of ISAF, General Dan McNeill. A veteran of Vietnam, Korea and Iraq, McNeill was an unknown quantity, although the Taliban had certainly noted his nickname, which gave them a strong clue about what to expect: he was known as 'Bomber' McNeill.

'I was in the middle of evening prayers and my mobile started ringing,' Mohammed recalled. 'It was embarrassing. I was with a lot of Taliban people, and I didn't want to answer it, but it kept going so I had to in the end. It was Manan. He was telling me to wait.'

'Why?'

'He said, "You're still welcome to come, but there's something going on. The Americans are bombing everything. You'll be OK when you get here, but I can't guarantee your safety on the road." He wanted us to wait another week.'

This confirmation that Operation Achilles (as I later learned it was called) was already under way was bad news for me. Another week in the Hotel Continental was not an enticing prospect, and there was no guarantee that Helmand would be calmer by the end of it. Indeed, the opposite seemed more likely. Taliban High Command, according to Mohammed, thought the Americans were trying to force the whole province, and they had been taken completely by surprise. 'We liked the British,' one of Obaidullah's lieutenants had complained to Mohammed. 'They negotiated, but these damned Americans just drop bombs. This McNeill – he's bad luck for us.'

Civilian refugees were streaming out of the towns in the north. Mohammed had met people in Chaman who had relatives who had been injured around Gereshk, Kajaki, Sangin and Now Zad. Jets and helicopters were reportedly destroying every half-suspicious vehicle that moved. That represented a serious danger to anyone travelling in the war zone – and it was not the only one. In Mullah Manan's view, the Taliban units we would undoubtedly meet along the way to him represented a greater threat by far. Some of these units, angry at and traumatized by their recent losses in battle, might just decide to ignore the orders from headquarters and kill me in revenge.

'Really?' I said. 'Even if we had the order in writing?'

'That's what Mullah Manan said.' Mohammed nodded gravely. 'They could say that they thought you were a spy, and that you'd forged it.'

The Taliban's grip on its troops, I was beginning to understand, was more tenuous than they would ordinarily admit.

'If anyone doubted us, couldn't we just phone Quetta or Chaman to verify my identity?'

'Not a chance. Everyone is worried about intercepts, so when there's fighting going on they keep their phones switched off. It was hard enough just to talk to Manan from Chaman.'

The Americans, it was thought, had deployed sophisticated jamming devices. Even the Afghans' normally reliable satellite phones were not functioning, or repeatedly cut the caller off after a few seconds.

I thought hard about going anyway. The risk of travelling to northern Helmand just now was impossible to quantify. Mohammed and I talked it over for an hour but he kept insisting it was up to me. I reflected on the weeks of planning, the psycho-logical preparation and all the money this trip had already cost me. And then I decided to cancel or at least postpone the Helmand visit. Discretion was the better part of valour. In the end, if a Taliban field commander reckoned it wasn't safe to join him, it seemed sensible to listen to that advice.

I was not ready to give up on meeting the Taliban, though. I knew that the movement's activities were not confined to Helmand. As the British had discovered, the Taliban were adept at rotating their troops through the front line, and I wondered if it might be possible to visit them in some rear area. Mohammed, Jeeves-like, had already thought of this, and after a carefully coded phone call he announced that I was welcome to visit Wardak, a province just south-west of Kabul. Mohammed said his family originated from there, which was reassuring. He would be known to the locals, and by travelling with him I could probably count on a measure of protection. The following morning, therefore, we hired a car and driver and set off on the long drive north.

I had spent just a week in the south, yet I was no longer worried about taking the Kandahar–Kabul highway. There was always a risk of bandits, but it seemed so much less than the one I had just contemplated taking in Helmand. Besides, I was travelling in a local car, a beaten-up Toyota Corolla, and I was in local dress, with two Afghans for company. It was the safest way. Indeed, the journey passed without major incident, although we were stopped three times by venal policemen as we left the environs of Kandahar. The driver handed them money, even though Mohammed insisted that he should not.

Once out of city limits we bowled across the desert in an arrow-straight line at seventy miles per hour. There was little traffic on the road, as expected, and the tarmac was new. At Qalat and the few other small market towns along the way I kept my head down in the back, wrapping my face in a borrowed shawl. We stopped once for petrol, which prompted Mohammed to tell me how the Taliban had recently killed a pump attendant suspected of planting tracking devices on their vehicles on behalf of American intelligence. We passed wretched encampments of Kuchi nomads, and then two ISAF convoys of Humvees coming the other way, their goggled turret-gunners hunched against the wind. The road rose into a glittering flat snowfield, and fell again before Ghazni.

Finally, in a forbidding landscape of low rocky hills about thirty miles from Kabul, Mohammed signalled the driver to pull in. At the side of the road a car was waiting for us, its driver lounging against the door. This, I presumed, was our Taliban contact. Mohammed got out of the car and hugged him three times.

'My cousin,' he announced, grinning.

'Your cousin?' I said, startled. 'Is he Taliban?'

'No, no. But he knows them. And they know him. It's the way of things around here. It's the best kind of security.'

We switched cars and headed off towards a distant range of mountains along a muddy and steeply undulating track. The district's name was Chak.

'After five o'clock, all this territory belongs to the Taliban,' said the cousin.

It was an impressive claim. If Karzai's grip on the country was really so partial this close to his home base, it was no wonder that the Taliban felt the country was theirs for the taking.

We bumped along the road for almost two hours. It rose gradually, narrowing into a fertile valley hemmed in by immaculate white peaks up to 5,000 metres high. The valley, I learned, was an enormous cul-de-sac with a reservoir and hydro-electric dam at its head. It was a principal source of power for Kabul, and struck me as a very likely battleground of the future. British troops had died to defend the dam at Kajaki in Helmand, yet it was not nearly so important strategically as this one. If the Taliban ever gained full control of this valley, they would be able to hold the capital and the entire national programme of economic development to ransom. Unlike Kajaki, furthermore, this place seemed impregnable. The road we were on was the only practical means of access. The Russians had understood the valley's importance and fought fiercely for control of it, losing dozens of tanks and hundreds of men in the process. Wrecked Russian vehicles were still on view here and there. At one point we drove over the barely visible carcass of an eight-wheeled armoured personnel carrier, so deeply buried that in a few more years it would be completely subsumed by the road. The Pashtun community here looked and felt as though it had never been conquered or pacified.

We passed lush meadows, and houses of stone behind high mud walls. The villages were neater and better kept than anything I had seen in the south. The entire valley was more ordered, more sure of itself than the region we had left behind. I kept my head carefully wrapped up now, more anxious than before to conceal my foreign face from the villagers, who stood about in little knots and watched us pass with undisguised curiosity. I presumed that the Taliban were watching us, from up above or down below – a presumption that was confirmed when Mohammed's mobile rang.

'Is that you in that white vehicle?'

Mohammed said that it was.

'You're early. We told you not to come until after dark. What are you doing here now? Our people were about to shoot you.'

Mohammed apologized and said that we would wait at our driver's house until dark.

'And who is your driver?'

Mohammed's answer was obviously satisfactory. He had not been exaggerating: in this valley, a recognizable family name acted as a laissez-passer.

His cousin's house was a fortress, with iron entrance gates twelve feet high. Inside was a muddy farmyard. We stepped out into an icy wind and crunched our way through the frozen clods to the house. A kindly greybeard, the cousin's father-in-law and head of the household, fussed over us. *Malmastia*, the Pashtun code of hospitality, was strong here. We were ushered into the guest room, the usual carpeted, white-painted box with cushions ranged around the sides. Tea, home-baked bread and a huge bowl of sugared, newly churned butter was rapidly produced.

'Is the *feringhee* [foreigner] cold?' said the greybeard. 'Does he want a blanket?'

I knew from experience that it was useless to protest. I was tucked up in a thick acrylic tiger-rug while the room's only working appliance, an antique single-bar electric heater, was carefully turned towards my feet.

Nightfall was a couple of hours away. Men of various ages came and went, sometimes to make desultory conversation, sometimes to pray, sometimes just to sit and watch in easy silence. A clock on the wall, the only decoration in the room, was permanently stopped at 10.33. Cocooned in the tiger-rug, I felt my eyelids droop as the shadows lengthened on the mountains through the window.

The greybeard looked alarmed when at last we got up to leave. He followed us out to the frost-caked car, chattering shrilly. It wasn't easy for Mohammed to soothe him.

'What was all that about?' I asked as we bumped our way back through the iron gates into the night.

'He thought we were staying. He wanted to know where we were going.'

'And what did you tell him?'

'I told him we had an appointment with some other cousin-friends,' Mohammed replied with a smirk, 'but then he said he would accompany us for our safety. He said it wasn't safe here because there were Taliban around.'

'Do you think he guessed the truth?'

'Probably. I don't know. It doesn't matter.'

We drove slowly back the way we had come, through one frozen deserted village and then another. On the outskirts of the second, our headlights picked out a cloaked figure at the side of the road. This spectre stepped forward as we approached, and a pair of dark eyes appeared briefly at my window, the rest of his face muffled in the folds of a woollen *patou*. He set off at a brisk pace down a rough side-track, motioning us to follow.

The track wound and dipped through trees and shrubbery and was barely passable in places. Our guide pressed on regardless, his bobbing, shrouded form wreathed in the vapour of his breath. At length we reached a cluster of farmhouses where the road was blocked altogether by a heap of branches. A pair of dogs, unseen in the darkness, began to bark fiercely as our guide dragged the obstacles out of the way. We had arrived at last at the Taliban's secret lair.

The mountain cold was harsh now, perhaps ten degrees below zero, although we didn't have to endure it for long. We were led into a farmhouse and up a steep earthen staircase to a room as hot as a sauna thanks to a wood-burning stove in the centre that hissed and clicked gently to itself. A man was seated next to it, alone. He rose as we entered and greeted each of us in the normal Pashtun way: a double hug, a solemn handshake, the right hand placed across the heart, and a long, falling murmur of salaams. He was a burly man of about forty, tall for an Afghan, with a glossy black beard and a handsome face.

'This is Commander Abdullah,' Mohammed said with satisfaction. I realized that he hadn't been quite sure whom we were going to meet tonight, either. 'He is the head of the Taliban in this province. His lieutenants are all on their way to see you.'

'Please tell him that I'm very pleased to meet him.'

Abdullah looked me up and down with his head to one side, sizing me up like a bird from a branch, before silently ushering me to the cushions next to the stove.

A stopped clock hung on the wall, just as at Mohammed's

cousin's place. This one said 12.48. Given the old cliché about the Taliban wanting to drag Afghanistan back to the seventh century, the symbolism suddenly seemed quite ridiculous.

Abdullah's lieutenants began to arrive almost immediately. They entered in ones and twos, dropping Kalashnikovs, RPGs and light machine-guns in a heap by the door, metal clanking on metal, until there were a dozen men sitting around the edges of the hot little room. At each arrival, everyone stood and performed the ritual of hugs and handshakes. Form was important, but it was also evident that these people had known one another intimately for years. Many of them, I was to learn, had fought together against the Russians. They were all from Wardak, although not necessarily local; some had walked for three hours to attend this meeting with a single foreign journalist. The order from headquarters to look after me was obviously being taken very seriously.

They stared at me with frank curiosity.

'The *feringhee* really came,' Mohammed overheard one of them say to the man next to him. 'Look at him – he's really one of them. Why don't we just kidnap him?'

'Shh,' his friend replied, 'don't even joke about it. He's here on orders from Quetta.'

As soon as everyone was assembled it was time for dinner: a communal heap of rice and a plate of oily, orange-coloured mutton. Once I had been served, the others fell upon the food with an enthusiasm that said much about how they usually ate. This was a special occasion. Abdullah had scooted around the circle beforehand with a pewter basin and a jug of warm water – a hand-washing ceremony that was usually performed by the youngest son of the family, not the most senior man present. It was a deliberate act of self-abasement, an expression of humility and comradeship more eloquent than any words. I knew immediately that I would be safe in Abdullah's hands. The *malmastia* tradition to which I had entrusted my life was solid among these Pashtuns.

They were all what the British Embassy in Kabul termed 'Tier 1 Taliban' – warriors motivated by ideology rather than angry poppy farmers or opium dealers, who were classed as Tier 2, or the adventurers, impoverished peasants and other hired guns who made up Tier 3. They were fighting, their leader explained with disarming simplicity, because it was their religious duty to resist the infidel invaders – just as they had fought the Russians, and as their fathers and grandfathers in earlier times had fought against the British. They were dressed like everyone else in Wardak, a necessity of the clandestine war they were waging. Before 2002, they confirmed, all of them had worn the black turbaned uniform of their movement. 'We drop the turbans here,' Abdullah said, 'but the time for black will come again.'

He had 700 men under arms – the precise number required, he claimed, to take and hold Wardak when the order came. Every province in the country, he said, had an underground cell of the requisite shape and size. They kept themselves in a state of constant readiness for the order from Quetta to attack a police station, or an American convoy, or even to take over the province. They slept during the day and did everything, including training and live firing exercises, by night. 'Night-time is Taliban time here,' Abdullah told me.

In Wardak, the Taliban were already an alternative government. Farmers came to them to settle land disputes. Even the police asked their permission before going about their business. 'If it wasn't for American air power,' Abdullah added with sudden bitterness, 'we could take half the country in a single day. What we need more than anything is missiles to shoot their planes. We cannot fight them in the air. But, insha'allah, we will get these missiles very soon.'

I asked about the wisdom of gathering so many Taliban commanders in one place. A laser-guided bomb through the roof above us would obviously serve ISAF well. Abdullah replied that they seldom gathered together like this, and never in the same place twice. Even separately, they tended to sleep in a different place every day. Then he added, with cheerful sang-froid, that a bomb through the roof was perfectly possible, since our location was no secret to the Coalition's intelligence community.

In a show of strength the previous year, Abdullah's men had taken over Wardak's local government district centre. 'We were ready to sell our lives to hold on to it, but headquarters said the time was not right, that there was nothing to be gained from our dying then. We were ordered to retreat.' Mistaking this move for weakness, US Special Forces had pursued Abdullah to this very farmhouse, surrounding it and demanding his surrender. There was a tense Mexican stand-off that ended, for reasons still obscure to them, when the Americans withdrew.

'Does that make you scared?' someone said when this story was finished.

I pulled a doubtful face, and everyone laughed.

'Don't worry,' Abdullah said quietly. 'If the Americans come again tonight, we will defend you with our lives.'

The laughter subsided; suddenly, everyone was nodding seriously. I smiled in gratitude – it seemed the appropriate response – although I was secretly bewildered by this pledge and the strangeness of my situation. Whose side, ultimately, did they suppose I was really on?

The talk turned naturally to Helmand. Musa Qala, they said, had been bombed again that morning. Fighting throughout the province was intensifying for the third consecutive day. Much of Abdullah's talk was bombast. The Taliban, he claimed, had 10,000 fighters in Helmand, with a further 2,000 suicide bombers standing by. They were concentrating on the south, he said, because this was where they had 'broken the back' of the British the last time; history, another Maiwand, would shortly be repeating itself. All of these men had fought the Coalition somewhere or other in Afghanistan the previous year. Wardak, I understood, was a designated safe haven, a place for the fighters to rest and reorganize before being rotated back to the front lines. In many ways they operated just as the British Army did.

I asked if any of them had themselves fought the British last summer. Abdullah nodded. He had been in Musa Qala in July.

'Were you there when the tank was blown up?'

Abdullah nodded again.

'Were you involved in that ambush?'

Mohammed's seamless translation suddenly stalled. 'I can't ask him that,' he said quietly. 'It's too close.'

There was an awkward silence as Abdullah glanced from Mohammed to me and back again, his eyebrows raised in amusement, perhaps guessing what was going on.

'There were lots of things happening in different places all the time,' he offered. 'The situation was very confused.'

'But . . . are you *ghazi*?'

Ghazi, an Arabic word, was a kind of honorific in Afghanistan that denoted someone who had killed an infidel in the service of jihad.

'Not yet,' Abdullah replied solemnly, 'but I know in my heart that I am very close to it.'

Mohammed was reluctant to go on with this line of enquiry. It seemed best to return to the generalities of killing the British.

Our Army boys, Abdullah conceded, were not bad soldiers. He said he was in a position to know, since he had got to within thirty metres of some of them at Musa Qala. 'They are not cowards. They do not cry, or shout "Oh-my-God" in the front line as the Americans do. But still, they don't stand and fight like us.'

'What do you mean?'

'I have a video of British soldiers surrendering. I can show it to you if you like.'

This could only be the Taliban version of the Musa Qala deal. Of course the British had not 'surrendered' in the conventional sense when they left that town on 17 October. There was never any question of the Paras and Royal Irish giving up their weapons. The garrison had withdrawn in fighting order, in a manoeuvre General Richards very carefully described as 'a redeployment'; but to these men the departure looked quite different. The Taliban had naturally filmed the spectacle for propaganda purposes. The video was probably on sale in every bazaar from here to Rabat by now.

'The British were defeated at Musa Qala,' Abdullah continued. 'Everyone knows this. We were going to slaughter or capture them, but we let them go out of respect for the elders. It suited us because it gave us a chance to destroy Karzai's spy network in the town.'

Abdullah and his men were against the presence of all foreign invaders in their country, but the British had special status. Most of their ancestors had fought the *gora feringhee*, as they called them – the red-faced foreigners. Every man in the room knew how they had beaten us in the 1840s. The long entanglement of Britain and

Afghanistan was evident even in the clothes these Taliban wore: it was no coincidence that they wore waistcoats, or that the Pashtun word for the garment is *wezcot*. I had long suspected that sending the British Army to win modern hearts and minds in the Pashtun south was one of the worst decisions Nato had ever taken, and now Abdullah seemed to confirm it. 'There's a strong connection,' he said. 'Fighting the British feels like unfinished business for many of us.'

The British death toll in southern Afghanistan had reached forty-five that week, a figure that included the fourteen victims of the Nimrod accident in early September. The Taliban did not believe it: they reckoned that there were well over a hundred British dead. I explained that there was no possibility in the British Army of manipulating the figures for propaganda purposes, but they remained sceptical. They were equally certain that the Coalition had inflated their estimates of Taliban dead, and in this they were probably right.

'Perhaps your figures don't include Nepalis?' wondered one lieutenant.

I assured him that any Gurkha dead would certainly be included in the body count – had there been any. He shook his head in a way that made me wonder what he thought he'd seen, presumably at Now Zad. It was plain he did not believe me; he just wasn't quite certain whether this *feringhee* was lying, or merely wrong about the facts.

The assumption of British racism behind the lieutenant's question about the Gurkhas was interesting. But however disdainful of other races he believed the British to be, they all seemed to prefer the UK to the US. These Taliban hated the Americans more than anyone, even more than the Russians who had brutalized their country twenty years earlier. 'The Russians fought man to man,' Abdullah said, 'but when one American soldier gets hit, a whole village gets razed by bombs in response. The only difference is that America claims to drop bombs with pinpoint accuracy, but that isn't true. I've seen many dead villagers. Their bombs are too big. It was easier to respect the Russians.' The Americans, Abdullah complained, were heavy-handed in other ways. 'The Russians just killed people, but these people enter our houses without permission and dishonour our women. To an Afghan, that is worse than being killed. Dishonouring us is the fastest way of ensuring your defeat.'

His was one of those Afghan points of view that made no sense whatsoever to the military planners of the West. The whole idea of the American military machine, with its reliance on long-range technology and air power, was antagonistic to these fighters. Their attitude to war was pre-industrial. To Western soldiers, it seemed almost insanely old-fashioned. These Taliban yearned to fight on the terms of a mythical past, when men were honourable and wars were won through courage and faith, not superior weaponry. This war, to them, was a holy duty: the object was not necessarily to win, but to resist. Abdullah was quite specific about that. 'We are against war,' he said. 'It creates nothing but widows and destruction. But jihad is different. It is our moral obligation to resist you foreigners. One year, a hundred years, a million years, ten million years – it is not important. We will never stop fighting. At Judgement Day, Allah will not ask, "What did you do for your country?" He will ask, "Did you fight for your religion?"'

'What we can't understand,' said a voice from the back, 'is why you allow yourselves to be the puppets of America.'

It was a question asked just as often back at home. The man

asking it was the group's Mullah, a straight-backed, scholarly man with piercing eyes who had said little so far, but who found his voice as the evening went on. He gave his name as Qari Abdul-Basit. *Qari* means 'Reader', a title given to specialists in the sung recital of the Koran. It was an obvious nom de guerre: Qari Abdul-Basit Abdul-Samad, from Egypt, was the first president of the pan-Islamic Reciters' Union, a legend in the Muslim world who died, rock-star like, in a car crash in 1989. The others, Abdullah included, deferred to the Mullah whenever he spoke. He was, I realized, the real spokesman for the group, their spiritual guide and mentor in their Holy War.

'You British are clever people,' the Mullah went on. 'It makes no sense. You were beaten here before, and you will lose this time, too. Why do you think it is any different now?'

'Maybe we believe in the superiority of our technology,' I said. 'We have bombs and planes with chain guns that can fire sixty-five rounds a second. You only have Kalashnikovs and RPGs.'

The men looked at one another.

'But we had even less than you the last time,' Abdullah said. 'Only swords and *jezails*.* But still we beat you.'

'A clever man does not get bitten by a snake from the same hole twice,' said the Mullah, to nods all round.

'But we're not in the same hole,' I persisted. 'It is different this time. We are not here to occupy your country. We are here to help your government to secure economic development.'

'Then why do you come here with guns and bombs?'

---

* A *jezail* is a crude but highly effective long-barrelled sniper's rifle of the nineteenth century, celebrated in Rudyard Kipling's poem 'Arithmetic on the Frontier' (1886): 'A scrimmage in a Border Station / A canter down some dark defile / Two thousand pounds of education / Drops to a ten-rupee jezail'.

'Are you saying that it would be different if we had come here unarmed?'

'But of course!' said the Mullah. 'In that case you would have been our guests, just as you are our guest now. If your engineers and agriculture experts had come to us and explained what they were trying to do, we would have protected them with our lives.'

'But our soldiers are trying to protect the engineers! That is what the fighting around Kajaki is about. The engineers cannot mend the generators unless there is security.'

'Mending the generators is a good thing to do. But the government has done nothing at the dam for the last five years. And now your soldiers have emptied the villages for miles around with their bombs and fighting. They are killing innocent people.'

'What about Panjwayi?' one of the lieutenants added, rolling an RPG around on the carpet with his foot. He was referring to Operation Medusa, five months earlier. Much of the fighting then had centred on Panjwayi, a district just west of Kandahar, where up to a thousand Taliban fighters had been killed. 'The Canadians have announced a huge aid package, but the people say it is all useless. One minute they're bombing us to death, the next they're promising to rebuild. That's a disgrace. Do they think Afghans are stupid?'

'What about al-Qaida?' I said. 'Bin Laden attacked the West. Don't you think we had the right to hunt him here?'

'Al-Qaida were our guests,' said the Mullah. 'We had no connection with them beyond that. We knew bin Laden as a jihadi in the time of the Russians. He is a good Muslim, an honourable man.'

'9/11 was not honourable.'

'There's no evidence that 9/11 was planned in Afghanistan.

Those martyrs didn't learn to fly here. Besides,' he added, emphasizing his bitterness with a solitary raised finger, 'you destroyed our whole government for just one man.'

'What about poppies? My government says that you exploit the opium trade to buy weapons.'

'How can they say that when we are the only ones who managed to reduce the harvest? Poppy-growing is *haraam* ['forbidden' – the opposite of *halal*]. Mullah Omar issued a fatwa against it. We were succeeding in abolishing it. We couldn't stop it all at once – the process is slow, like weaning a child off breast-feeding – but we were getting there when the Americans came.'

'And now?'

'And now we make no money from poppies,' he insisted. 'What little money we have is entirely donated by the people.'

'They say you are against economic development. They say you are against women's education.'

'That is not true. There are girls' schools here in Wardak, set up under the Taliban, that are still running.'

'But many girls' schools have been burned.'

'Some have, it's true,' he said, 'but only those schools with Western curricula, where girls were being taught pornography.'

And so it went on. I pressed as hard as I could, yet found no chink in the Mullah's ideological armour. I knew I was being spun a very slanted version of reality. The accusation that girls were being taught pornography in Western-funded schools was backward and absurd. More than 1,100 girls' schools were said to have been attacked or burned down in Afghanistan since 2002. A dozen girls' schools had been destroyed in Wardak alone; by September 2006 there was just one still open in the entire province. I was also aware that as 'Tier 1' Taliban, these men were far from typical of

314

the average fighter who opposed the British during Herrick 4. They presented themselves as defenders of the national interest, yet only a quarter of the public openly supported them, at best. They were not quite the populist movement they claimed to be.

On the other hand, support for them did seem to be growing.* And it was hard, in the end, not to sympathize with some of their grievances, or to disagree wholeheartedly with their central contention that the West had no business being in their country. America, they said, were hypocrites when they claimed to cherish human rights. Collateral damage caused by bombing was one thing, but what excuse could there be for Abu Ghraib, or for Guantanamo, where dozens of innocent Afghans had been held for years without trial? In Kabul I had met the Taliban's former ambassador to Islamabad, Abdul Salaam Zaeef, who had spent more than three years in detention, most of it in Cuba, enduring strippings and solitary confinement and endless psychological bullying by bone-headed GIs. He was a gentle, bespectacled, dignified soul, a religious moderate who publicly and repeatedly condemned the 9/11 attacks before his arrest. I had read a translation of his account of his experiences at Guantanamo, a bitter little book that sold over 200,000 copies in Pashto, and I had to agree with him that his incarceration without trial or charge was a disgrace.

My Westerner's conscience was troubled, and it was no comfort to recall that Captain Bladen Neill recorded something very similar as long ago as 1845. 'Does the review of the past in Affghanistan

* According to the Senlis Council, which conducted a survey of 17,000 Afghans in March 2007, when 26 per cent of respondents said they 'openly supported the Taliban'. Spokeswoman Norinne MacDonald commented, 'A couple of years back, such support was just three per cent.'

[*sic*] justify us in maintaining that our conduct there was without reproach?' he wrote. 'Was there no breach of faith, no disregard of promises, to cause doubts of our integrity? It must ever be borne in mind that the rights of the Affghans, as a nation, had been cause-lessly assailed, their feelings wantonly insulted ... They had grounds for the indulgence of revengeful passions; and had their cause not been stained by [the massacre of the Kabul garrison in 1842], they must have claimed the admiration which would have been due to a people combating to the death for their assaulted freedom.'

It was past one o'clock in the morning yet the meeting showed no signs of breaking up. Abdullah and his men had been asleep all day, and seemed to be enjoying the novelty of this exchange with a *feringhee*. I was enjoying it too. I was susceptible to the romance of that lonely farmhouse, and could almost imagine being one of them.

'Tell me,' said one of the lieutenants, leaning forward and shyly clearing his throat. 'Please don't take this as an insult or anything, but ... supposing thousands of Afghans had invaded *your* country, and bombed *your* villages, and killed *your* wives and children, what would you do?'

'I'd fight,' I found myself saying. 'Of course I'd fight.'

The throat-clearer paused, considering this.

'And tell me, in such a situation, do you think it would be possible for an Afghan journalist to come as you have come to us now, to meet and talk and eat with fighters from the British resistance?'

His question had an edge to it. It was, of course, inconceivable that this surreal meeting could ever have happened the other way round.

'Probably not,' I said.

'So, why aren't you scared now?'

'Because I understand that you are good Pashtuns. I have faith in your respect for Pashtun Wali, for *malmastia*.'

'Yes,' he nodded equitably. 'Without *malmastia*, we would certainly kill you.'

It was hard to imagine these people ever being defeated. I recalled reading an interview with a Para whose patrol had been ambushed by a single gunman, who popped up with an AK at close quarters with no earthly possibility of survival. 'You do wonder what goes through their little minds sometimes, don't you?' the Para told the reporter.

Incomprehensible courage was often married to military prowess. I didn't doubt this as one of the lieutenants began to explain his technique for doctoring an RPG warhead to improve its ability to pierce armour – including that of a British Scimitar, I thought darkly to myself. He said that RPG warheads were readily available in the markets for 400 Afghanis – about £4. 'I'll show you how to fire one if you like,' he said cheerfully. 'You have to keep your mouth open when you pull the trigger, otherwise your eardrums will burst.'

There was something genuinely moving about their revolutionary fervour, however naive or wrong-headed it might have been. The Mullah's argument that, had we only asked them, *they* would have provided security for Western engineers and developers was hard to resist while I reclined on their cushions in the warmth of their stove. As Pashtuns, of course they would have treated unarmed foreigners as honoured guests! If the Mullah was telling the truth, it meant that an opportunity for dialogue with these extraordinary people had indeed existed before the battles of

Herrick 4. It implied that the resort to bloodshed had been at best premature, at worst wholly unnecessary; and that by taking a fight to the north of Helmand, the British had thrown away a precious chance, however small, to reach an acceptable compromise.

I wondered if it was not too late for international dialogue with the Taliban. At the very least, better communication had the potential to benefit everyone, right away. If, for example, they truly believed that girls were being taught 'pornography' in Western-funded schools, might this not simply be because no one had explained the curriculum to them? (I checked later and discovered that Chak district's only girls' school, in the village of Sheik Yassine, had been torched in April 2006, six months after it opened its doors. It had been built by an American-funded NGO called Afghans4Tomorrow with the consent of Chak's tribal elders but, as I suspected, without direct consultation with the Taliban – although there were of course many other complex local political factors at work in the decision to destroy the school.)

I also wondered whether it was not they but I who was being naive. There was no telling, in the end, how honest the Mullah was being with me. In any case, although he might possibly have been the voice of the Taliban in Chak, or even in Wardak, he was not Mullah Omar. He did not set his movement's policy towards the West. It was also an easy thing to promise security for Western engineers and aid officials, a much harder one to guarantee it in a land as intrinsically violent as this one. But, still, didn't any chance of peace deserve the benefit of the doubt?

I asked if I could be photographed with them. Abdullah, wary at first, gave his permission on condition that his men's faces were covered. Two men scrambled forward, as eager as children. They arranged an RPG and a couple of guns in the foreground, and hustled in on either side of me as Mohammed took the shot. Someone lent me their hat and turban, insisting I put them on. There was general hilarity as I bungled it, and the badly wound cloth slid down over my face.

'How about that?' someone cried when the turban was properly adjusted at last. 'He looks exactly like someone from Dara-i-Noor!'

There was more laughter. Mohammed, still taking pictures, explained that Dara-i-Noor was a district near Jalalabad whose people were noted for their pale skin and blue eyes.

When he had finished I passed the camera around the room for everyone to enjoy the results on the little screen, and also to allow Abdullah to check that his men's masks had not inadvertently slipped. The pictures were as ambivalent as my feelings for these people. They made me look, almost, like their comrade-in-arms; yet they might just as plausibly have been released to the Western media as evidence of an all too successful kidnap operation.

Qari Abdul-Basit suddenly announced that it was time to pray. The men lined up towards Mecca, switching with bewildering speed from pranksters into soldiers of God. I sat alone on the cushions and watched the line bow, kneel and kiss the ground in perfect unison as the Qari's singing filled the air. His voice was extraordinary. I listened in a state of semi-hypnosis as his mournful crescendos reverberated in the silences in between. There was spirituality here, a transcendental sense of peace and purpose and closeness to death and God seldom experienced in the modern West. This, for me, was Islam at its most appealing. It was marvellous how these people were able to plug instantly into such rapturous oblivion, five times a day, and for a brief moment I frankly envied their serenity.

And yet, for all its strength and purity, I was not seduced but saddened by the Taliban's belief, and the destructive, un-compromising way in which it displaced everything else in the world. Faith came before everything, even love of family, as I discovered later when I asked Abdullah if he had children. The Mullah and the lieutenants had left by then, and apart from Mohammed we were alone.

'I have two sons, aged two and four,' he replied.

'I have a daughter aged two,' I responded with a smile. 'How often do you get to see them?'

'Sometimes. Not often. I don't give them the father's love that I could because when I am killed it will be much harder for them.'

'But that's one of the saddest things I've ever heard! How do you know you will be killed?'

His expression didn't even flicker.

'Listen,' he said. 'My father, grandfather and great-grandfather all died by the bullet. I will die in the same way, and no doubt my sons too. It is not so sad.'

'But . . . do you actually wish to die by the bullet?'

'Of course! It is glorious to be martyred. To die in the service of jihad is the ambition of all of us here.'

The chasm between our cultures yawned again. In the West we are taught to put love of family before everything. It is our most cherished value, the bedrock of our civilization, a shared assumption that underpins the plots and endings of a million Hollywood movies.

'Allah gives us children, so it is our duty to give to Allah before we give to our family,' Abdullah went on patiently. 'Life has no taste without faith, no matter how much you eat of it. But dying in jihad is like having a full stomach without eating. It is peace and perfection.'

320

The meeting had not broken up until three. The Taliban left as they had arrived, shuffling out into the cold night in ones and twos, their weapons across their shoulders. Abdullah warned that he would wake us at first light, when we would have to move on.

'James,' Mohammed whispered as we crawled into our sleeping bags. 'There's something I must tell you. You know that phone call I got?'

'Yes – what about it?'

A couple of hours earlier, Mohammed's mobile had rung and he had answered it, interrupting a particularly complicated exchange with the Mullah. I had shot him an irritated look, for I had asked him to ensure that his phone was switched off during the meeting. When the call was finished he carried on translating for me as if it had never happened.

'It was a friend in Helmand. He was confirming some news. Mullah Manan was killed last night.'

I sat up in my sleeping bag, wide awake again.

'They dropped a laser-guided bomb through his compound roof near Kajaki. Ten or eleven Talibs were killed. Some civilians also.'

'But – how did they know where he was?'

'I don't know. Spies, probably. What does it matter now?'

He had a point. Had we gone ahead with the visit to Manan we would have been in the compound with him when the bomb struck – most probably in the very same room. His warning to Mohammed that he couldn't guarantee our safe passage across Helmand, together with my decision to heed it, had probably saved our lives.

'Does Abdullah know?'

'He knows. He told me about it the moment I got here. He also told me not to tell you. Manan was his friend from Soviet times. All of the people here knew him. We were praying earlier for Allah to accept his martyred soul into Paradise.'

This detail explained a lot about the mood of the evening's meeting: the earnest talk about martyrdom, the flashes of bitterness about Coalition air power. Abdullah and his men were still in shock. It was extraordinary, the strangest Pashtun paradox, that they were able to separate the blame for Manan's death from their guest of the evening, an emissary of a country whose air force might well have been responsible.

And then I fell asleep, confident that among these people my vulnerability would protect me better than any gun or body armour. Apart from the threat of another Coalition bomb, I could not have been safer.

Postscript

Eighteen months have passed since I began this book project. The title, *A Million Bullets*, was the idea of my publisher, Doug Young at Transworld. I liked it – it seemed to strike the right sardonic note in the wake of John Reid's expressed hope for a bullet-free campaign – but felt bound to point out that, actually, only half that number of bullets had been fired during the Herrick 4 period I was writing about. Doug immediately replied that *Half a Million Bullets* didn't sound catchy enough. 'Besides,' he added, 'I bet we've fired a million since then. Why don't you find out?'

This was more easily said than done. In late 2006 the MoD abruptly stopped advertising the amount of ordnance being expended in Afghanistan. The generals themselves now agreed that the firing of hundreds of thousands of bullets was probably not an indicator of a successful hearts and minds campaign. I asked Adam Holloway, the ex-Army MP, who offered to try to extract the figures via a written parliamentary question. A fortnight later, rather to his amazement, he received the answers he had asked for.

My worry that my title was an exaggeration was splendidly misplaced. The British, led by the Marines, fired more than a million bullets during the six months (October 2006 to March 2007) of Operation Herrick 5 alone – 1,295,795 of them; in the course of Herrick 6 (April to September 2007) 12 Mechanized Brigade, led by the Royal Anglians, fired 2,474,560. Those figures excluded bombs, artillery rounds and 30mm cannon shells, and of course all the bullets, rockets and RPGs fired at the British by the enemy (for which no statistics will ever exist). Results for Herrick 7, which began in October 2007, had yet to be collated.

What next? At the time of writing, Operation Herrick 8, the first 'roulement' of 2008, is about to begin – and it is a Para-led operation once again. This time, however, 16 Air Assault Brigade will be spearheaded not by a small battle group but by two whole battalions of Paras, along with elements of a third – the first time that so many Paras have fought together since World War Two. Firepower has been stepped up, with more armoured vehicles and new Merlin troop-carrying helicopters at the troops' disposal. The RAF is also expected to deploy its new Eurofighter ground attack aircraft for the first time. There are now almost 8,000 British troops operating in Afghanistan – the biggest deployment there since 1880.

International attention was once again drawn to Musa Qala at the end of 2007. The Taliban – 2,000 of them, according to their own figures – had been dug in for ten months since the collapse of the controversial deal there. It was their last significant urban base in the region, and now a large Coalition force succeeded in throwing them out again. The operation was led by the Afghan National Army, and much was made of the symbolism of their victory. Des Browne, the Defence Secretary, called Musa Qala 'iconic'. But the

ANA could not have succeeded without the close support of 300 US Special Forces and fully 2,000 regular British ones – itself the largest single British operation in years. The Taliban occupiers did not defend the town but slipped away as usual, regrouping in the mountains to the north in order to fight another day. The British military, anxious to impress upon the locals how different this occupation would be from the last one, quickly announced plans to build a new mosque, road, clinic and school. 'Securing Musa Qala is a major blow to the Taliban,' Brigadier Andrew Mackay told reporters as he rode on the back of an ANA truck through the town. 'The most important part of this operation is the reconstruction and development ... that is how the operation should be judged.'

But will new roads and buildings be enough to convince the people? In the course of their house-to-house clearance operation, troops of 2nd Battalion, The Yorkshire Regiment, discovered an estimated £150 million worth of opium piled in eighty-five sacks against a wall, along with a pile of white powder, suggestive of a makeshift heroin factory. However intolerant towards the drugs business the Taliban might have been in the past, their attitude here was evidently quite different. A trade of such immense value will not be given up lightly, either by the farmers, heroin manu-facturers, smugglers and associated workers who depend upon it for their livelihoods, or by the Taliban who tax them to fund their insurgency. The challenge now for the ANA is to hold the town against counter-attacks. The world is watching. If they fail, the prognosis for an early British exit from Helmand looks poor indeed.

As Musa Qala was reconquered, Gordon Brown, the Prime Minister, announced what his officials called 'a shift of emphasis' in

Britain's Afghan strategy: from now on, he would support President Karzai's bid for reconciliation with middle-ranking Taliban who were prepared to lay down their guns and abide by the constitution. As 2007 came to a close, it emerged that British officials had in fact already been talking to the Taliban in an unofficial way for perhaps six months – so unofficially, indeed, that it seemed that the Afghan authorities themselves did not always know about it. Soon after Musa Qala's recapture, the Governor of Helmand, Assadullah Wafa, complained to Kabul that two senior foreign diplomats – Michael Semple, the acting head of the EU mission, and Mervyn Patterson of the UN – had travelled to the region for secret talks with the Taliban without telling him. President Karzai, apparently incensed at the perceived undermining of government sovereignty, promptly expelled the pair from the country. The details of how, precisely, the Taliban should be engaged in dialogue remain unclear. A negotiated settlement for Afghanistan will remain elusive for as long as such confusion continues; but at least the prospect of talks is closer than before.

Gordon Brown's new strategy was sugared by the promise of an extra £450 million of development funds between 2009 and 2012. It may be too little, too late. To date, despite some improvements since 2006, not enough has changed for the people of Helmand. Development and reconstruction work, even in Lashkar Gah and Gereshk, is still far from what it should be. As Paddy Ashdown, the former High Representative for Bosnia, pointed out, in mid-2007 the amount of aid being spent per head of population was precisely one-fiftieth of what the international community put into Bosnia and Kosovo, 'less, in terms of resources, than has ever been put into a successful post-conflict stabilization and reconstruction effort'.

Meanwhile, opium production remains at record levels – the British and Americans are still arguing about counter-narcotics strategy – and suicide bombings are on the rise across the country. A record 140 such bombs exploded in 2007. In February 2008 in Arghandab, the idyllic-looking district north-west of Kandahar I had visited a year earlier, a bomber killed more than a hundred men and boys who were attending a dog-fighting festival. There are more suicide bomb attacks over the border in Pakistan, too, where democracy itself seemed to falter at the end of 2007 when elections were postponed following the assassination of the leader of the Pakistani People's Party, Benazir Bhutto.

With a few notable exceptions, the Afghan National Police are as corrupt and indigent as ever, and quite unready to take over. Doubts also remain over the ANA, despite some notable improvements in its performance since 2006. Worst of all, thanks in part to Coalition reliance on air power, hundreds if not thousands of innocent civilians continue to be killed in insurgency-related violence, with a potentially catastrophic effect on public relations. An estimated 6,200 people were killed in violence related to the insurgency in 2007 – an estimate that one very senior officer told me privately was far too low. Whatever the true figure, no one doubted that the 2007 fighting season was easily the country's deadliest since the US-led invasion of 2001.

The British Army looks certain to go on paying a heavy price. At the time of writing, sixty-five young soldiers had either been killed in action or had died subsequently from their wounds, and more than 300 had been injured, 101 of them seriously or very seriously. The Prime Minister declared in December 2007 that troop levels would settle at about 7,800 for the long term, but declined to set a time limit for this commitment – unlike General Dannatt, who in the summer of 2007 warned of a 'new great game' in central Asia, and ordered his commanders to prepare accordingly. Sir Sherard Cowper-Coles, the British Ambassador to Kabul, specified that stabilization of Afghanistan could take thirty years. The Home Front seems unlikely to have the patience for that if, as seems likely, the violence continues at the present intensity. As they say in Afghanistan, 'You may have the watches, but we have the time.' The American experience in Iraq has hardly been encouraging, and domestic British support for Operation Herrick remains elusive. According to the most recent poll, a third of respondents thought that British and Nato troops could never win in Afghanistan, and 62 per cent thought that all British troops should be withdrawn either immediately or within the year.

And what will happen to Britain's Armed Forces? Between June and November 2007 more than 5,000 military men and women quit their jobs, 1,300 of them officers; another 2,000 were waiting to have their resignation applications approved. Such a rate of attrition cannot be sustained for long. A 'broken' Army could spell the end of the government's ability to project or protect national interests anywhere abroad. Our relationship with the US would be greatly weakened, along with British influence in Europe, the UN and the world.

But where is relief to come from? Despite pleading, Britain's chief European partners are still refusing to commit the necessary troop reinforcements to Afghanistan's dangerous south. Nato, a military alliance that has underpinned Western security for fifty years, could well end up being buried in Afghanistan, a country long known as 'the graveyard of empires'. 'I think [southern Afghanistan] may be the death knell of Nato unless we're very careful,' said Lord (Peter) Carrington, a former Nato secretary-general. 'I mean, when we get a situation in which so many countries are not prepared to join in. Really only the Canadians and the Americans and the British and the Dutch are fighting there. I think this is very dangerous for Nato. I think we ought to ask ourselves, if this doesn't work, what on earth is Nato for?'

Osama bin Laden once taunted the West for its unwillingness to fight, and it may indeed be that some of Britain's main Nato allies have lost their appetite for it. As one of the *Spiegel* journalists I met in Kandahar pointed out, just one person has been shot dead by a German soldier since the end of World War Two, a guerrilla in Kosovo who unwisely attacked a UN peace-keeper there in 1999. The soldier responsible, the journalist added, was instantly taken off duty and sent off for psychological counselling, despite his protests that he didn't need it. The modern German Army is a very different beast from the Wehrmacht of popular memory.

Britain seems to have bitten off more than she can chew in Helmand; and her Army – brave, proud and uniquely professional, but scandalously under-resourced by government and tragically under-appreciated at home – is looking ever more isolated internationally. The Dutch and the Canadians are under intense domestic pressure to reduce their military commitments. In Washington, outgoing President George Bush and his neo-con supporters are on the back foot, with presidential elections pending. Despite the reconquest of Musa Qala, a jihadist wave partly set in motion by British policies is still building in the wider region. The 'kinetic' nature of Operation Herrick 4 set the tone for Britain's Afghan engagement for, very probably, years to come. Was it really worth the risk?

Edinburgh, April 2008

Notes

Introduction

3: A professor at the Royal Statistical Society ... comrades in Iraq: Professor Sheila Bird, quoted in the *Independent*, 1 October 2006.

5: By the end of the year ... 320 non-combatants: *Observer*, 12 August 2007, 'Civilian death toll rises in the bloody battle of Helmand'.

7: 'They looked on with astonishment ... enter the field as competitors': Henry Havelock, *Narrative of the War in Afghanistan 1840*, quoted in Patrick Macrory, *Kabul Catastrophe* (1966; reprinted 2002, Prion Books), p. 124.

10: 'We are running hot ... I say "just"': *Guardian*, 4 September 2006.

12: In November 2007 ... required strength of 101,800: *Guardian*, 23 November 2007, Richard Norton-Taylor, 'Under-strength and under strain as experienced soldiers queue to quit'.

13: 'I don't see how any Muslim ... they can't be like us': *Guardian*, 5 July 2006, 'Muslim soldier's family condemn "terrorist" claims'.

14: The objectors' self-interest was widely condemned: see, e.g., *Sunday Telegraph*, 5 August 2007, Jenny McCartney, 'There are some news stories that force you to question just what Britain has become'.

17: 'It's the man who is the first weapon of war ... even quicker by overuse': *The Times*, 10 October 2006.

331

Chapter 1: In Kandahar
39: 'As we cleared the pass ... in complete disorder across the plain': J. Martin Bladen Neill, *Recollections of Four Years' Service in the East with HM Fortieth Regiment* (1845; reprinted by the Naval and Military Press), pp. 160–2.

Chapter 2: Aya Gurkhali!
51: Around Now Zad ... in only three years: see www.aims.org.af/afg/dist_profiles/unhcr_district_profiles/southern/helmand/naw_zad
51: In 2006, according to the UN ... responsible for almost half of it: Senlis Council, *Helmand at War*, June 2006.
52: The province is on the way ... and even Colombia: UNODC World Drug Report 2007.
81: Most worrying of all ... cannot begin to police itself?': *Newsnight*, BBC 2, 26 October 2006.

Chapter 3: The Dragon's Lair
90: 'Hero Dean' ... THIS is what our boys face': *Sun*, 1 November 2006.
111: Taken together, the stories ... according to plan: see *Daily Mail*, 22 September 2006.
123: It can carry ten tons of ammunition ... bullet casings from the aircraft floor: see Dan Mills, *Sniper One* (Michael Joseph, 2007), p. 140.
123: The accusation spilled over into the press ... hearts and minds: *Guardian*, 10 August 2007, Declan Walsh and Richard Norton-Taylor, 'UK officer calls for US Special Forces to quit Afghan hotspot'.
136: The twenty-fifth anniversary ... in the conflict itself: *Sunday Times* magazine, 10 June 2007, Michael Bilton, 'Lions Bled by Donkeys'.

Chapter 4: The Joint UK Plan for Helmand
145: 'Well, we will offer an alternative ... he does not question me further: Leo Docherty, *Desert of Death* (Faber & Faber, 2007), p. 145.
146: 'What's the form?' ... we're doing fuck-all about it!': ibid., p. 175.
149–50: Yet it was not until June 2007 ... a meeting closed to the public: *The Times*, 28 August 2007, Michael Evans, 'Army chief predicts

"a generation of conflict"'.

152: 'It's all very well having bombers . . . the insurgency': Noel Barber, *The War of the Running Dogs* (Collins, 1971), pp. 62–3.

161: 'Brigadier Ed Butler has it all . . . a man ready-made to lead': Michael Evans, in *The Times*, 19 May 2006.

163: Yet when they reached the chief's son . . . some pain-killers: Patrick Bishop, *3 Para* (Harper Press, 2007), p. 110.

164: Some of those who dealt with the Governor suspected that he was prone to 'flap': ibid., p. 110.

167–8: It was not until January 2007 . . . a two-mile security perimeter: see *Observer*, 28 January 2008, Jason Burke, 'Dam holds back force of the Taliban'.

173: According to the journalist Christina Lamb . . . 'the Maiwand thing': *Sunday Times*, 9 July 2006, 'Death Trap'.

173: In 1998, in the Panjshir Valley . . . the legend 'VR 1840': see *Kandahar Cockney* (Harper Perennial, 2005), p. 45.

181: In 2001, hundreds of bright yellow MRE . . . public relations disaster: see, e.g., http://www.thirdworldtraveler.com/Landmines_html/ClusterBombs_Afghan_HRW.html

181: In 2007, another attempt to curry favour . . . the World Cup in 2002: this story was widely reported, but see, e.g., Brian Whitaker in the *Guardian*, 28 August 2007.

183: 'establishing relations . . . [we] would be dealing with': Patrick Bishop, *3 Para*, p. 30.

Chapter 5: The Chinooks Push the Envelope

191: 'I want to know exactly . . . and they are not': see http://news.bbc.co.uk/1/hi/scotland/north_east/6303011.stm

191: That summer a suspected SAM-7 . . . the following July: *Daily Telegraph*, 29 July 2007, Tom Coghlan.

192: The results then were devastating . . . aircraft were lost: Defence Research Paper, Advanced Command and Staff Course, Number 9, Sept 2005–July 2006.

193: 'parallel-parking a car with your eyes closed': see *Milwaukee Journal*

Sentinel, 7 April 2003, Katherine M. Skiba.

197: Hasler, suspecting that some spare 'chicken fuel' might be useful . . . the engines to burn up: Patrick Bishop, *3 Para*, p. 173.

209: 'Clearly we could generate a higher tempo . . . reconstruction and development': BBC News, 8 October 2006.

211: But the reporter chose not to mention this . . . twenty-five years earlier: *Daily Telegraph*, 4 October 2006, Tom Coghlan.

216: One egregious example . . . bikinis: *Sun*, 27 March 2007, 'Does my bomber look big in this?'

Chapter 6: Apache: A Weapon for 'War Amongst the People'

221: Early on in Herrick 4 . . . gutted alive: *Independent*, 1 October 2006, Raymond Whitaker.

221: The threat to aircrew . . . a mole working at the MoD: *The Times*, 31 January 2007, Daniel McGrory.

222: 'The Brits are good . . . Lieutenant Jack Denton: *Sunday Telegraph*, 29 April 2007, Gethin Chamberlain, 'US aircrews show Taliban no mercy'.

Chapter 7: Tom's War

236: The report, broadcast on *Newsnight*, generated much controversy: BBC 2, 26 October 2006.

237: 'I was always happy to read-hear-watch interviews . . . which was advantageous': see www.arrse.co.uk/cpgn2/Forums/viewtopic/p=913822. html#913822

239: There wasn't much the squadron could do . . . the majority of them unmarked: see http://www.landmines.org.uk/270.php

242: 'Inside I could see one body . . . they are going to kill us" ' / 'I could see it was one of the lads . . . he screamed': *Guardian*, 18 November 2006, Audrey Gillan.

254: The press later reported . . . in some way during their tour: *Daily Telegraph*, 22 August 2006.

259: 'They were running out of food . . . a bunch of colonials!!': *Independent*, 1 October 2006, Raymond Whitaker, 'Blood & Guts: At the front with the poor bloody infantry'.

Chapter 8: The Royal Irish and the Musa Qala Deal

267: In Brigadier Butler's view . . . every time a man had to be casevac'd: Patrick Bishop, *3 Para*, p. 254.

270: When one of the .50 cal machine-guns . . . held together with Superglue: *Independent*, 3 September 2006, Cole Moreton and Tom Coghlan, 'The war the world forgot'.

288: Talking to the Taliban . . . eventual negotiation was inevitable: *Guardian*, 6 September 2006, Simon Jenkins, 'Talk to Mullah Omar, if it saves British soldiers' lives . . . Hamid Karzai admits what our leaders can't: to achieve security in Afghanistan, he must do a deal with the Taliban'.

289: I was sure that the standard Western view of the Taliban . . .: some of the material that follows this first appeared in the *Independent on Sunday*, 16 December 2007, 'Muscle alone won't solve Afghanistan's problems'.

291: In December 1997 . . . Omaha's Super Target discount store: *Sunday Telegraph*, 14 December 1997, Caroline Lees, 'Oil barons court Taliban in Texas'.

Chapter 9: Amongst the Taliban

314: More than 1,100 girls' schools . . . in the entire province: according to the American NGO Afghans4Tomorrow (private correspondence).

317: I recalled reading an interview . . . the Para told the reporter: *Guardian Weekend*, 14 October 2006, James Meek, 'In their minds, all they want to do is kill English soldiers'.

Postscript

324: This time, however, 16 Air Assault Brigade . . . Eurofighter ground attack aircraft for the first time: *Sunday Times*, 30 September 2007, Michael Smith and Louise Armitstead, 'Biggest blitz by Paras since WW2 to crush Taliban'.

325: 'Securing Musa Qala . . . the operation should be judged': Fisnik Abrashi, Associated Press, 15 December 2007.

325: In the course of their house-to-house clearance operation . . . a makeshift heroin factory: *The Times*, 13 December 2007, Nick Meo.

326: As 2007 came to a close ... expelled the pair from the country: *Guardian*, 27 December 2007, Declan Walsh.

326: As Paddy Ashdown ... stabilization and reconstruction effort': see *Guardian*, 19 July 2007.

327: In February 2008 in Arghandab ... a dog-fighting festival: Allauddin Khan, Associated Press, 17 February 2008.

327: An estimated 6,200 people ... the insurgency in 2007: *Independent*, 12 December 2007, Colin Brown.

327: sixty-five young soldiers ... 101 of them seriously or very seriously: MoD figures, 30 March 2008.

328: Sir Sherard Cowper-Coles ... thirty years: *Daily Mail*, 20 June 2007.

328: According to the most recent poll: YouGov/*Sunday Times*, 13–14 December 2007.

328: Between June and November 2007 ... resignation applications approved: *Guardian*, 23 November 2007, Richard Norton-Taylor, 'Under-strength and under strain as experienced soldiers queue to quit'; see also *The Times*, 18 February 2008, Melanie Reid, 'If the recruiting officer's job is becoming impossible, no wonder'.

328: 'I think [southern Afghanistan] may be the death knell of Nato ... what on earth is Nato for?': GMTV, *The Sunday Programme*, 10 December 2006.

Appendix: Maps

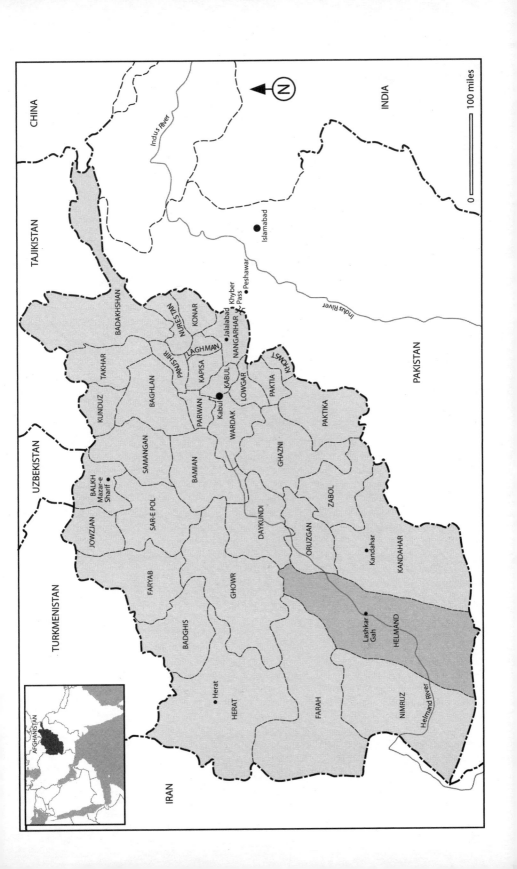

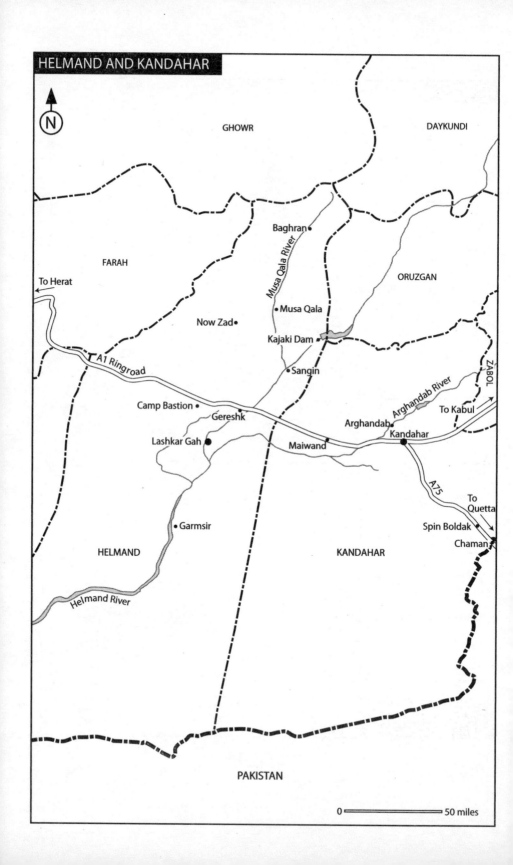

HELMAND AND KANDAHAR

N

GHOWR

DAYKUNDI

FARAH

Baghran •

Musa Qala River

ORUZGAN

To Herat

• Musa Qala

Now Zad •

Kajaki Dam •

ZABOL

A1 Ringroad

• Sangin

Arghandab River

To Kabul

Camp Bastion •

Gereshk

Arghandab •

Lashkar Gah ●

Maiwand

Kandahar ●

A75

To Quetta

• Garmsir

Spin Boldak •

Chaman

HELMAND

KANDAHAR

Helmand River

PAKISTAN

0 ══════ 50 miles

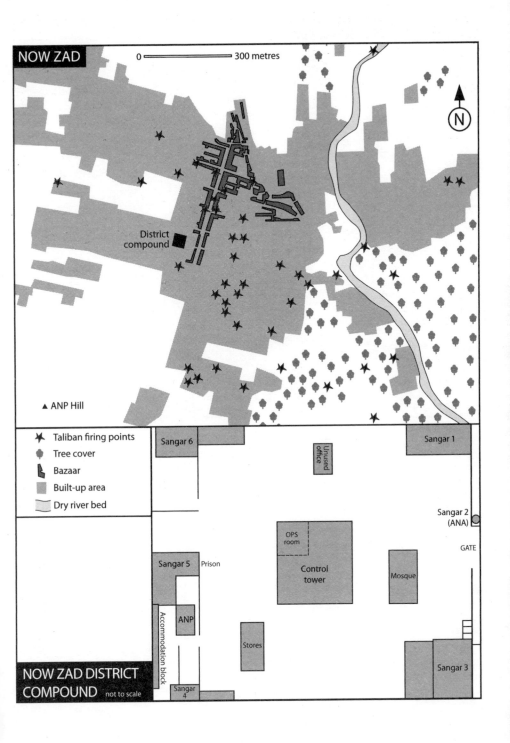

NOW ZAD

0 ⸻ 300 metres

N

District compound

▲ ANP Hill

✹ Taliban firing points
⬡ Tree cover
⬧ Bazaar
▨ Built-up area
▨ Dry river bed

Sangar 6

Unused office

Sangar 1

Sangar 2 (ANA)

GATE

OPS room

Sangar 5   Prison

Control tower

Mosque

Accommodation block

ANP

Stores

NOW ZAD DISTRICT COMPOUND not to scale

Sangar 4

Sangar 3

Picture Credits

Endpapers [hardback edition]: An aerial view of Camp Bastion in Helmand, 2006: Johnny Green/PA photos

Picture section

All photos are courtesy of the author, except where otherwise credited.

Poppies in Helmand: Patrick Allen/DPL; Taliban pose with an RPG, Zabul province, south of Kabul, 7 October 2006: AP Photo/Allauddin Khan

Lieutenant Colonel Stuart Tootal during an operation to secure the village of Musa Qala, 6 August 2006: Reuters/Corporal Rob Knight/Crown Copyright/Handout (Afghanistan); Governor Mohammed Daoud, November 2006: Mirrorpix; Defence Secretary John Reid at Camp Bastion with Brigadier Ed Butler: Johnny Green/PA Archive/PA Photos; Leo Docherty on patrol: courtesy Leo Docherty

Mobile phone shot taken during Operation Mutay: Paul Wood/DPL; Gurkhas in a Land Rover; Major Dan Rex under camouflage nets: both

Index